One More Victory Lap

Wishing you great success in
FreeLife!

One More Victory Lap

*"My personal diary
of an Olympic year"*

CARL LEWIS

written with
JEFFREY MARX

ATHLETICS INTERNATIONAL ❦ SANTA MONICA, CA

ISBN 0-88497-005-1

Typesetting and design by
The Manifestation-Glow Press
Flushing, New York

Published by
ATHLETICS INTERNATIONAL
1801 Ocean Park Blvd., Suite 201
Santa Monica, CA 90405

*This book is dedicated to the people
who have been with me every step of the way
throughout my entire career,
and especially to the friends and fans
who have offered such incredible support
during my final run to the Olympics.*

— CARL LEWIS

*These pages are written for
Wendy, Kelly, and Carl,
all of whom keep reminding me
that absolutely anything is possible.
They are also written for the heroes
who save lives through
organ donation and transplantation.*

— JEFFREY MARX

INTRODUCTION

There are so many elements to an Olympic year. The physical and mental preparation. The private doubts and public challenges. The glare of the media spotlight. The intensity of the competition. Then there is finally the joy that comes with doing your absolute best – no matter what the order of finish in any particular event.

Ultimately, though, my 1996 Olympic season was really about one single element more than any other. It was about humanity. It was about reaching out and connecting with other people, touching their lives, and being deeply moved by what I felt coming back in return.

Right from the outset, I knew that my fifth and final Olympic year was going to be special. I wanted to document and share the complete story of it. So I decided to keep a diary. The entries often move from day to day in disjointed fashion, much like life itself, which I think helps to keep things interesting. Yet there is also an unyielding direction in which these entries move: toward the Games in Atlanta, and the final days of my career.

"You half expect him to be in a rocking chair by now, working at his needlepoint, a pair of battered corduroy slippers on his famous feet."

– MARK MCDONALD

"As a man grows older, he often comes to realize that the most veracious triumphs are determined not by others, but by oneself; that the only lasting victories are won when a person defines his own goals. He need not announce what those goals are; sometimes, when the pursuit begins, he need not even know."

– BOB GREENE

Sunday, December 31, 1995 – Atlanta

Running and jumping in the Olympics at the age of thirty-five? Have I totally lost my mind? I know there are a lot of people who think so. Especially when they take into consideration the fact that my last strong year of competition was 1992. But there are reasons for everything. There are reasons why I've had a few down years. There are reasons why I feel I'll be myself again. Still, I hear it all the time: You're going to Atlanta? Really?

I guess I can understand why people might be surprised. They wonder if there is anything left for me to gain by putting myself and my record on the line yet again. They want to know if I fear going out a loser – after being a winner so many times – and if that would somehow put an unnecessary blemish on my achievements.

But that is entirely missing the point. The way I see it, this whole experience will be about so much more than just winning and losing. It will be about the journey itself. It will be about pushing myself to see what I have left. It will be about my sheer determination to walk away from my final year of international competition knowing that I have given it the absolute best that I have to offer.

In other words, unlike other Olympic years I have been through, this one clearly will not be defined solely by what happens on the fields of competition. Not by me, anyway. I will ultimately judge the outcome by answering this one question: Did I do everything possible to represent myself to the best of my abilities at this stage in my life? That does not require me to match any of my past accomplishments. It only requires me to be the best I can be right now.

No question, there are times when I too find it hard to believe I'm getting ready for a shot at my fifth Olympic team. Back when I was starting out, the Games were something you'd think about as once in a lifetime, if that. I was eighteen years old when I made my first Olympic team, the 1980 team that ended up boycotting the Moscow Games. Then I actually competed three times: Los Angeles in 1984, Seoul in 1988, Barcelona in 1992. Eight gold medals in all — that's the number everyone always talks about. But I tend to think more about the number of years than the number of medals.

If someone had told me at the outset I was going to be competing this long, I would have just laughed. *Yeah, right, and I'm also going to jump from here to the moon.* There have been so many times along the way that I have thought about retiring. And forget the number of times I've been written off as too old. I couldn't possibly count that high.

So Atlanta at the age of thirty-five? I mean, being thirty-five offers you the constitutional right to run for president of the United States, not World's Fastest Human. I'm not even sure exactly when I decided to set my sights on Atlanta. In fact, I'm not really sure I ever did. It's just something that evolved over time. Running and jumping is what I do for a living. It's the best job I'm ever going to have. So I've stuck with it. Simple as that. And one other thing: I've kept returning to the idea of just how much I enjoy a good challenge. I have always enjoyed creating challenges, going after them, and making good on them. I absolutely love pushing the limits and then seeing what happens. Always have. Always will.

The entire process is made all the more enjoyable by the fact I'm able to experience it with my best friends, my Santa Monica Track Club teammates, with whom I train and travel and share just about everything in my life, just as they share so much of themselves with me. Leroy and Michelle Burrell. Mike Marsh. Floyd Heard. My sister Carol. We've all been together forever, it seems, and our lives have become so unmistakably intertwined both on and off the track. Imagine going to work every morning with your best friends there to laugh and struggle and explore right along with you. If more of us could do that, we would certainly see a major decrease in the number of people preoccupied with the thought of early retirement. So many more of us would be perfectly comfortable with the idea of staying right where we are.

Sure, there have been times when my motivation has dwindled a bit— whose doesn't? — and especially the last few years. I'm a human being, though, not a machine, so there is nothing wrong with that. The fortunate thing is that I constantly find something new to get me motivated again. And my current motivation — my final motivation as an athlete — just might be the most powerful I've ever felt. I want to leave track and field on my own terms, want to go out with a bang, with passion, because I want people always to remember me at my best. It is difficult to imagine a better place than Atlanta to refresh those memories of who and what I am when I'm at my best.

One more victory lap. That's the way I'm looking at it now. If all goes just right, it would be incredible beyond words to finish my Olympic career the same way it began — with a victory lap on American soil. From Los Angeles to Atlanta. But that's not all I mean by one more victory lap. I want to approach the entire year as a lap for everything that has come before it. I want to share it all with the people who have been behind me every step of the way. I want to enjoy all the people and the places between now and the Games. Most of all, I can't wait to see and feel the excitement of an entire nation supporting its own. It was one thing to experience that energy in my early twenties, as I was still finding my way in the world. It will be something else altogether to see and feel it as a grown man, when I can appreciate and understand it with a more complete perspective.

Please, though, don't get me wrong. This is not going to be some sentimental journey without purpose. Not at all. To be sure, I want to win as much as ever. Maybe even more. I still turn to one of my favorite quotes as an injection of fire: "All athletes should bear in mind that they are competing not with other athletes but with their own capacities. Whatever I have already achieved, I have to go beyond." And I will.

So here we go. Of all the possible ways to begin an Olympic year, though, this one definitely fell into the category of unique. My 1996 started a day early because I was part of a live television broadcast to celebrate the beginning of the New Year in Japan. Late morning here was midnight in Tokyo. I don't exactly make a habit of starting an Olympic year, or any year, by standing in the middle of an empty stadium with my image and voice being bounced off a satellite to the other side of the world. Usually I'm just with friends and family at home or out at a party in Houston. But I guess this was meant to be my own day in the life of Dick Clark — nothing but smiles and good feelings for all the viewers celebrating with their little noisemakers and bottles of champagne.

We were live from three cities. Most of the guests — Japanese entertainers and celebrities — were right there in Tokyo. Magic Johnson was live from Los Angeles. And I flew to Atlanta because they wanted to play on the Olympic theme. It was kind of strange standing there alone in Fulton County Stadium, right where second base would be when the Atlanta Braves are playing, and doing the New Year countdown into a television camera. But I pulled it off the best I could. We also had a good time with a song they asked us to do. Narada Michael Walden, a Grammy Award-winning musician and good friend of mine, played the drums and fired up his band while Patti Austin carried me through a duet of "Georgia on My Mind."

Then the host in Japan asked me something about my preparation for the Olympics. I tried to keep it simple — training is going great, the excitement is building, America is going to put on a tremendous show for the world — because it would have been impossible to squeeze much more than that into a quick answer. Especially with them translating into Japanese. Although now that I think about it, maybe I should have added one more teaser: *Stay tuned. We'll be right back in Atlanta with opening ceremonies of the Games.* Because as quickly as an Olympic year tends to fly by, that is the way it will seem, like all we're doing is taking a commercial break before we start running and jumping for real.

Monday, January 1, 1996 – Houston

My manager, Joe Douglas, started in on me even earlier than usual this time. Months ago, he was already saying he was booking me for some event to get me out of Houston for the first day of 1996. Of course, I kept telling him the same thing I always do when it comes to New Year's Day: "Joe, you can schedule whatever you want, but I promise you, I'm not going. You know where I'll be."

It's been the same song and dance for years now. Joe tries to get me out of Houston so I'll miss our annual New Year's Day football game, but no matter what he pulls, I always end up playing. And Joe ends up worrying. He spends too much time imagining me crumpled up in the cold grass with some career-ending injury. "And for what?" he always wants to know. "Why do you want to take a chance like that?"

Joe obviously has a good understanding of the risks involved when any athlete, even a finely-tuned professional athlete, starts messing around beyond his or her normal realm of activity. In fact, it was just four years ago, during the last Olympic season, that one of my teammates, a promising hurdler named Courtney Hawkins, pretty much wiped out his chances of making the U.S. team by taking a nasty spill and badly spraining his ankle in practice. While trying to pole vault!

I have to admit, this football game is the one time a year I go totally against the best interests of someone who relies on healthy legs, healthy everything, to earn a living. But I play because it's tradition, and I love it. Don't we all, no matter what we do for a living, deserve at least one day a year when we throw caution to the wind? I think so. And especially when it can be so much fun.

One of the best things about the Santa Monica Track Club (the SMTC), my club since Day One on the international circuit, is the way we enjoy doing so many different things together. Not just training and traveling and competing, but so many other things as well, such as the annual gridiron bash. The way the SMTC works, the sprinters train here under Tom Tellez, my coach ever since I went to the University of Houston. The runners specializing in longer distances, 400 meters and up, train in Santa Monica with Joe, who doubles as coach and manager, and actually triples as founder and general caretaker of the club.

So it's gotten to the point that Olympians and other friends come from all over the country for this football game. Sometimes we have as many as a dozen world-class sprinters on the field at once. It's eleven-on-eleven on a regulation field, not exactly flag football, not officially tackle, sort of a combination. We call it *flackle*. It is extremely competitive. Of course, the game itself is only half the fun. The other half is talking and laughing about it when it's over. Who made the best hit? The worst cheap shot? The best catch? We argue and laugh about it for weeks.

This being an Olympic year, we did make one concession. We all agreed to cut down on the tackling. With blocking as physical as always, though, there was still plenty of hitting to go around. I managed to escape with a sore thumb and an aching shoulder. The hit of the game was on Mike Marsh. Mike is best known to outsiders as the 1992 Olympic champion at 200 meters and world-record holder on several relay teams, but he has also established quite a reputation in our football games. Everyone knows he is the guy most likely to get in an extra jab or hit when you least expect it – all in fun, of course. This time, though, it was Mike who ended up on the wrong end of a blow. After making a good, clean block and falling to the ground with the guy he was blocking, someone else (still unidentified) hit Mike from behind, knocking him silly. "Felt like a pipe in the back of my head," Mike finally said after lying there moaning for a few minutes. "It's like my brain was just sloshing around in there." The tradition continues. No touchdowns for me this time around, but we still beat Mike's team, 31–14.

A bunch of us went to Mike's house for the post-game dinner, but it was hardly the most lively of get-togethers. We ate. We watched a real football game on television. We complained to each other about all our bumps and bruises. I don't care what kind of shape we're in from all the running and lifting and training, all that blocking and tackling and hitting the ground takes a toll. I was so sore and tired I could hardly move. But we survived. Joe Douglas can finally stop worrying.

Tuesday, January 2 – Houston

It would have been nice to just forget about training for a day and give my football-abused body a rest. But this is not the time for that. No skipping anything unless there is a very good reason (injury or illness) and simply being sore does not qualify. One thing I know about training at this stage in my career: with Father Time tugging on my legs, I need to be more focused than ever. And I have been. In fact, this has been the hardest I've ever worked in the months leading up to an Olympic year.

It was all the way back in the middle of last summer — alone in a hotel room in Sweden — that I started considering the changes I wanted to make in my overall preparation for 1996. We were in Goteborg for the World Championships, but there was plenty of time to think because I was injured – strained hamstring in my left leg. Not exactly Bosnia or the federal deficit in the broader scheme of things, but I guess the cocoon of track and field is no different than any other. We tend to exaggerate the importance of relatively meaningless developments. Gives us something to talk about. And so there was plenty of speculation in Goteborg that my bad leg was more than just a bad leg. Maybe it was really the end of my career. Obviously, I got extremely tired of such talk, but I also could see why so many outsiders were down on my chances: I hadn't really performed up to my abilities since all the way back in 1992. I had not run 100 meters in less than 10 seconds, even my long jumping was off, and now the entire 1995 season seemed to be turning into a non-year for me.

The World Championships are always the most important event in a pre-Olympic year. Results determine everything from the way your competitors look at you and the media treat you to the support you're going to get from corporate sponsors. So I certainly had incentives to compete. But the one thing I absolutely would not do was take a foolish chance just to prove a point – and then end up doing the kind of damage to my leg that really could end a career. So after an entire week in Sweden, a week that included light workouts and a few promotional appearances but mainly a lot of time cooped up in a hotel room, I finally pulled out of the World Championships without once setting foot in the stadium.

It would have been so much better to close out the summer with a big performance that would carry me into the beginning of the Olympic year on a positive note. How often, though, do any of us actually hold the power to define the beginnings and ends of such significant periods in our lives? Not very often. We only hold the power to react to them, to choose what we do with them.

What I needed after pulling out of the World Championships was some time alone to reflect. It was the second week in August – less than a year until the opening ceremonies in Atlanta. I needed to think about where I was and where I wanted to be. Most of all, I needed to figure out how I was going to get there. Forget how many times I'd already been to the Olympics. Forget the medals I'd already won. It was time to start all over again. And that would mean everything: new attitude, new diet, new fitness and training program.

Once I was back home in Houston, with everyone else still com-

(PHOTO: F. CARTER SMITH)

This is the hardest I've ever worked in the months leading up to an Olympic season.

peting on the regular European circuit that continued after the World Championships, I felt like a kid who'd been let out of school early and hardly knew what to do with himself. But I soon decided where to start. Taking the advice of a close friend, Mary Cullen, I went to San Diego to see a doctor named Barnett Meltzer, a nutritionist who specializes in natural healing and stresses healthy living as the best possible form of preventive medicine. Mary had heard that Dr. Meltzer was known for his ability to pinpoint the source of allergy problems – which had been dogging me for a few years – and trying to control them through both diet and behavior.

After sticking little needles in my arms and doing all sorts of tests, he offered two immediate conclusions: my lymphatic system was very clogged (which was slowing down my metabolism) and he thought an allergy related to flour might be part of the problem. I had been a vegetarian since 1990, but I do eat a ton of bread and pasta, so maybe there was something to it.

The first thing Dr. Meltzer did was put me on what he called a cleansing diet – which I soon learned was the near equivalent of health by starvation. Here is what we had on the initial menu:

Breakfast: Eight ounces of fresh juice (grapefruit). Fruit salad. Twenty almonds (no salt). Alfalfa sprouts (as much as I'd like). Herbal cleansing tea.

Snack: Eight ounces of fresh juice (watermelon). Two celery sticks with almond butter.

Lunch: Large green salad. Half an avocado with salsa on corn tortilla. Two celery sticks. Herbal tea.

Snack: Eight ounces of fresh juice (watermelon). Herbal tea.

Dinner: Eight ounces of fresh vegetable juice. Large green salad. Large bowl of vegetable soup. Baked potato with salsa. Herbal tea.

Not exactly a diet to bulk you up. I went to San Diego to see Dr. Meltzer every Wednesday for five or six weeks, making adjustments to the diet as we went along, and other than starving, I felt great. I also ended up looking like a high school kid or something – skinny as I've been in a long, long time. I was down below one hundred and seventy-five pounds, way too light for competition (want to be around one hundred and eighty-five) but right where I wanted to be, clean and fresh, for the initial phase of my new fitness and training program. From there we started adding back things I could eat at the same time we were increasing the difficulty and duration of my workouts.

The entire structure of my fitness and training program was new as well: all sorts of new exercises, including plyometrics and a variety of drills with a medicine ball, but the most significant addition has been lifting weights. Not to bulk up, but to get strong. There is a big difference between the two. The effectiveness of lifting for runners has been argued for years. Until the 1960s, most runners stayed away from too much lifting because they were afraid of becoming "muscle-bound" and forfeiting flexibility. But almost all top runners do at least some lifting now, in large part because of the relatively new field of biomechanics, which has offered a variety of documentation supporting the importance of maximizing certain muscle groups. I've dabbled with weights before, but never much, and the one year I did the most lifting, 1986, I probably ran the worst. I was definitely one of those people who felt that the lifting took away from my flexibility, so after that I was always scared of using weights.

Now, though, I was dealing with a new set of circumstances. I'd missed so much work the previous three years that I'd lost the physical edge I used to have. Sure, I had to consider age as a factor. But I also knew I'd gone three straight years without a fall training season. Fall of 1992, I was totally burned out both physically and emotionally after the Barcelona Olympics, so I chose to take a few months off. Fall of 1993, I was still having back problems after a car accident earlier in the year. Fall of 1994 was totally wiped out by a lingering stomach disorder acquired from that wonderful Russian cuisine during the Goodwill (Badfood) Games in St. Petersburg.

Fall is your only real chance for serious strength training before you get out on the track to start running and jumping. So missing three straight years has been a huge issue for me. It wasn't just a matter of wanting to lift weights this time around. It was a matter of necessity. I simply need the strength. And flexibility is not as much of a concern anymore because yoga more than takes care of that. I've been doing yoga for a couple of years now and will continue with it to help regulate my flexibility.

So far it seems I'm getting exactly the results I wanted. My entire body is cut like never before and I feel absolutely great on the track — strong and fit and confident. Part of the confidence comes from knowing that Coach Tellez was so much a part of setting up this program, and he's the one person who knows both me and our sport better than anyone. He always has me ready when I need to be. And yet there are still moments when I wonder if I'm doing all the right things. I'm executing this plan without wavering. But a mighty big question remains: Will it work?

Wednesday, January 3 – Houston

It's amazing what we'll do to promote a track meet. Especially when it's our own — right here at the University of Houston on the third of February. That's about the only way Leroy Burrell and I would have agreed to be in the commercial we just did. Leroy is a teammate, close friend and the current world-record holder in the 100. We're going to run the 60-meter dash in the Gallery Furniture Games, which will be our first competition of the season. It will also be the first time I've run indoors in years – but that's a whole different story. The issue for now is how to act completely silly while you're selling something.

We've all seen those commercials for an electronics store or maybe a used car lot where it's all about gimmicks and decibels. As if the value of a sale is defined by how loud and fast the salesman can talk. Well, in Houston we have Jim "Mattress Mac" McIngvale, owner of Gallery Furniture and the driving force behind some of the most ridiculous stuff on the air. Put it this way: He got the nickname by wearing a mattress suit in a commercial. Need I say more? Actually, yes, one more thing: As goofy as Mattress Mac can be on television, he's also a great guy, always doing a lot of positive things in the community, always supporting others. And I know he won't mind me poking a little fun – because fun is the name of his game. Fun advertising has helped him transform a pile of mattresses into an incredibly successful business.

Anyway, Leroy and I pointed fingers at each other, according to script, and talked trash, with Mattress Mac standing between us as the peacemaker. "I'm the fastest man alive," I said, leaning across Mattress Mac to get to Leroy. "No, I'm the fastest," Leroy shot back, jabbing me in the chest. And then came Mattress Mac with the voice of reason: "OK, guys, for the last time, no more running in here. Save it for the Gallery Games." We each had a line about the meet and information on how to get tickets. Then Mattress Mac closed by waving a wad of bills and turning up the volume: "Remember, Gallery Furniture saves you *money!*"

Which is something they also did on this commercial – saved money. Definitely one of the least expensive productions I've ever seen. One camera. One angle. A few talking heads. Grand total of maybe thirty minutes in a local television studio. I couldn't help but think of the last commercial I was in – part of a high-tech campaign for Pirelli tires in which they had me running on water and jumping on top of the Statue of Liberty. It took several months to plan, shoot, create special effects, edit, and get the final product on air all over the world. The Gallery Furniture spot starts running this weekend.

By then Mattress Mac will have thrown one more gimmick into the mix. Leroy and I are scheduled to join his press conference tomorrow by driving a Ferrari Testarossa right into the fieldhouse and up to the starting line. Mattress Mac will then announce that anyone who breaks a world record gets the car. He certainly knows how to grab your attention and generate excitement. Exactly the kind of guy we need to help promote American track and field out of the Dark Ages. Maybe we ought to just nominate Mattress Mac for executive director of USA Track & Field.

Thursday, January 4 – Houston

It looks like this will be the first time since before World War II that every country affiliated with the Olympic movement — now one hundred and ninety-seven nations — will actually be competing. That's because North Korea, an outsider for so long, just accepted an invitation to participate in Atlanta. For once, no politics getting in the way. That would be a nice touch, and a welcome change from the past.

Unfortunately, there is a long history of nations either being banned or choosing to boycott the Games because of politics. Germany and Japan, for example, were excluded from the 1948 Games in the aftermath of the war. And then there was South Africa, consistently and rightfully shunned during the worst of the apartheid years, but now, thank goodness, a changed nation and back in the Olympic family. The first of two major boycotts came in 1980 when President Jimmy Carter, protesting the Soviet invasion of Afghanistan, refused to send American athletes to the Moscow Games. The Soviets retaliated by pulling out of the 1984 Games in Los Angeles.

It seems almost impossible now, in my mid-thirties, to look back at 1980 and realize how clueless I was about the whole boycott issue. I had no real understanding of the degree to which the political landscape so directly affected the lives of so many dedicated athletes. People like: Al Feuerbach, the great shot putter, who would never get another chance; little Tracee Talavera, the thirteen-year-old gymnast, who would never again be the focus of such great expectations; Anita DeFrantz, a rower and one of the most outspoken critics of the boycott, who now serves on the International Olympic Committee; and Isiah Thomas, the basketball star, who forever lost his chance to play in the Games.

Then again, how could I possibly have related to what these people were going through? I was so young, eighteen years old, the first time I qualified for the Games. I made it in the long jump and as a member of the relay team. Equally exciting was the fact that my sister Carol also made it as a long jumper. And she was only sixteen at the time!

We knew that a lot of the older athletes were angry about the boycott, but we certainly were not mature enough to understand the implications. All we understood was having a good time, enjoying what we were doing, and we were definitely having a blast. I mean, how often do a brother and sister get to make an Olympic team together? It was no big deal that we couldn't go to Moscow. We just figured we'd go to the Games next time.

In fact, back then I thought of the Olympics as something you do only once. You do it and then you move on with your life. So I actually figured we might even be best off waiting for 1984. Neither one of us was ready to win an individual event in 1980. Maybe I'd have a shot at gold in the relay. But if I was going to compete only once in the Olympics, I knew I'd be more prepared both physically and emotionally by 1984. Maybe I'd be able to do something significant by then.

Of course, the participation of the North Korean athletes this year would be more symbolic than anything else. It's not like they're going to be marching off with a bunch of medals. But sometimes a symbolic gesture is enough to make a difference. And why not? There's certainly more than enough negative energy floating around in our world. Why not reach out for something positive and embrace it when we have the opportunity?

Friday, January 5 – Houston

I'm finally all the way back from the New Year's Day football game. No running today, but my body fully cooperated with me through an extensive lifting session. There were no more extracurricular aches and pains.

The highlight of the day had nothing to do with training, though; it was watching the last of the "Planet of the Apes" sequels. Carol and I have been watching one movie a night since Monday. Talk about cable channels struggling to fill the airwaves. But I love old movies — no matter how hokey. What I enjoy most is seeing how much the production techniques and quality have improved over the years. Once I got started this week, I was hooked. I had to see all five in the series or I would have felt like I was missing something. The original, with Charlton Heston, was definitely the best. After that, they went downhill fast. But at least we laughed a lot.

Carol and I have been laughing together for so long now. In fact, we've been doing just about everything together for so long. Carol is my only sister (we have two older brothers) and my best friend. We played together as kids, trained together as teenagers, both attended the University of Houston, and both went on to the Santa Monica Track Club. Carol is also a world-class athlete – former national champion and two-time Olympian as a long jumper – so we've been everywhere together. She is easily the one person with whom I've spent the most time.

Carol is hilarious. That would be a good place to start a description of her. She is incredibly straight to the point – no sense playing games with Carol because she's always going to tell you exactly what she thinks. She's extremely competitive, and fiercely loyal when it comes to family and friends. Then there is her incredible ability to carry on a conversation about practically anything, and with just about anyone. Carol and I have been teased that we'd both be definite medalists if they had talking Olympics. "Of course, I'd win," Carol says, showing that competitive side of hers, and also probably correct with her assessment.

Carol has been such an integral part of the international track scene for so long, she's like an at-large ambassador of goodwill. She knows everyone, everywhere, and keeps up with foreigners as if they live just down the street. A Swedish jeweler, a German journalist, a Spanish marketing executive – you never know who it's going to be when Carol gets a call. A few years back, it was an Armenian long jumper, Robert Emmiyan, calling unexpectedly from the airport in Houston. Would it be OK if he visited for a few days? Would she come pick him up at the baggage claim area? He ended up living and training with us for several months, and had the time of his life, temporarily becoming part of an American family. It was business as usual for Carol, the at-large ambassador, always entertaining, always keeping things interesting.

The last few years, after suffering a broken foot while jumping, Carol shifted away from the track and into the broadcast booth. She's

My sister Carol will definitely win the talking competition as a network analyst for the Games.

(PHOTO: NBC)

done an excellent job as a track and field analyst for the networks and has also prepared feature stories for *Entertainment Tonight* and other shows. But now she's back in the transition game. She is still doing television, but Carol has also been training with us since the fall, working her way back into shape, and will soon decide if she's going to take one more shot at the Olympic trials. In the long jump. Not the talking competition. We're still waiting for that event to be officially sanctioned.

Saturday, January 6 – Houston

Here's an issue we've been dealing with for years: trying to change the track and field schedule for the Olympics. One of the biggest challenges of competing in four events is staying both physically and emotionally prepared all the way through the Games. That is an expected and accepted challenge at this level. But why make it even more difficult than necessary by lumping certain events right on top of each other? We've never had success with any of our schedule requests, though, and maybe there have been legitimate reasons for that, but this year is different. This time we're not just talking about how difficult something would be; we're talking about impossible.

The 200 and long jump are scheduled for the same time in Atlanta. That means I'm out of at least one event before I even have a chance to train through the spring and decide which events I want to enter in the Olympic trials. So back in September, Joe Douglas wrote Primo Nebiolo, president of the International Amateur Athletic Federation (IAAF), to request that the 100, 200 and long jump be separated. After reading a newspaper report that Nebiolo had initially responded favorably to our request, Joe wrote him again and offered specific changes that would allow me to compete in all three individual events plus the relay. The proposal would also separate the 200 and 400 – an important point because I'm no longer the only one lobbying for a change. Michael Johnson, who won both the 200 and 400 in the 1995 World Championships in Sweden, wants to go for the double again, but his events, with preliminary rounds and all, currently overlap on the schedule.

The rationale for allowing late changes – changes that really don't hurt anything – has always seemed so simple to me. The best athletes should be able to compete in their best events. That's what makes for the highest level of competition, the best performances, and, ultimately, the best Olympic stories. That's what the fans want. That's what television wants. That's what we all should want. So why keep it from happening?

The reason I bring it up now is that this morning we picked up a positive sign that the changes might eventually be approved. A newspaper in Italy is quoting Nebiolo as saying organizers would try to ensure that both Michael Johnson and I will be able to compete in all our events. They'd *try*. Of course, if the changes are made, Michael and I could end up facing each other in the 200, which would certainly be one of the marquee events. But we'll just have to wait and see what happens. I know I'd be much more confident about the changes being made if Nebiolo were to contact us directly to discuss the issues, as opposed to sending cryptic messages through the media.

Sunday, January 7 – Dallas

I'm usually glued to the big screen television on a football Sunday. Give me the clicker, and I'm fine. Trust me, I'll find my favorite team, the Philadelphia Eagles. If they're not playing a network game, I'll get them on the special NFL programming package I ordered at the beginning of the season. Today, though, it was the playoffs, and so close to home, so I couldn't help myself. I took an early morning flight with Leroy Burrell to see the Eagles and Cowboys in person.

I've been a huge Eagles fan going all the way back to my days growing up in Willingboro, New Jersey, a suburb of Philly. As a spectator, I think I've always been more drawn to team sports than individual sports. The strategy. The ups and downs of a long season. The drama of the playoffs. The personalities. All of it.

I know my friends get sick of hearing me talk about the Eagles, but I can't help it. I study my weekly *Eagles Digest* newsletter, which I get in the mail, and I'm totally absorbed by the games. At home, I yell like a complete psycho at the television. At the stadium, I try to control myself a bit more, so the guys in white jackets don't come looking for me.

Leroy is also from just outside Philly and has always pulled for the Eagles. All we wanted to talk about last week was the playoffs. And we were fortunate that our new friend Mattress Mac happened to notice that. After listening to us go on and on about the Eagles throughout those days we did the commercial and the press conference, he was nice enough to make a few calls and find us tickets to the game.

Unfortunately, the Eagles went down, 30–11, but the Cowboys played well. Nobody's going to beat them if they keep playing the way they did today. The only thing that bothered me was some of the Dallas fans. Not because they were against us. That's fine. In fact, it was kind of fun mixing it up with them. But there was this one group of idiots near us that just loved making fun of the Eagles. You know, we're *Dallas*; the Eagles are *nothing*. It was especially annoying because I thought the Eagles played hard. As an athlete, I respect the preparation and the effort, no matter what the outcome. Why would you laugh at a team that puts up a good fight but loses? Makes no sense to me.

There was this one guy sitting near us who was wearing a Cowboys scarf and ragging on us the whole time. Friendly ragging, I guess. But then he turned to me near the end of the game, holding out the scarf, and, with an ugly tone, said, "Here, here, you can hide behind this." I looked him dead in the eye, and said, "Oh, you must think I'm a quitter, huh?" And he didn't know quite how to respond. He just turned back toward the field. And then two minutes later he was turning toward me again and asking for an autograph. Which I gave him. But I can't say I was overly excited about doing him any favors. It would have been more enjoyable to just tattoo an Eagles logo on his forehead.

Monday, January 8 – Houston

Judging by the questions and comments I get all the time from people outside our sport, and even from people in it, there's a general misperception that we must spend morning, afternoon and night at the track. For some reason, people want to think we train by quantity: run, run, run, and then run some more. But actually the best sprinters are much more concerned with quality than quantity.

Take our workout this morning. We call it a breakdown. Four hundred meters in less than 51 seconds. Then five minutes to rest. Three hundred meters in less than 39 seconds. Five minutes rest. Then 200 meters in less than 25 seconds. We call it a breakdown because it's guaranteed to break you down. Great way to start the week. We'll usually alternate what we do on Mondays: breakdowns one week, repeat 200s the next. Repeats are when we do back-to-back 200s, usually six of them, maybe 24 to 26 seconds each, with just 90 seconds to rest between finishing one and starting the next. Try it next time you're out for a little exercise. Won't take long to figure out what I mean by quality over quantity.

I've heard it said many times that our workouts look more like an actual track meet than a training session. And I can see why visitors are left with that impression. For years, our club has been stacked with talented sprinters, and we don't like to mess around. We're not out on the track long, but when we're out there, we're rolling. Helps to make the real meets feel like just another day at the office.

The last few years I've generally trained with Leroy Burrell and Mike Marsh. The past few months have been somewhat different, though, because Leroy has been off on his own more than usual. It's been kind of strange. I mean, I'm so used to having him around. When he was in high school, I helped recruit Leroy to Houston. When he was an undergrad, I usually went with him to the collegiate meets. And we've been training together ever since. Leroy has had his greatest successes, including two world records in the 100, when he, Mike, and I have worked as partners. We've always been so together in everything. But Leroy has struggled the last two years with a foot problem — plantar fascitis, a painful inflammation of the band of tissue running the length of the foot — and I don't think he wants to "race" as much in practice anymore. He's adjusted both his running and his overall training program. It's somewhat hard for me to understand why he'd want to get away from what has worked so well for him in the past, but I also have to believe Leroy knows what's best for himself. He's the same person he's always been, intelligent, thoughtful, great sense of humor, the best of friends. But now he's doing his thing and we're doing ours. Floyd Heard, the fourth member of our relay team, has joined Mike and me on the practice track.

The rest of a regular week, this time of year, anyway, goes something like this. Tuesdays we'll lift weights and practice starts. Wednesdays we'll lift and do plyometrics (bounding exercises, such as stadium steps, and a variety of other strength and fitness drills in which we propel our own body weight instead of pumping iron), and then sometimes I'll work on the long jump. Thursdays are the easiest. We'll usually do six or eight 150s or flying 100s, which means we start from a jog instead of from the blocks. Fridays we'll lift, take starts, and, depending on how the rest of the week went, maybe I'll take some jumps.

Of course, all of this changes as we go along. For example, we'll soon go from running two days a week to three days, and then to four, and finally five. We always have an overall plan, with the emphasis on being ready when it counts the most. This year, that would be mid-June for the Olympic trials and second half of July for the Olympics. But even though we have a plan, we're always willing to make adjustments based on factors such as time of the year, the number of days before a meet, and how we feel.

Only one thing remains an absolute constant: quality over quantity.

Tuesday, January 9 – Houston

There's one more big change at the practice track that I should have mentioned yesterday. I'm not coaching the college kids anymore. The last few years, Leroy and I have been helping Coach Tellez with the Houston relay teams. Leroy's been working with the women, I've been working with the guys. And I've really gotten into it. In fact, I've been told I get more worked up about their performances than I do about my own. Probably because I have a lot more control when I'm the one competing. With them, I'm helpless once they're on the track.

But no more. Not this year, anyway. It just got to be too much of a drain on me. Part of it has to do with the whole Generation X attitude, or whatever you want to call it. Much as I believe in having a good time, enjoying what you do even while you're working hard at it, there are certain things I just don't understand and can't accept about the young athletes of today.

Maybe it's my background – growing up with the guidance of two strong parents who also happened to be school teachers. My mother and father ran a household full of love and support but also one that might as well have been a factory cranking out a steady and unyielding supply of discipline. Believe me, that leather strap hanging behind the door in their bathroom, the one my father used to sharpen his razor, well, that leather strap and the behinds of the Lewis children got to know each other pretty well during the early years. I'm sure that has a lot to do with the way I now feel about discipline. Maybe it also helps explain why I have no appreciation for these young athletes who want all the benefits of being an adult but too often fail to act accordingly.

The one thing that's really been bothering me is the way some of these people handle themselves while representing the university. They're all good people, for the most part, and overall they make me proud to be associated with them. But it's the little things that get on my nerves. Wearing hats – backwards, of course – in restaurants. Headphones on and blasting music at all the wrong times. Funky language. And here's the one that really gets me: carrying those beepers. That's fine on their own time; no problem with that. But some of them actually carry beepers right onto the track during a meet. Who in the world does a college kid need to be hearing from in the middle of a track meet? That's not caring about your team. That's socializing. That's trying too hard to be cool.

I know some of this might make me sound like a grumpy old man or something, but sometimes I can't help it. Back in the fall, Coach Tellez asked me to stop by for a team meeting. He wanted me to welcome back the student-athletes, and that gave me a chance to get some things off my chest. Guess you could call it my "Time to Grow Up" speech. Time to make a commitment to yourself and your teammates. Of course, soon as I left, some of them probably drowned out my words with their headphones and beepers. That's just the way it is these days.

Maybe next year I'll go back to coaching again. For now, though, I'm taking a break. I'm still one hundred percent behind the team. But if I'm going to perform the way I want to this year, I can't afford the energy it takes to keep fighting through the headphones, the beepers, and the attitudes.

Wednesday, January 10 – Houston

I shared my workout with a shadow. Every move I made, lifting weights, throwing the medicine ball, practicing starts, doing box drills, running stadium steps, the shadow was there. It was a film crew preparing footage for my next step into the digital world. I've already been writing columns and participating in chat sessions, which are like live online interviews, for a service called NetNoir, which is available on America Online. Now I'm working on the official U.S. Olympic team CD-ROM, which should be in stores by April.

The CD-ROM will serve as a comprehensive guide to the Games, all sports, but it's interesting that Jackie Joyner-Kersee and I, both from track and field, were selected as the spokespersons. That told me two things: One, even with the extreme exposure of the Dream Team in basketball, and no matter the expectations of any other individual athletes, track and field remains the centerpiece of the Summer Games – even in spite of the overall failure of our sport to market itself in non-Olympic years. Two, maybe longevity does indeed count for something, because Jackie and I have been around forever. Anyway, our images will soon be seen training, running and jumping across computer screens all over the place. We'll be demonstrating and explaining both our training techniques and our specific events.

First, though, comes the production process. That's how I got the temporary shadow, a crew from Dallas-based Archimedia Interactive, which is handling the CD-ROM project. Wendell Holloway, the producer, wanted spontaneity, not a totally scripted show, and that made it very easy to work with him. I guess he's going to include all the grunting and groaning of training right along with the step-by-step descriptions of what we do and why we do it. They'll be back tomorrow to film us working on handing off the baton, the crucial exchange in a relay, and a few other drills. Then we'll finish up with an interview segment and audio to be placed over certain portions of the video we shot. It should turn out to be an attractive product. I think people will enjoy it.

Thursday, January 11 – Houston

Sometimes the Olympics make for pretty good entertainment even months before the opening ceremonies. Exhibit A: a behind-the-scenes corporate collision between a major Olympic sponsor and its number one competitor. It's Visa against American Express – with the Atlanta Committee for the Olympic Games (ACOG) stuck right in the middle.

The credit card companies have been going at it for years with high-profile advertising campaigns tied into the Olympics. As an official sponsor (i.e. major contributor), Visa highlights the angle that only its cards will be good at the Games. American Express has countered with some creative ambush advertising of its own.

But now we have a new twist. Contrary to what we're used to seeing in the Visa commercials, the Atlanta Olympics will in fact be taking American Express. ACOG is making it known that starting next month you'll be able to buy tickets by phone with either one of the credit cards. Let the Games begin!

Technically, it appears the Atlanta organizers can do whatever they want on this one because apparently Visa secured exclusive rights only on ticket sales by mail and not on telephone orders. But talk about turning your back on a friend. The Visa people have to be going ballistic. John Bennett, a marketing executive for Visa International, has in the past talked about the "halo effect" that comes with being an Olympic sponsor. Wonder how it feels to be wearing that halo now. ACOG officials make the point that with more than $400 million expected from ticket sales alone, they don't want to hurt the potential market for remaining tickets by limiting sales to people with Visa cards. But, oh, what tangled webs we weave.

I make note of this situation partly because I find it kind of amusing (can't wait to see how Olympic officials wiggle out of it) but also as a reminder of what the modern Olympics are really all about: pure business. Visa is one of more than thirty corporate sponsors paying some $628 million to be affiliated with the Atlanta Games. NBC television is paying more than $1 billion to broadcast both the 1996 and 2000 Games – and will profit handsomely from the deal. It's nice to think that the purity of running and jumping and throwing still counts for something. And it does. But anyone who fails to realize how the Games have been transformed by money has been asleep way too long. Wake up and smell the dollars.

Friday, January 12 – Houston

A few good practice jumps into the pit after lifting weights, and there might as well have been lights and bells and sirens going off to signal this major revelation that finally dawned on me. By jumping the way I did, feeling quicker and stronger than I have in so long, getting a really good pop off the board, it finally hit me just how far out of synch I've been the last few years. Not that I've been totally blind to the situation before now. Sometimes, though, you have to do something right again before you can fully appreciate the comparison with doing it wrong. And there are so many things I'm doing regularly now – doing the right way – that I didn't do at all the last few years.

It sure feels good to be whole again, both physically and emotionally, back with passion and purpose. When it comes to fitness and strength and confidence, you can't just turn them on and off like a light switch when it's time to compete. No, first there must be passion and purpose, and a plan, long before it's time to reach for the run-fast-and-jump-far switch.

This time of year, I normally would not even be taking practice jumps yet. And especially after a full lifting workout. But this is a whole new deal. Even Coach Tellez seemed to be somewhat impressed today, and that is definitely a rarity for him. He is not exactly one to get excited about practice. All he cares about is getting the job done when it counts.

And speaking of which...

I'm setting a goal right now, three weeks and a day until our first meet. Obviously, I'm not exactly Mr. Indoors. I never have been. Sprinters are confined to running shorter distances indoors than outdoors. As a strong finisher, I'm much better outdoors in the 100, where I have enough room to pick off people in the last part of the race. As Ian Thomsen of the *International Herald Tribune* puts it: The way I run, 60 meters is like being cut off in mid-sentence.

I think 1992 was the last time I even ran the 60. But my goal is to run a personal record, anything under 6.60 seconds, first time out of the blocks. It's nothing I'm going to mention to anyone else. But I'll be thinking about it. *Carl Lewis ran his best 60 ever in his first meet of the year.* That's what I want the story to be. That's how I want to set the tone for things to come.

Truth is, though, I can hardly even believe I'm looking forward to an indoor meet.

Saturday, January 13 – Houston

Item in this morning's newspaper: No more American Express for ticket purchases. Only Visa. Seems there was an urgent meeting in Atlanta between top executives of Visa and Olympic officials. Now that would have been an event worth the price of a ticket – no matter how you paid for it.

Monday, January 15 – Houston

Had the Reverend Martin Luther King, Jr., survived the struggles of the civil rights movement and gone on to lead a long, healthy life, he would be waking up this morning to his sixty-seventh birthday. Instead, we have a national holiday in his name, and we celebrate his memory.

Martin Luther King Day offers an ideal opportunity to reflect on the past, and the significance of that past means a great deal to me. But we're also living in a time when we need to be doing so much more than looking back. We need to be addressing the needs of where we are now, and where we are headed, because otherwise we in the African-American community face the unthinkable risk of moving backward instead of forward.

I guess I come at the issue of race relations from a somewhat unusual perspective. In many respects, my success in athletics and business has allowed me to go where I want to go and do the things I want to do. Yet I am well aware life still does not work that way for many African-Americans. And, like any other person of color, I've had my own brushes with racism. In that respect, I will always be a man of color before I am a man of sport, a man of corporate America, or a man of anything else. Arthur Ashe, the late tennis star, put it this way: "In my world, as privileged as it can be at times, there is absolutely no escape from race....I am almost always aware of race, alert to its powers as an idea, sensitive to its nuances in the world."

It was my parents who made it so natural for me to share those sentiments, because I have been forever touched by the fact they were so personally involved in the civil rights movement. They were right in the middle of it, living in Alabama, when I was just a baby. My parents knew and marched with King, and he baptized my brothers Mack and Cleve. Like anyone else my age, most of what I've learned about our history has come from books and television. But the feelings of people who actually experienced the bus boycotts, the fire hoses being turned on them, the senseless beatings and killings, those are the intense feelings I picked up from my parents at a very young age.

Once I was old enough to understand, my mother would tell me: "It was a time of sacrifice. But sometimes if you want to make things better, you have to sacrifice first." Some of the sacrifices were unspeakable. One of my father's closest friends was a man named Chris McNair. His little girl, Denise, was one of four children killed in a 1963 bombing of the 16th Street Baptist Church in Birmingham.

A few years ago, I made a trip to the National Civil Rights Museum at the site of the old Lorraine Hotel in Memphis, where King was shot and killed. The exhibits were so powerful; incredibly sad, of course, but also filled with the hope of all those dreamers. It's hard to describe what it felt like to sit in that replica of the bus on which Rosa Parks protested. It would be impossible to explain the emotions stirred up by being in that room where King spent his last night. We even stood on the balcony where he collapsed in his own blood, and I tried to imagine what it must have been like to hear and feel that gunshot from across the street. I was so affected by the whole experience, I later sent my mother to Memphis so she could see the museum for herself. The most amazing thing for her was finding pictures of so many friends on the walls. Which obviously goes a long way in explaining why this is such an important holiday for us.

So many people these days start talking about race relations, and they soon fall into a conversation that somehow links the O.J. Simpson case with the Million Man March. Next thing you know, they're solving the world's problems by taking sides on a bloody glove and a racist cop and the Nation of Islam. I'm less inclined to enter that kind of discussion, because the issues I see are so much broader than those. Actually, the way I see it, there is really one issue and one issue only when it comes to the future of our community. That issue is education.

Martin Luther King would be very proud of the way some African-Americans have stressed school. But he'd probably be disappointed as a whole. I mean, back in the 1960s blacks were not even allowed to participate in the political process, but they sure knew the issues of the day. Now we can vote all we want, but do we even have the education to understand the issues? Our young people should not be offended by the idea of books. They should be embracing them. But here we've gone all these years, all these years since people like my parents and their contemporaries fought so hard for all of us, and yet so many of us still have not accepted the importance of education.

It sure is a lot easier to be divided and conquered when you're not educated. That's the unfortunate reality we now face when issues such as affirmative action are debated in the political arena. We hear African-Americans complaining all the time about certain politicians, always whites and usually Republicans, who want to do away with affirmative action: "They're taking away our jobs." But if we want to attain our fair share of the jobs, we've got to start doing *our* job, too. We absolutely must educate ourselves.

Sometimes I wonder what Martin Luther King would have to say about where we stand now. In fact, thanks to my parents, thanks to both the historical perspective they shared with me and the intellectual curiosity they instilled in me, I often wonder how someone like King would have evolved through the years and the decades.

Tuesday, January 16 – Houston

A British film crew was here to shoot workout and an interview for a half hour show they're doing on my career. It will be one of about a dozen, I think, in a series the International Olympic Committee is producing on former champions from a variety of sports. Funny thing is, I'm the only one still competing. Guess they figured I'd be done by now.

Anyway, I'm glad they were able to schedule my part so early in the year, because Joe Douglas has already been getting swamped with pre-Olympic media requests. We're trying to handle as many as we can now, before the season starts, so they do not become too much of a distraction. Obviously, it still will not be possible to schedule them all, but we hope to take care of at least the major newspapers, magazines and television networks with one-on-ones, and then anyone else is welcome to attend our regular press conferences before and after meets.

Of course, I've been around long enough to know that no matter how accommodating we try to be, no matter how positive the majority of the coverage, there will always be someone who finds a reason to rip me. There were times early in my career that it bothered me when that happened, especially when I was unfairly portrayed by someone who hardly even knew me, if at all. But my entire perspective has changed so much over the years. Now I realize that I've had it both ways. Some of the positive stories build me up to the point where I'm made to look like a much better person than I really am. Some of the negative stories make me out to be worse than I could possibly be. Nature of the business, I guess, and it really serves no purpose to be unduly affected by any of it. Because life moves on.

Wednesday, January 17 – Houston

How do I get into these things? One minute I'm preparing for an upcoming event at my house — a fundraiser for a non-profit group called Best Buddies — and the next minute I'm on the phone with someone telling me to stick clumps of human hair outside in my flower beds. Never can tell how one thing will lead to the next. Guess I better back up and explain.

Best Buddies is a college-based volunteer program designed to promote special friendships between students and people with mental retardation. The idea is to help integrate individuals with retardation into the mainstream of society. And it works. The organization was created by Anthony Shriver, youngest of the five children of Sargent and Eunice Kennedy Shriver, one of the most prominent power couples in Washington, D.C. Sargent was founding director of the Peace Corps and George McGovern's vice-presidential running mate back in 1972. Eunice, in addition to being part of the most famous political family in America, created the Special Olympics. I've known the Shrivers for years, have worked with Best Buddies since 1989, and now serve on its board of directors.

Last fall Anthony asked if I'd be willing to have a fundraiser at my house. Our original idea was maybe fifty people for a reception. Months ago, we settled on a date, which is two weeks from tomorrow, but that's about the only thing that has not changed dramatically. Everything else has grown way beyond anything I'd imagined. We've got major corporate sponsors. We're going to conduct an auction with incredible items: sports memorabilia, tickets to the Olympics, travel packages to Europe, a few works of art. The local gossip columnist has been plugging the event. And now it looks like we'll have maybe *two hundred* and fifty people instead of fifty. I'll be very surprised if we clear anything less than $100,000 for Best Buddies.

Thank goodness for Carol and the rest of our planning committee. My primary job is preparing the house — and that in itself is enough of a job. That's where the clumps of hair came into play. I spent the afternoon planting flowers because I want the yard to look good for the guests. But I've been having a problem lately with rabbits. I plant something in the day. They eat it at night. So I put in a call to the state Department of Agriculture and was passed along to some expert on rabbits or flowers or whatever.

"Just have to fence in the flowers," he told me.

"Trying to avoid that," I said.

"Do you have a dog you can keep in the yard?"

"I do, but he's young." Ramses, my Rhodesian Ridgeback, has only been around since October. "Don't really want to leave him outside all night."

"How about bright lights? Rabbits don't like bright lights."

"I don't either, and I have a lot of windows."

"Well, then you might want to try mothballs or...hair. You put human hair in the beds, the rabbits smell humans and stay away."

So at least I learned something new today. But I guess I'm just going to take my chances with the rabbits. Don't really want clumps of hair all over the yard. Not exactly the look I'm after.

Thursday, January 18 – Houston

Give us an issue with some bite to it, in or out of sports, and it never takes us long to transform the gym, an airport, a restaurant, wherever we are, into a debate club. That's a major part of what makes it so enjoyable to spend as much time as I do with my training partners – the overall intelligence and interest levels. Politics. Business. Social issues. Religion. We pretty much cover the gamut. This morning, though, we got stuck on a track topic: the questionable future of American sprinting.

I've been sounding the alarms for years now, warning people that unless we initiate major changes, and soon, we're headed for a drought. How bad will it get? I've been saying no American medalists in the 100, no gold, no silver, no bronze, by the Olympics in the year 2000, which would be huge, because we've always dominated the 100. Well, it turned out I was wrong. The shutout came even sooner than I thought it would. Five years sooner. It was last summer at the World Championships in Sweden when we came away empty for the first time anyone could remember.

Unfortunately, I did nothing to help. I ran so poorly at the U.S. national championships, I only qualified for the Worlds in the long jump, and then I had to pull out anyway with that hamstring injury. Leroy Burrell was also out, dogged by the same foot problem that had been bothering him for two years.

And then look what happened: Dennis Mitchell, who usually performs well in the big meets, pulled up injured in a preliminary heat. The second American, Maurice Greene, a decent newcomer but too inexperienced, got knocked out early. So we were down to just one sprinter, Mike Marsh, in the final field of eight, which never happens. We always have at least two Americans, if not all three, in the final. And then even Mike, who I was picking to win the gold, ran a disappointing race. After a bad start, he finished fifth. First and second went to a pair of Canadians, Donovan Bailey and Bruny Surin, and third went to a guy named Ato Boldon from Trinidad. When the final rankings were released, 1995 went down as probably the worst year in the history of American sprinting.

So where do we go from there? First, we need to examine how we have managed to lose the depth of young American talent we used to take for granted. We need to start with kids. It used to be that everyone wanted to be the fastest kid on the block. Fastest from here to the fire hydrant. Here to the street corner. But now it's different. Kids just want to dunk a basketball or score a touchdown. That's what gets all the attention on television. Most kids don't even bother with track and field anymore. And it's all about a lack of marketing. We lose kids, or never even get them, because we have done such a horrible job of getting them excited about our sport.

And what about the young athletes who do initially gravitate toward track and field? We lose too many of them on the way to college. Proposition 48 and other NCAA eligibility rules are claiming way too many of our student-athletes as victims — both African-Americans and whites, but, unfortunately, a disproportionate number of African-Americans.

What happens to their spots on the team? Too many of them are handed over to foreign athletes — many of whom are older and more mature than our typical college freshmen. The foreigners are valuable to coaches who are more concerned with winning on the collegiate level than they are in building a strong pool of American talent for international competition. Don't get me wrong. I'm all for open borders. But our college coaches are too quick to bring in foreigners. We need to spend more time and effort locating talented young Americans and more scholarship money working with them.

After what happened at the World Championships, I think people are finally realizing that the old guard — Leroy Burrell, Mike Marsh, Dennis Mitchell, and me — will not be around forever. So I hope we will finally do something to develop a new generation of American sprinters. The first thing we need to do is accept that our current system is crippled by major flaws. Then we must be willing to make the changes necessary to eliminate them.

Friday, January 19 – Houston

Bob Knight, the Indiana basketball coach, has an indelible way of reminding his players to concentrate on the important things: "Don't fight the rabbits. Because, boys, if you fight the rabbits, the elephants are going to kill you." I read it once in a magazine piece by Frank Deford, one of my favorite writers, and what a perfect line to help us keep things in perspective. It means nothing at all, though, when it comes to my yard — because I still can't get my mind off the rabbits!

I was walking into my room this evening, happened to look out a window, and there was a rabbit right there in the middle of the yard. Just standing there. Probably thinking about which one of my new flowers he wanted for dinner. So I starting banging on the window and yelling at him, like some crazy guy, and the poor rabbit nearly jumped out of his skin. He took off into the woods. But that was it for me. Can't keep fighting the rabbits. Tomorrow I go with the mothballs.

Saturday, January 20 – Houston

When we were kids, both our parents were track coaches, so they used to take Carol and me to practice with them and let us play in the long jump pit. It served as our baby-sitter. Most of the time we just played in the sand, building castles and then smashing them, while Mom and Dad were working with the older kids. Sometimes, though, we'd also imitate the drills everyone else was doing. So, naturally, once we were old enough to get in on the real action, we gravitated back to the sand and started jumping into it, and the long jump has been our favorite event ever since.

When either one of us is jumping in a meet, there might as well be two of us out there on the runway, because we're always in it together. Believe me, unless Carol is broadcasting, if she's anywhere else in the whole stadium, even with sixty thousand people in the place, that piercing voice of hers will find a way of reaching me. I always hear Carol screaming for me, and then I hear about it from friends and athletes who remain in awe of her ability to make sound waves travel impossible distances.

I'm certainly not as loud as Carol when I'm watching her jump, but I'm nonetheless involved every step of the way. I study her approach and form, especially keeping an eye on her checkpoints along the runway, and then report to her between jumps, helping her to make adjustments, especially when Coach Tellez is not around. I've missed that part of being at a track meet the last few years, once Carol broke her foot and stopped jumping, so it's great to have her back again. This afternoon was her first competition since 1992. I went with Carol to watch her jump in a predominantly collegiate meet at the University of Houston.

She was much more nervous than she used to be before a meet. Part of that comes from being away for so long. Part of it comes from knowing she's still not entirely ready yet. But nothing spectacular is going to happen all at once. Carol understands that. Her timing was a little off. She said her approach felt strange. But I think she got more and more comfortable with each jump. Carol ended up in second place, which was fine, but that's not even the important thing. What's important now is getting the feel of competition again, sticking with her training, losing a few more pounds, and then being ready for the outdoor season.

Sunday, January 21 - Houston

Normally my day of rest and relaxation. But today I went out and did the Houston-Tenneco Marathon. Twenty-six-point-two miles on the road. Luckily, I did it in a car. I went along as a spectator to cheer on a friend, Ellen Todd, whose boyfriend John Rodriguez does massage therapy for me.

Ellen certainly was not a threat to win the race or even to finish anywhere near the front. But she's exactly the kind of person who makes an event like this so enjoyable – your average person striving to meet a goal. Ellen is a legal secretary. Forty-one years old. Says she can think of a hundred different things in her life she has started without finishing, but now she wanted to finish something most people would never even start.

It takes a certain degree of confidence to set yourself up for a challenge like that, the willingness to take a risk and possibly fail. It's no different, really, than the mentality required of an athlete trying to win an Olympic medal. In either case, the greatest challenges are those that come from within, and the results will ultimately be measured internally as well, no matter what it says on the external scoreboards or clocks.

First half of the race, John and I drove to different points where we could catch up with Ellen and encourage her. Second half, John stayed out and ran with her. Not me. I'll stick to 100 or 200 meters at a time, thank you. I stayed in the car and continued to meet them along the way.

The finish was incredible. An Ethiopian runner almost made a wrong turn near the finish line but recovered just in time to beat a guy from Wales. By one second. To run all those miles and then have it come down to the last few yards like that – unbelievable.

And our friend Ellen was a champion as well. Which means she finished. She just missed her goal of four hours – and kept telling us how sorry she was about that – but worrying about a few minutes would be entirely missing the point. The point is she ran the thing. She finished.

People ask me all the time: What's it like at the Olympics to stand on that podium with a gold medal around your neck? Well, I believe it's the same as anyone setting a goal and achieving it. Anybody can experience the intensity of that emotional high – it's just that more people share in the celebration of it when you're talking about the Olympics. Maybe nobody else was watching now, but I wanted Ellen to feel like she was standing on one of those podiums. Often it's the people like her, ordinary people challenging and extending themselves, who are the most inspiring athletes of all.

Monday, January 22 – Houston

This is the second time I've kept a diary. The first was just a two-week period during the summer of 1989. I did it while traveling on the European track circuit, for a chapter in my 1990 autobiography, *Inside Track,* because I wanted to give people a glimpse into the nomadic nature of international track and field. During those two weeks I spent time in England, France, Switzerland, Germany, Sweden, and Norway, competing in five meets, promoting another, and filming a television commercial.

And there was really nothing unusual about that trip. I'm all too familiar with way too many airports and hotels. Even when I'm home in the States, I'm not usually home for too long at a time. I'm always going out of town for an event of some kind: an awards banquet or television show, an appearance for a charity or a sponsor, a photo shoot or filming a commercial. There's always something.

So that's the only thing that's been really strange so far about writing these diary entries the last few weeks. I can't believe how many times I've actually been able to put "Houston" at the top of an entry. I can't believe how much I've been home lately – and I love it. That's not the reason Joe Douglas and I have made a concerted effort to keep me here as much as possible, though. The real reason is to stay focused on my work, the only work that matters now, which is preparing myself for the months ahead, getting and staying ready for Atlanta. Everything else needs to be on hold until after the Games. Of course, I'll still make a trip when I must, but I've cut way back, and you'd have to knock me out cold to get me on an international flight. No way I'm going overseas until after Atlanta. It takes too much out of you, both physically and emotionally.

John Lott, the strength and conditioning coach at the University of Houston, who's been working with me on my training program, is a big believer in what he sees as a triangle of fitness. Each side of the triangle, healthy diet, adequate sleep, and proper training, is equally important. Each side affects the others, and only with consistency do we have a chance to reach peak performance. Of course, it's a whole lot easier to maintain that consistency at home than it is on the road – just as it is for any business person who is used to a routine. It's so much more stressful to be on the road. And that's why I'll be perfectly content to keep on writing "Houston" above these diary entries for a while. It's an intentional and integral part of the overall plan.

Tuesday, January 23 – Houston

It has to be one of the true blessings in this world that the cycle of the summer Olympics, once every four years, happens to coincide with the presidential election cycle. No matter how consumed we become with our own efforts, our own passion, we always have an outlet. We can always turn to the campaign trail for the ultimate diversion. What could possibly be more entertaining than the highest form of political theater? And tonight we were offered the opening act of the year. It was the State of the Union address, with President Bill Clinton at center stage, and then the response of Senator Bob Dole, who's looking like he'll be the Republican nominee to face Clinton in November.

I've always been drawn to politics. For one thing, it's the most obvious forum in which to debate the vital issues that both drive and divide us as a nation, and I've always been intensely interested in public policy. I have a great deal of respect for the elected officials who genuinely devote themselves — some of them actually do — to making positive contributions. But that alone would not be enough to keep me glued to the campaign trail. It's the pure entertainment value of it all that keeps me glued. The scheming and scamming. The open attacks as well as the blind hits. Hilarious sound bites. The spin doctors. Polls. Debates. Where else could we find characters and plots like we find in national politics?

Take tonight. The red, white, and blue ceremony of it all. Clinton enters the arena as the reigning champion. One side blows kisses. The other throws darts. The president pays tribute to his wife, Hillary, who's been target of the week because of Travelgate and Whitewater. He salutes the veterans of World War II, and then singles out one of them by name: Bob Dole, of all people. Clinton even introduces us to a couple of heroes who helped save lives after the bombing in Oklahoma City. Talk about tugging on the heartstrings.

And when it finally came time to talk policy, Clinton might as well have been setting off some chemical reaction on the Republican side of the aisle, because there sure was plenty of squirming going on. What could those Republicans possibly do about the fact Clinton was so obviously in total control? Nothing. Not tonight.

Maybe the Republicans would have been best off just hiding from the cameras. I mean, Speaker of the House Newt Gingrich? He looked so pasty and pouty, as one pundit described him. Senator D'Amato from New York? Couldn't tell if he'd been sniffing smelling salts or just needed a visit to the restroom. Then there was Dole, bless his heart, so stiff and old-looking. Sure seemed bitter in that Republican response, didn't he? The way he pushed the word "liberal" off his lips, targeting Clinton with it, it was as if the mere mention of such a label carried with it some mysterious and lethal connotation. It gave Dole such pain to say that word — liberal— but not as much as it gave the rest of us to watch him struggle with that TelePrompTer.

Oh, am I giving myself away here? Not too tough to figure out which side I'm on, huh? That's what makes the campaign season so much fun — taking sides and conducting your own mini-debates with friends and family.

Summer of 1992, we were on the road in Europe for almost six weeks before, during, and after the Olympics. I don't know how I would have made it without the presidential campaign to keep us going. Every night I'd call around the hotel to make sure my Santa Monica Track Club teammates were awake to watch *Crossfire* on CNN. Every day we'd talk and argue and laugh about what we'd seen. Which reminds me of a major problem I'm already having with the current Olympic year. Michael Kinsley recently left *Crossfire* to work with an online company. How am I supposed to get through an Olympic year without him?

Wednesday, January 24 – Houston

"No Pain, No Gain."

It actually made me cringe when I saw that on a T-shirt someone was wearing at the gym today. The whole premise of it – that training your body must make you hurt to make you better – has always been a pet peeve of mine. Because it's so wrong.

Take the guy wearing that shirt this morning. Probably in his early thirties. Maybe working out simply to be fit and healthy, or to stay in shape for a recreational basketball league or something. Pretty much your average person. For someone like that, working out should be something to enjoy, not something that hurts.

Even for a professional athlete, I still don't buy into the theory of push, push, push, until you drop. You need to be smarter than that, or else you're not going to be around very long. It is often more important to rest than it is to drive yourself to the point of pain. Because pain can also mean injury, maybe now, maybe later.

Here's what I think makes the most sense: Your workout schedule should include hard, medium and easy days, and you should never have two hard days in a row. You must allow for recovery between your hard workouts. If you're on a six-day cycle, for example, the order of your workouts should be hard, medium, hard, easy, hard, medium. Believe me, you'll be ready for a day off after all that.

"Get the Rest, Do Your Best." Maybe that's what we ought to have printed on T-shirts we wear to the gym.

Thursday, January 25 – Houston

Talk, talk, talk.

I've been doing a lot of that the last few days, and more is already scheduled for next week. Television shows. News radio. Sports radio. It's a shame they always want us so early in the morning. But such is the life of a meet promoter – doing whatever I can to let people know about the Gallery Furniture Games. Hope to see you there!

Luckily, I don't have to do all the local shows. Leroy Burrell is covering some of them. I sure hope all this talk turns into ticket sales, though, because if there's any correlation between sound waves generated and people in the stands, the place is going to be packed.

Friday, January 26 – Houston

Big breakthrough at the track. We were working on starts, coming out of the blocks and running anywhere from 30 to 60 meters, and Coach Tellez pulled me aside because he'd noticed something I was doing wrong. It was a technical mistake, and he wanted to make sure we corrected it right away.

It was not the start itself. I was reacting pretty well to the gun and was fine the first 15 meters. But then, instead of opening up and really running, instead of lengthening my strides the way I should have been, I was continuing to take short strides. Short, quick strides are exactly what you want in the initial drive out of the blocks. That's what it takes to get going. But once you reach about 15 meters, you need to be opening up that stride and accelerating. I was waiting too long to enter the acceleration phase. It's like rolling a ball across the floor. The sooner the ball builds momentum, the better it'll roll all the way to the wall.

You'd think by now, after all these years, I'd know better than falling back into such a basic error. But it happens. Everyone gets into a bad habit from time to time. And it's amazing how much of a difference something like that makes. Such a subtle thing, but worth maybe a tenth or even two tenths of a second when you're running the 100 – which could easily be the difference between not even making the Olympic team or ending up the gold medalist.

Needless to say, I was very pleased that Coach Tellez had figured

(PHOTO: UNIVERSITY OF HOUSTON)

Thank goodness we've always had Coach Tellez here to lean on. That is 1988 gold medalist Joe DeLoach on the left.

out what I was doing. He said he thought he'd noticed the problem last season but wasn't certain. Now, though, now that I'm bigger up top from all the lifting, he said it was more visible. It looked as if I was trying to muscle my way through, the way shorter, quicker starters do, instead of using one of my natural advantages, my height, which allows me to really open up my stride. I could see where this might sound unduly technical to an outsider, but the very existence of a sprinter is defined by evaluating and tinkering with details like this.

Once you identify and fix a problem, you feel great about it because you know you're improving. So today gave me a tremendous boost of confidence. And the whole process was such a good reminder of how lucky I am to have Coach Tellez. I don't care who you are or how talented you might think you are – you better have a coach who knows what he's doing. You always need someone who can be your eyes when it's impossible to see something yourself.

Monday, January 29 – Houston

We all felt flat this morning. Usually, if we're running 400 meters, I'll know by the 200 mark what kind of a day it's going to be. On a good day, I won't really feel anything at 200, and I'll know I'm going to be fine from there. This morning, though, my legs were screaming at me even before the midway point.

When we were finished, and Mike Marsh wanted to know how it felt, I said, "Hate to admit it, but horrible! My legs were getting tired at about 190."

"Me, too," Mike said. "Actually, I was about the 180 mark."

It was probably an indication that we made a mistake last week. In anticipation of our first meet, which is this Saturday, we adjusted our lifting program, cutting back on the amounts of weight and increasing the numbers of sets and repetitions. We figured that would lessen the stress on our muscles, and help us stay rested and sharp. Now we know better. Unfortunately, what was meant to be easier on the body actually turned out to be harder. Even the weekend off was not enough time to fully recover.

We continue to learn as we go.

Tuesday, January 30 – Houston

When you're hurting, there's no such thing as running through it. Not if you're smart. So, after the way we felt yesterday, Coach Tellez suggested a day of rest, and we agreed. No lifting. No running.

First time I've missed a workout since we started the fall program. Actually, there was one Friday I didn't train. I had to be out of town on business. But I did that Friday workout on Saturday instead. I probably haven't had a stretch of total commitment like this my entire career. Ever. Skipping today made total sense, though, because we can't be trying to recover at the same time we're running in a meet.

Wednesday, January 31 – Houston

In addition to my overall respect for Jesse Owens, my respect for both his athletic accomplishments and the way in which he carried himself through the most difficult of times, there is something else about him that has always stuck in my mind. It is the indignity he suffered not only on Nazi soil while competing on Hitler's playing fields in the 1936 Olympics, but also on his own, where even his post-Olympic celebrity failed to enable him to earn much of a living.

He was eventually forced to make ends meet by racing in exhibitions against horses, dogs, and motorcycles.

Jesse was put through the grind of an incredible shrinking machine, temporarily reduced from the status of Olympic hero to something of a freak show participant, because before anything else, he was still the grandson of slaves. No matter how many medals he collected or how much pride he generated, he was still a black Olympic hero in a very white society. Not even the best sprinter on the planet could run away from the reality of that.

It is with direct attention to the irony, then, that I view one of the most bizarre developments of this pre-Olympic season: the aggressive marketing of the late Jesse Owens. I mention it now because I just received a promotional piece in the mail – the announcement of a plan to capitalize on the memory and image of this man who has been dead for sixteen years. General Motors, Kodak, adidas, even the U.S. Olympic Committee, which never did enough for him when he was alive – they all want a piece of him now. Corporate folks are placing Jesse in advertising around the world, using old footage and photographs, and that is only one component of the deal-making.

His name and likeness are also being licensed for sale on a vast array of products: T-shirts, mugs, water bottles, trading cards and telephone debit cards, to name a few. There is even a special Jesse Owens logo to denote "brand" status. Talk about the power of creativity. CMG Worldwide, an Indianapolis firm that actually specializes in the marketing of dead athletes, movie stars and other celebrities, has represented the estate of Jesse Owens since 1987. But this year brings a new twist, because CMG has packaged it as the sixtieth anniversary of the 1936 Games.

Now, don't get me wrong, we should all know and accept by now that the Olympics are big business. Huge television contracts. Corporate sponsors with public relations tie-ins. Endorsement deals for the athletes. Everyone trying to cash in on the hype that comes with the quadrennial spectacle. But the sixtieth anniversary of the year Jesse Owens won his four gold medals? Sure, we're all in the habit of celebrating an occasion as memorable as the sixtieth year since a sporting event, right?

As a youngster, I had a chance to speak with Jesse, then fifty-seven years old, when I was competing in one of his youth meets. The mem-

As an Olympic hero, Jesse Owens had to earn a living by running in exhibitions against horses. Years after his death, he stars in a corporate marketing campaign.

ory of our brief conversation, the emphasis he placed on both having fun and working hard, has always stuck with me. Jesse has always been an inspiration to me. But I definitely don't remember him sharing any advice about telephone debit cards.

It all makes good sense, I guess, because it was just last year that CMG had so much success with its campaign to sell the one hundredth birthday of the late Babe Ruth. There were hundreds of products and promotions, and a healthy bottom line, with a Ruthian estimate of twenty-five million dollars in retail sales. Next year it will be the fiftieth anniversary of the season Jackie Robinson broke major league baseball's color barrier. Yet another opportunity to bring together the drama of yesteryear and the cash register of today.

Of course, none of this would have meant a whole lot to me back when I first met Jesse and learned, from my parents and from books, about the magnitude of his achievements. Now, though, with the benefit of time and perspective, there is something satisfying to me about the current popularity and marketability of Jesse. It is something deeper than the initial chuckle brought on by the idea of the so-called sixtieth anniversary celebration – because it's almost like Jesse is finally getting his fair share.

In terms of the history books, the wrongs of his past were corrected long ago. He has already been afforded his due as one of the greatest champions of all time. But now he's getting his fair share as well. There is a distinct difference between the two. I'm pleased because of the financial benefits this will offer his family. It will also help refresh, and even elevate, our collective memories of someone they loved very much. And, who knows, maybe even Jesse Owens himself is looking down on all of this with pride, with a knowing smile, with a clear understanding of the historical significance.

One of the most consistent struggles throughout the course of my career has been working to push the entire sport of track and field from the Dark Ages of amateurism into the enlightened arena of professionalism. Dead men selling was never what I had in mind. Yet I can't help but marvel at the whole concept.

Obviously, we can use this anniversary campaign as a yardstick of just how far the commercial side of the Olympics has raced ahead since Jesse Owens made his name, or his brand, or whatever it was. We can also use it to gauge the incredible advances in the overall scope of sports marketing. Finally, though, this Jesse Owens campaign might even be worth celebrating on a much broader scale. Because, ultimately, it sends a pretty strong message about our society as a whole. It tells us that sixty years after Jesse was all but ignored by the overwhelmingly white world of corporate America, sixty years after he was reduced to running against those horses, we are finally at the point where it is perfectly natural for a black man to be held up as a role model not only for his own people, but for all people.

Thursday, February 1 – Houston

No matter how many times I'm asked the same questions about the same subjects – running in the Olympics, the age factor, drugs in sports, whatever – I try to keep it at least somewhat stimulating by including new anecdotes. But there's only so much you can do to keep it fresh and interesting. That's why the most enjoyable interviews, especially those on live radio or television, are usually the ones where the host or another guest comes up with something totally off the wall.

Exhibit A: one of those in-studio shows I just did on local television to promote the meet Saturday. The host was challenging the audience to answer two impossibly obscure trivia questions. Who was the tenth-round pick of the Chicago Bulls in the 1984 NBA draft? And who was the twelfth-round pick of the Dallas Cowboys in the 1984 NFL draft? Next thing I knew, the monitor was filled with hilarious action footage. First it was my head placed on the body of Michael Jordan playing for the Bulls. Then it was my head on the body of Michael Irvin playing for the Cowboys. Because I was the answer to both trivia questions. Of course, I never played a minute for either team. Drafting me was basically a publicity ploy, I guess. But reacting to that goofy-looking footage, which caught me completely off guard, that had to be about as hard as I've laughed on a television show.

Still, it was nothing compared to the most creative stunt someone pulled on me during a radio show. It was late last summer, shortly after we returned home from the World Championships in Sweden, and it started out innocently enough. Jim Dent, the host of a syndicated show on Prime Sports Radio out of Dallas, was asking about the Olympics and other stuff I could talk about in my sleep. But then he wanted to take just one phone call. Some guy had been bugging him to get on the show.

"Mister Carl," the caller screeched in a strange accent. "Mister Carl, this is Harashi."

Harashi?

He said he was calling from Bangladesh. He was so happy to hear I had met his daughter in Sweden and that we had hit it off. He was so happy to hear we were engaged.

"And we want very much to meet you," Harashi insisted. "We hope you have a big family, and we want to let you know we love you very, very much."

I was speechless.

"Carl, do you have any idea who that is?" the host interjected.

"No clue," I said, knowing someone was playing a game with me, but struggling to figure out who it could be. So I offered Harashi a deal: "If you can get Sinatra to sing at the wedding, it's a go." And that just cracked him up. It cracked him up so much that he finally went to his normal voice and revealed his real identity. "Harashi" was Dale

Brown, the longtime Louisiana State University basketball coach and a friend of mine. The producer of the show had arranged with him to call in while I was on.

Of course, knowing Dale, I doubt he bothered to tell anyone what he was going to do once he was on the air. But that's Dale. He's not exactly the most predictable person in the world, but definitely one of the most entertaining. He'll do almost anything for a laugh. And his energy level — always exploding with positive energy — is incredible. It's like he's Norman Vincent Peale with a whistle and a clipboard, and also a game plan to help his athletes grow in ways that extend well beyond the basketball court. That's what makes him so special.

It was nice of him to call in. But Harashi better watch out. He needs to remember what they say about paybacks — or do they have that saying in Bangladesh?

Friday, February 2 – Houston

I'm not sure why, but I'm much more relaxed than I normally am for the start of a new season. I usually get pretty worked up about the first meet of the year because it can feel almost foreign, like the first day of school. I mean, someone will actually be timing our performances and announcing the results to the world. No matter how long I've been doing this, no matter how much experience I bring to the starting line, I am nonetheless beginning all over again, just like anyone else.

So why am I so relaxed? Tomorrow night I'll be up against a very strong field, including two of the fastest men in the world, and I still have that goal I set a few weeks ago. I want to run a personal best right off the bat. Yet I find myself pretty low-key about the whole thing. I'm fixed in a position where I'm trying to be enthusiastic. I want to get into it, but I'm also stuck with being realistic. It's still indoors, which makes it impossible to fool myself into thinking this will be anything more than a glorified training session. Leroy Burrell is the only one in our group who has even geared his workouts to prepare for the 60, so I'd have to pick him to be the favorite.

No doubt, a fast time and a victory would be a big plus for me as far as starting off on the right foot. But I don't know. With all the promoting Leroy and I have been doing, all the energy we have put into presenting a first-class, entertaining meet, I almost feel less of a burden as a runner and more of a responsibility in terms of making sure we put on a great show for the fans.

Saturday, February 3 – Houston

The inaugural Gallery Furniture Games go down as a split decision. The meet was tremendous. I was terrible.

First the good news. What a feeling it was to walk into our new fieldhouse on the Houston campus and see a capacity crowd of almost 4,500, with everyone totally into it. The whole idea was to get away from being just another track meet, to pump it up with lively entertainment. Sure, we wanted great races, and had them, and without ever letting the action slow down, because we limited the number of races and kept the program tight. But in addition to great races, we also wanted to make sure we had the atmosphere of a bigtime special event, and that is exactly what we created.

Miss Universe sang the national anthem. We had a laser light show produced by the same guy who does it at the Houston Rockets basketball games, and another NBA-style feature, jock rock music booming between races. The Ferrari was sitting right there on the infield as an incentive, begging for someone to break a world record. And once the competition was over, the top athletes were seated to sign autographs and pose for pictures. All that for the price of admission! No question, the fans experienced a meet, an event, they will always remember.

As did the athletes. It was one thing to hear Leroy Burrell, Mike Marsh, or any of the other locals going on and on about how great it was to be part of something so new and exciting (not exactly commonplace for American track and field). It was even better, though, to hear it from the world-class competitors who came here basically as a favor to us, to see if they could help us start something special. People like Dan O'Brien and Roger Kingdom and Ruth Wysocki. "It was like a European meet because the fans were really into it," said Suzy Hamilton, a U.S. Olympian who ran away with the 800. "A meet like this, a new one in a new location, gives me hope that we can help bring the sport back in this country." It was music to my promoter ears.

I just wish I could be nearly as excited about the way I ran. But I'm hardly in the habit of celebrating a last-place finish. I felt like I cleared the blocks OK, but then I made some very bad mistakes. I stayed too low. It took me way too long to be up and running, and the 60 is much too short a distance to be wasting time. Everyone just got out and left me, like I was standing still. Leroy won with a time of 6.64 seconds, nowhere near the world record of 6.41, so the Ferrari was safe, as it remained throughout the evening. Mike was second in 6.71. I was fifth – last – with a turtle time of 6.84. Even though I knew I was dead meat right from the start, at least I only had to go 60 meters to take my beating; outdoors, I would have had to endure almost double the distance before getting drilled.

Most people are somewhat apprehensive about saying much to me after such a lousy performance. I guess they don't want to hurt my feelings or offend me. Thank goodness, though, I can always count on the people closest to me to come right at me with their thoughts. No pulling punches for someone like Joe Douglas. After the meet, we went straight out to dinner, and I was so thirsty, the first thing I did was down a huge glass of cranberry juice in about two seconds flat. When I came up for air, Joe was just cracking up.

"What Joe?"

"Faster than your 60," he said.

I laughed along with him. But knowing Joe the way I do, it will not be long before his laughter turns into concern. Or perhaps making light of the situation was just his way of putting a temporary mask on that concern. Because no matter how early in the year it is, no matter the fact it was just an indoor 60, Joe will make more out of this than he needs to. He probably won't sleep too well tonight because he'll be trying to figure out what I'm doing wrong, and he'll be worrying about the months to come.

We sprinters and the people around us definitely tend to analyze and overanalyze way more than the average bear – and Joe even more so than the average track person. If someone outside our little world ever observed the way we spend hours on end dissecting something as simple as running from point A to point B, he'd almost have to conclude we're absolutely nuts. But that's us. That's the world in which we live.

Sunday, February 4 – Houston and Atlanta

As expected, the laughter quickly gave way to the concern, which was of course accompanied by a far-reaching search for explanations. Joe Douglas had any number of theories. I'm not running enough. I'm lifting too much. I'm just not into it – still not where I need to be as far as emotional commitment.

Talking to another SMTC insider, Joe then offered the harshest assessment of all: "I just don't want Carl to go out with half an effort. He's too good for that. There's too much at stake. If he's not going to be focused, he needs to just forget the whole thing. He can just go to NBC and be a commentator or something." Sometimes Joe forgets I'm always going to hear the whispers. Or maybe that was precisely his intention.

Anyway, all I could say was: "Let's not overreact. I'm training well. I feel good. The only disappointment is that I didn't go out and run a technically sound race. I made mistakes. But I certainly don't see that as any reason to panic."

It's not like I run one bad race and all of a sudden I'm just obsolete. We're still in this thing for Atlanta – June, July, August – not a little indoor meet in Houston. Ultimately, people are going to remember one thing, Atlanta, which is where we headed for a Nike dinner this evening and then promotional work all day tomorrow.

Monday, February 5 – Atlanta

Never in my wildest dreams did I ever imagine I'd be back with Nike. Not after the way our relationship ended the first time around. But time has a way of healing bruises, good business is still good business, and now that we're back together, it is once again a very comfortable fit.

Some background is in order. Throughout the early and mid-1980s, I was under contract to Nike, my first major endorsement deal. Actually, it was a consulting agreement that put me in their shoes and clothing, and their advertising as well. I was able to spend some time with Phil Knight, the founder and president, and many of the other top executives, and was always impressed with their innovative approaches to both design and marketing. Unfortunately, they allowed the shortcomings of one certain Nike representative, no longer there, to create some major communication problems. Next thing we knew, a combination of negatives pushed the relationship beyond repair. We

(PHOTO: NIKE)

Unveiling the new Olympic uniforms at the Super Show in Atlanta.

even ended up in court, in 1987, before finally settling our differences, and by then I was already with another shoe company, Mizuno.

With that in mind, you can imagine the reaction from people in the know when I peeled off my Santa Monica sweats just before the long jump finals at the 1995 national championships. Because, amazingly enough, I was once again wearing the Nike swoosh on my uniform, the first public indication we had just agreed to rejoin forces, through the Atlanta Games and beyond. It was the result of incredible patience and persistence on the parts of both Joe Douglas and a number of Nike people throughout more than a year of discussion. It took that long to put our previous differences completely behind us, and to forge a new understanding of exactly what would be expected of each other.

And what a pleasure it has been working with the new track and field people who had joined the company. The relationship has been perfect for both of us. We did an event for kids last summer in Sweden. We spent a few days together last fall at Nike headquarters in Oregon for the Olympic Summit, with athletes from all sports. We did a photo shoot in Houston for print advertising. We got together in New York for groundbreaking on the new Niketown store.

And now this: a day of big laughs and fun on the runway. Not the long jump runway, but the kind of runway usually reserved for fashion models. This was the big day at the Super Show, the annual sporting goods trade convention, and we were officially unveiling the 1996 USA Track & Field team uniforms. Five other Nike-sponsored athletes (Jackie Joyner-Kersee, Gail Devers, Sandra Farmer-Patrick, Michael Johnson, and Dan O'Brien) paraded around the stage with me in the new gear. And we had a blast. Lots of whistles, wild expressions, and lively reactions as we went through our exaggerated moves.

Once we were done with the show, and the interviews that followed, I had a chance to visit briefly with Phil Knight for the first time after all these years. He was extremely kind in welcoming me back. And I told him it was great to be home again.

Tuesday, February 6 – Houston

I was hoping the day away from home would give everyone a chance to put that first race behind us. It only took a few minutes back in the gym to realize nobody was ready to do that. This was not just about me. Everyone seemed a bit uneasy about the season opener. Even Leroy Burrell, who won, was eager to evaluate everything we're doing right and wrong.

Coach Tellez was off in Japan, speaking at a clinic, so we sat down with John Lott, our strength and fitness coach. It was Leroy, Mike Marsh, Floyd Heard, Mark Witherspoon (another training partner), and me, all crowded into John's office in the gym, and there was definitely some tension in there. We each had pretty strong opinions about where our training needs to go from here.

But the thing that bothered me most was: Why are we even considering changes at this point? Once everyone else was out of the room, I told John: "Look, you have a plan, Coach Tellez has a plan, I have a plan, and I still have total confidence in what we're doing. The way I see it, there's simply no reason to move away from our plans. We're in this far. We're committed. So we should stick with everything we're doing." And that is exactly what we decided on. Everyone just needs to chill.

Even Coach T. There was a message from him on my answering machine, from Japan: "Carl, I've been thinking about your race, and I just don't know what you're doing. It's like you're not even thinking. Like your mind is somewhere else. We'll talk when I get back." Man, I wish everyone would just chill.

Wednesday, February 7 – Houston

So Emmitt Smith of the Dallas Cowboys wants to make football an Olympic sport. At the Super Show in Atlanta, Emmitt said he wants in by the year 2000. Of course, we know it's nothing more than a publicity stunt. Reebok is going to feature Emmitt and his Olympic dream in a marketing campaign. But the mere mention of yet another Olympic sport, even as a gimmick, should remind us that we've already gone too far. It should remind us of ballroom dancing.

My initial response was: Kidding, right? But, no, the International Olympic Committee (I.O.C.) was absolutely serious last year when it declared ballroom dancing a "provisional" sport that might eventually be included in the Summer Games. Please, spare us. How exactly are we defining "sport" these days? Do we really want to see "athletes" in prom wear?

Ballroom dancing in the Olympics, however that would work, is a totally ridiculous idea. *Sports Illustrated* declared it a "sign that the apocalypse is upon us," and plenty of others took their shots. In addition to the well-deserved wisecracks, though, there is actually a substantive reason to avoid adding ballroom dancing, or anything else, for that matter, to the summer agenda. The Games are already feeling the crunch of too many sports. Athletes are crowded into inadequate housing. Competition venues are forced further and further outside the host city. Security becomes more and more of a problem.

I.O.C. leaders keep promising to do something about the size of the Games. But every "sport" or "event" or "hobby" wants in on the fun (i.e. the exposure and the money). Instead of subtracting, the I.O.C. keeps adding. Beach volleyball and mountain biking, for example, will be introduced in Atlanta, with badminton and table tennis making return appearances. All of which will help push the total number of competitors past the ten thousand mark.

So, no, we do not need ballroom dancing. We do not need Emmitt

Smith and his football buddies. What we need is population control.

Thursday, February 8 – Houston

Nothing like having a couple hundred people over for dinner to get things jumping. The Best Buddies fundraiser turned out to be everything we wanted it to be, and then some, for which I owe a huge thanks to the committee members who worked so hard. The house and yard looked great, with all the decorations and special displays, including old pictures and all sorts of Olympics memorabilia. The food and entertainment were just right. And the auction was incredible. We ended up clearing even more than our goal of $100,000.

Still, none of those things meant much at all in comparison to meeting and hearing from two young women named Suzanne Taylor and Leticia Gonzales, who are, in the ultimate sense of the term, Best Buddies. Suzanne is a 25-year-old with mental retardation who lives in a special group home, called the Intrigue House, in San Antonio. Leticia is a senior majoring in sociology at St. Mary's University, also in San Antonio. Together, they have shared a wide array of incredibly meaningful and enjoyable experiences since meeting through Best Buddies.

"The way I viewed mental retardation before meeting Suzanne, it was more of a fear than anything," Leticia says. "It was just a matter of not knowing, not understanding. Suzanne immediately broke that stereotype for me. First time I met her, she was sitting me down, asking if she could get anything for me, not the other way around, and she went and got us something to drink. She's very functional, and a lot of fun to be with. A real go-getter. More so than me, actually."

"Before meeting Letti," Suzanne says, using her nickname for Leticia, "if anyone ever asked me, 'Have you ever had a friend without disability?' I would have told him, 'No, I haven't. Only teachers, staff at the group home, parents, coaches with Special Olympics.' I mean, I have been knowing Letti now for almost two years, and our friendship has grown leaps and bounds.

"I've basically learned it is OK for me, as an individual with a disability, to be a friend with a person that doesn't have a disability. Of course, I know inside of me I am still a special person, with a disability, but it makes me feel so normal when I'm with Letti. If I can be

(PHOTO: HOUSTON CHRONICLE)

A night for Best Buddies. Carol is on the left. Eunice Kennedy Shriver and son Anthony join us.

involved with normal people, I'm going to do it. That not only teaches me, it teaches them also. They don't always have to be with people who don't have disabilities."

Together, Suzanne and Leticia go to dinner, to the movies, to the library, to clubs, to all the places young friends go. Together, they are leaders of the Best Buddies program at St. Mary's, sharing and spreading a beautiful picture of just how powerful it can be to reach out and participate. And so, both as a tribute to them and to educate everyone attending the fundraiser, we invited Suzanne and Leticia to speak after dinner. They both spoke with such passion and simplicity, and it was the one time all night that the place was absolutely silent, because the message was so unmistakably strong. Suzanne and Leticia simply owned us.

One of the most amazing parts of Suzanne's tale was the way she spoke of the time, soon after joining Best Buddies, when she was chosen to attend the organization's leadership conference in Miami.

"I was scared to death," is the way she put it. "Terrified. My first time being on an airplane my whole entire life. But I thought to myself, Maybe it will be worth it, because I am going somewhere new. I'm going to do something worthwhile. I will become a leader."

And she did.

"One thing I basically learned was how to work closer with people. And I also learned that it takes more to be a leader than to be a follower."

By the time Suzanne was done speaking, there were more than a few moist eyes in the crowd. It's one thing to help raise money for a good cause – another thing altogether to help raise the good cause itself. Thanks to Suzanne and Leticia, we were able to do both.

Friday, February 9 – Houston

It was no big deal to be putting away plates and chairs and all that type of stuff the morning after a party. Nothing unusual about that. But it was entirely something else to be packing away my gold medals – especially so soon after seeing them all out in one place for the first time. Well, all but one of them.

It was Anthony Shriver who suggested the medals ought to be displayed where guests could look at them. It was a natural way to build on the "House of Olympic Gold" theme. What Anthony didn't know when he mentioned the idea was that the medals had never even been out before. After each Olympics, I've tucked away the new medals in a bank vault with the others. It's always funny how kids, and sometimes even adults, will see me out somewhere and ask to look at one of the medals, as if I'd just be carrying them around in my pocket.

For the party, though, I agreed with Anthony. The medals would be a nice touch. We temporarily mounted them on a wall, in a display case, and below each medal we put a card with my memories printed on it. Now, I've never been one to sit around and dwell on the past, but this unexpectedly turned into an exception. Writing the messages for those cards, and then seeing them exhibited with the medals, a neatly organized row of ribbons and gold, I was surprised how deeply my emotions were touched. It really made me think about what was represented there – and I was genuinely moved. Based on comments I got during the party, it seemed that a few of the medals, and the stories attached to them, stuck out as crowd favorites.

1992 Olympics. 4 x 100 relay. Barcelona, Spain. *Our own version of the Dream Team. We put on a clinic. I'll always remember the roar of that crowd high above the mountain by the sea.* To this day, it amazes me how many people so clearly remember that race. Sure, it was a world record, but that was only part of the excitement. There was something extra that night, the energy of the crowd and the whole atmosphere, that carried us to another level. Maybe it was the fact it was the final night of the Games. It was like all these thousands of people in the stadium were celebrating together, all these people from everywhere in the world, because this was the perfect opportunity to share ourselves one more time before returning to our homes.

1988 Olympics. 100 meters. Seoul, Korea. *Notice the extra wrinkles in the ribbon. Pre-owned gold?* That one required some explaining, and also drew some laughs. Of course, most people remember the incident. It was the race after which Ben Johnson was caught on steroids and stripped of the gold, which then went to me. That's where the wrinkles came into play. I don't know what in the world Ben was doing with that medal while he had it, but it sure was a mess by the time he gave it back. I mean, the least he could have done was find an iron and do something about those wrinkles.

And then there was a special area above the display case in recognition of the missing medal — and in honor of my father. 1984 Olympics. 100 meters. Los Angeles. *My first gold medal. I was overwhelmed with excitement, joy, relief — all the possible good feelings wrapped up in one. This is the medal I later buried with my father.* Hard as it is to believe, it's been almost nine years since he died of cancer. I buried the medal in his hand because that first event in my first Olympics had always carried such a special meaning for him. I've missed my father so much since he left us in 1987, and think about him all the time, but it always gives me a good feeling to think of him with that medal in his hand the last time I saw him.

This morning, after returning the other medals to the vault, I took that card describing the first one and set it on a window sill above my bed. Next to it, I placed an old picture of my father on his way to a track meet, smiling, holding his camera, the rising sun of the Santa Monica Track Club logo proudly displayed on the chest of his shirt. Vintage Bill Lewis.

From now on, my father will be looking out at me from the window sill above my bed.

Saturday, February 10 – Houston

All it took was two and a half hours for Jenny Spangler, small and sweet but also relentless, to transform herself into a female Rocky. She began the day as a total unknown, a thirty-two-year-old computer systems analyst who just a few months ago did not even have anywhere to train. When she lined up for the U.S. Olympic marathon trials in Columbia, South Carolina, she was ranked number sixty-one in the field. Then she ran right past all the favorites, people who were actually asking each other who she was, and ended the day a champion. Her time of 2 hours, 29 minutes, 54 seconds was second best in the history of the marathon trials.

It will certainly go down as one of the great triumphs of the year, and just hearing about it by telephone made my whole weekend. Of course, I was hearing about it from Joe Douglas, who was so excited he probably could have gone out and run a marathon himself. See, Jenny had done it with the rising sun of the Santa Monica Track Club on her chest. She became our first member of the 1996 U.S.

Olympic team. And what a story.

Jenny once won a race called the Grandma's Marathon in Minnesota, setting an American junior record in the process, but that was all the way back in 1983, and she pretty much disappeared after that. She was thirty-third in the 1984 Olympic trials, and forty-ninth in 1988. Then she went back to school for a master's in business administration, still running when she felt like it, but only for herself, not competing. The comeback started in 1993 but almost came to an end last year when she suffered a painful stress fracture in her foot. Injured and almost broke, she was about to concede that maybe her body had not been built to house a champion.

That's when one of Joe's former runners, Willie Rios, started working with her. Willie was himself an Olympian, running the 1,500 meters for Puerto Rico in the 1968 Games. Now he's a Chicago lawyer who coaches on the side. But what was he going to do with Jenny and her training partners, several other Olympic hopefuls, when the brutal cold of winter hit the midwest? Willie turned to Joe, who offered the support of the club, temporarily moving Jenny and the others out to California. Of course, Joe is the eternal optimist, so I was never quite sure what to think of his regular updates on the progress Jenny was making. But now we know he was right all along.

I'm so happy for Joe, who works and works and works, always putting his athletes first, to make things like this happen. And I'm also thrilled for our new Rocky. I mean, Jenny. No doubt, the memory and impact of this day will be with her forever, and I can't wait to watch her run in Atlanta. I just know she's going to make the most of her Olympic experience.

Monday, February 12 – Houston

Imagine having a birthday party where a thousand admirers come from all over the world, Japan, Africa, India, Europe, and from all across the United States, and they come bearing so much more than gifts. They bring with them expression boatloads full of love and gratitude and joy-filled hearts, each vessel prayerfully and soulfully packed for the uplifting journey to its spiritual destiny port. Consider it in precisely those words because that is the way Sri Chinmoy himself might describe it — and because that is the only way I could even

(PHOTO: MARAL)

As my friend Sri Chinmoy (right) says, I should think young, and then I will run young.

try to capture the intensity of the feelings last August when I went to New York for the celebration of his sixty-fourth birthday.

Sri Chinmoy is a spiritual teacher with whom I have been close for years. He has been tremendously supportive of me in both my career and my personal life. He even gave me a new name, Sudhahota, pronounced Shoot-a-hota, which is a Sanskrit name meaning unparalleled sacrificer of immortality. Pretty heavy. (I never have asked Sri Chinmoy for a translation of that translation.)

Of course, as soon as I mention being close with someone I call "Guru" and consider a powerful source of inspiration, people with closed minds immediately look for a way to attack and reject what I'm saying. They wonder what in the world has gotten into me. But this is not a cult or anything like that. It is a collection of free and open-minded people drawn to someone with two primary goals: helping others find their own spiritual way, their own inner peace, and trying to steer the global community toward becoming what Sri Chinmoy calls a Oneness-World.

Sri Chinmoy is a native of India who first came to the United States in 1964 and has been leading meditation sessions at the United Nations for more than twenty-five years. He is himself, in a sense, one of the most prolific diplomats of the world, constantly praying, writing, singing, drawing, and teaching, all for the betterment of humanity. He is based in New York, borough of Queens, but often travels, working on a vast array of international programs with support from people such as Mikhail Gorbachev, Mother Teresa, Pope John Paul II, Nelson Mandela, Archbishop Desmond Tutu, and Queen Elizabeth II.

As an active Christian, raised in a Lutheran church but no longer associated with any particular denomination, I was somewhat cautious when I was first getting to know Sri Chinmoy back in 1983. But he has never once tried to take anything away from my relationship with the Lord. In fact, by fostering my spiritual growth, he has only enhanced that relationship. That might be difficult for some people to understand, an Indian guru having such an impact on a devoted Christian, but I've always tried to remain pretty open-minded in all that I do. Others, of course, are equally free to think whatever they want about my relationship with Sri Chinmoy. But none of that will affect me. None of it will affect what I think of him.

Anyway, I mention all of this now because I've been thinking about something Sri Chinmoy said to me during that visit for his birthday. It has always amazed me how often he knows just the right thing to say or do in my presence, and this was clearly one of those occasions. It was soon after I had pulled out of the World Championships with that hamstring injury, and there were so many people writing me off as being too old to compete anymore. Washed up. Time to hang up the spikes. But Sri Chinmoy, almost out of nowhere, it seemed, just blurted out his analysis of the situation one day at lunch, emphasizing the positive, as always, and even suggesting a game plan for the mind.

He said: "The media, when they say you are done, it is like they want to put negative ink spots on your heart. Ignore it. Do not even read it. You have to forget about your age. Be thirteen. Always think of this number, thirteen, and keep the energy and desire of someone who is thirteen. Then you will always be young. You will always run young."

After my first race of the year, that disaster in the 60, and then all the sniping and second-guessing that followed last week, I guess it should come as no surprise that those words of encouragement from Sri Chinmoy are once again fresh in my mind. I will keep reminding myself of the power and energy behind them. With the naysayers once again out in full force, I will continue to do whatever it takes to keep filling my thoughts with positives.

Tuesday, February 13 – Houston

I did what they call an on-line chat session for an hour this evening. It was part of my work with NetNoir, "the soul of cyberspace," which is an Afrocentric service available on America Online (keyword: NetNoir). NetNoir has been great because it's my first road map to the information superhighway, and it's incredible to see some of what's out there.

The chat sessions are live and interactive, meaning anyone with America Online can ask questions or offer comments. Most of what I got tonight was about Atlanta and the Olympics in general, and there were other interesting topics, such as civil rights, stories about my parents, advice for young athletes. But the question of the night had to be: If I were racing against Deion Sanders, how far ahead would I be at the 100-yard mark? Answer: I really don't know. But I do know and like Deion, and he might hear this, so I'll say it would be a good race.

I've also been writing a variety of general sports columns for NetNoir, everything from basketball to football to boxing. Of course, I sometimes write about track and field as well, but usually prefer when the topic is something out of the ordinary. Those are the columns I enjoy the most – both reading them in newspapers and writing them for NetNoir.

Wednesday, February 14 – Houston

I've been on a variety of sports trading cards put out by companies that sell baseball cards and other collectibles. But I've never been on one like this. I've never before been on one designed to save lives – because it's actually an organ donor card. The first sample, hot off the presses, just arrived by overnight mail, and I'm extremely pleased with the way it turned out. The purpose is to reach as many people as possible about the desperate need for organ and tissue donors, an issue on which I've been working for years.

The beauty and power of donation is the way it transforms the end of one life into the fresh beginning of another – or several others.

A friend in the transplant community recently showed me a T.S. Eliot quote: "What we call the beginning is often the end. To make an end is to make a beginning. The end is where we start from." And that is certainly the case when an organ or tissue is donated for transplantation.

I saw it myself back in 1989 when I shared the dramatic fall and rise of a special friend, Wendy Marx. She was twenty-two years old, happy and healthy, enjoying her first year out of college, Duke University, when she was hit with a severe case of Hepatitis B. The virus quickly destroyed her liver and she slipped into a coma. I'll never forget standing by Wendy's hospital bed and holding her hand while she lay so still and silent. The doctors were saying she had less than twenty-four hours to live. Then came the Gift of Life: an organ donor and successful transplant surgery.

Six months later, with Wendy back at full strength and eager to parlay her near-death experience into a powerful message of hope for others, we formed the non-profit Wendy Marx Foundation for Organ Donor Awareness. Wendy and I have been all over the country together to conduct a variety of programs. Inevitably, though, I end up talking about donation no matter where I am or what I'm doing; in stadiums and at media events around the world, of course, but even more so in private, one-on-one situations. At the barber shop. On the street. At the gas station. No matter where it is, I always tell people the same things: You can save someone's life later by making a decision now. Once you have shared that decision with your family, it is something that will never again affect you while you're alive.

We Americans do so much planning for birth. We decorate a room for the baby. We attend classes to prepare for the delivery. We read books about parenting. But we try so hard to ignore the other end of life. We do so little to prepare ourselves and our families for death. We need to reach the point in our society where a family discussion about organ donation gets at least equal billing with the decision about what color to paint the baby's room.

Unfortunately, the public campaign to save lives through organ and tissue donation continues to be an uphill battle. Back when Wendy needed a donor, she was one of almost nineteen thousand people on the national waiting list for a transplant of some kind. It was the severity of her condition that catapulted her to the top of the list and allowed her to be assigned a donor. But the list keeps growing and growing, with more than forty thousand people in the U.S. now waiting for a new kidney, liver, heart, or some other organ to keep them alive. Each and every day, on average, eight people on that list die waiting. It is a staggering statistic. But we can change that. We *need* to change that. We *must* change that.

The best thing about our own personal tale is that more than six years after Wendy had that liver transplant, more than six years after we were told she had maybe twenty-four hours to live, she remains with us, once again healthy, happy, vibrant. She remains on the West Coast, working for an Internet company. As much as anything, though, Wendy is living, breathing, smiling proof that organ donation works. She has inspired me so many times, in so many ways, and is certainly responsible for my commitment to this new donor card program. She and the family of Mickey Mantle.

Most of us heard at least something about Mantle, the baseball great, when he underwent a liver transplant but then died last summer as a result of cancer. It was about as high-profile a case as we've had in the history of transplantation, with a massive public debate about whether Mantle should have been given the organ in the first place. I firmly believe he should have. His drinking days were long gone, and, as was the case with Wendy, it was the severity of his condition, not his celebrity status, that allowed him to move swiftly up the waiting list. Despite the way certain journalists and medical ethicists chose to portray the situation, every indication was that the system worked exactly as it was designed to work.

Anyway, the most important legacy of the whole ordeal has already proven to be the commitment of the Mantle family and friends to make a longterm impact on the public campaign for donors. It was that immediate commitment that brought me together with Mickey's widow, Merlyn Mantle, and their three sons, Danny, David, and Mickey Jr. It was last August, just two days after the funeral. Knowing of my longtime interest in organ and tissue donation, the Mantles invited me to work with them. I was honored to join the family in Dallas, where Mantle was treated, for the announcement of the new Mickey Mantle Foundation.

The first project was the printing and distribution of millions of Mickey Mantle donor cards. It had been one of Mickey's final wishes. We also decided that similar cards with my picture and signature would be distributed in the months leading up to the Olympics. And we're hoping that other athletes and coaches will join the effort so we can turn it into a series of sports donor cards. As I've always told Wendy, and now I've been telling the Mantles as well, we're definitely in this for the long run.

Thursday, February 15 – Houston

We just got word that Pirelli, the Italian tire company, is about to start running our commercials in the States again, which is great because it's one of the most successful advertising campaigns I've been in. Right up there with the Nike stuff from early in my career and the 1992 Panasonic campaign. But I've got to give Pirelli the nod for most creative.

First they put me in high heels to make the point that power is nothing without control. I don't know how many hours I spent on the track that day, leaning down in a posed starting position, red stiletto pumps all shiny and killing my feet, with Annie Leibovitz, probably the number one celebrity photographer in the world, shooting away from all angles. That was a couple years ago. The picture made for a highly successful advertising campaign in Europe and also made quite a splash in the U.S., with newspapers and magazines wanting to know what I was doing in high heels. Simple answer: making a memorable ad. Still, some of the imaginative comments I got, from both men and women, were hilarious.

Of course, the people at Pirelli loved all the attention, so they came back with plans to continue and expand what we were doing. The next idea was to make me look like a high-performance tire that could handle the toughest of conditions, so they squeezed me into a rubber suit with actual treads cut from top to bottom. Maybe you saw me last year dressed as the Pirelli P6000, running on water, and on the Statue of Liberty, and then jumping to another New York landmark, the Chrysler Building. It was by far the most talked about commercial I've been in. And worldwide sales of Pirelli tires jumped dramatically.

We've done several other print advertisements together. The wildest is a tight shot of me growling, wearing silver fangs and claws, pretty nasty looking, as if I'm a tiger gripping the road. But it's the Statue of Liberty commercial that's being slated to run again throughout the spring and into the summer. I'm just thankful we don't have to climb all the way back up to the top of Lady Liberty again. I mean, you believe everything you see on television, right?

Friday, February 16 – Houston

Last day in the gym. No more weights and medicine ball after this. Only running and outdoor work.

While we were winding down our final session, knocking out those last sets of stomach-crunching throws with the med ball, John Lott, our strength and fitness coach, was reminding us just how far we have come. Day One was August 11, 1995. We started with a six-pound ball, doing two sets of fifteen repetitions each, and eventually progressed to a fourteen-pound ball, doing three sets of seventy-five.

And that was just the med ball. Back when he was introducing me to some of the weightlifting exercises, John was concerned that I might feel embarrassed with how little I could do, so he started me on a junior bar. Now look where I am. I even catch myself looking in the mirror to check out the new muscles.

Sunday, February 18 – Houston

People often ask me about some old athlete or a particular track and field event as if I'm a walking encyclopedia of Olympic history, as if being an athlete for so long automatically makes me a dedicated student of the Games. It does not. Sure, I am pretty well versed in the story of Jesse Owens, for good reason, and have picked up plenty of other tidbits here and there, facts and figures and assorted stories. But I'm certainly no expert. No way could I answer all the questions I get. But I have often thought it would be nice to learn more about the athletes and events of the past.

I'm finally acting on that desire. Every now and then, I'm just picking a topic and reading about it, my own continuing education, History of the Olympics 101. The timing is somewhat appropriate, I guess, because Atlanta is being celebrated as the Centennial Games. There will be so many links to the past.

This afternoon I did some reading on Paavo Nurmi, who was a runner from Finland. No matter how many times I've heard his name and been told how great he was, I've never known much about anything he did, not even what events he ran. His name has been coming up lately because he was the only runner to win more gold medals than I have. People often ask me about that: Am I the alltime leader in gold medals, and if not, do I still have a chance to be?

I found several books with long passages on Nurmi, and what I learned was incredible. First, it turns out there was another athlete, Ray Ewry, who actually won more golds than Nurmi. Ewry won ten, all in standing jump events that were eliminated long ago, but two of them are not officially recognized because they came in the disputed 1906 Games. Nurmi won nine golds. I'm next with eight.

But the things I discovered about Nurmi go so far beyond the medal count. He was undoubtedly one of the most remarkable athletes ever to perform in any discipline. The way he is described in one of the books, Volume 8 of *The Olympic Century*, Nurmi was all business: "He was short and barrel-chested, a pale-haired man with pale, cold eyes." He usually ran with a stopwatch in the palm of his right hand, and with a style that set him apart from the others: "So long was his stride that his feet hardly seemed to touch the ground." He was known as the Flying Finn. Nurmi set twenty-nine world records at distances from 1500 to 20,000 meters. He won the nine golds, as well as three silver medals, in the three Olympics from 1920 through 1928. And some of the stories behind them...

Back then, for a while anyway, the Games included a cross-country race. In fact, four of Nurmi's golds came in just two of those races. The first individual across the line was awarded a gold, and then members of the best national team also got one. In both 1920 and 1924, Nurmi was the top individual and the Finns collected the team medal. Too bad we can't collect golds two at a time anymore!

The wildest of all the Nurmi stories unfolded in the second of those cross-country races. It was July 12, 1924, one of the hottest days ever recorded in Paris, the temperature reaching 113 degrees. Forty-two runners started, but they soon began dropping out, many of them *passing* out. Only eighteen made it into the stadium for the last lap. Just a dozen actually made it across the finish line, and even the survivors are described in *The Olympic Century* as "a grotesque trickle of heatstroke-maddened zanies." Of course, Nurmi was absolutely fine as he claimed first place. But he still needed his teammates for a shot at that second gold.

As it says in *The Complete Book of the Olympics*: "In order for Finland to win, at least three men had to cross the finish line. Nurmi and Vilho Ritola finished easily, but Heikki Liimatainen, staggering along in the oppressive heat, halted 30 meters short of his goal. Delirious, he turned around and began staggering back the way he had come. The crowd shouted at him and he stopped. After standing for a while with his back to the finish line, he finally regained control of his senses, turned around, and walked across the finish." Talk about a bizarre twist. If the guy had stayed down for the count, Nurmi and I would be tied with eight golds. (By the way, the cross-country race was forever excluded from the Olympic program after the heat-induced horrors in Paris.)

There was one other thing about those 1924 Games that immediately brought a smile to my face. Nurmi had to lobby for a late change in the schedule – and got one. The 1500 and 5000 were originally separated by only half an hour, but after the filing of a formal protest and much debate on the issue, organizers finally agreed to expand the interval to almost a full hour. Amazing! Not only did Nurmi go on to win both events, he even established a precedent for the type of change I have always fought to allow.

Finally, years later, Nurmi even ended up in a dispute with the international track federation concerning the rules of amateurism. Once again, sound familiar? Nurmi was disqualified prior to the 1932 Games on grounds that he allegedly charged "excessive expenses" for his travels to various competitions. Bless his heart, on top of everything he achieved on the fields of competition, the Flying Finn was also way ahead of his time when it came to the business of sport.

Monday, February 19 – Houston

When I was pulling out of the parking lot after workout, I could still see Leroy Burrell lying down on the track, flat on his back, hurting and hoping. Hoping he would soon stop hurting from our breakdown. Remember, though, that's why we call our first workout of the week a breakdown. It'll get you every time.

Mondays are even tougher now than when I first described our training schedule, six weeks ago, because we've picked up the pace.

Back then we were running 400 meters in less than 51 seconds; now we're at 48. We were running 300 meters in less than 39 seconds; we've dropped to 33. And we were running the 200 in less than 25 seconds; we're down to 21. Which is rolling. Four, three, two, just like that, with recovery time in between, of course, but it was also the hottest day of the year, already up in the eighties, and it always takes time to adjust to the heat.

No wonder Leroy was knocked out. I was hurting too. Big time. But I refuse to lie down on the track. I'd sooner drive around the corner and then pass out than let anyone see me down on the track, although today was definitely a test of that mettle. When we're lifting weights, I'll admit when I'm hurting. But never on the track. No way. Maybe I'll joke about hurting on the track. But I'll never just come right out and admit it.

Tuesday, February 20 – Houston

I was over at the University of Houston alumni center and unknowingly walked into a bizarre experience. It happened while I was passing by the athletics Hall of Fame, in which there is a larger-than-life statue of me out by the front window. That in itself is a bit strange. There is nothing normal about being a statue while you're also a living, breathing human being, and especially while you're still working at your profession. Statues are usually for dead people. Or at least retired folks.

But this morning we hit a new high on the abnormality scale. It was the first time I happened to wander by while someone was really studying the statue. This woman was examining the USA top and the 1984 gold medals (replicas) hanging from my neck. She was reading the imposing words engraved under my name: "He doth bestride the narrow world like a colossus...We shall not look upon his like again." She was staring so intently into my eyes – I mean, the eyes of the statue – that I almost had to say something. Like: What are you doing all up in my face?

No question, it was quite an honor to be chosen for the only statue in the Hall, especially when you consider some of the other athletes celebrated in the exhibits: Hakeem Olajuwon, Clyde Drexler, Elvin Hayes, Fred Couples, Flo Hyman, Andre Ware, and Leroy Burrell, to name a few. I've always been struck by how permanent the statue seems to be. That, and the fact it makes me look big as a house.

But now I have something else to think about – how strange it felt to watch someone studying me like that. And here was the weirdest part. After a minute or two, this woman happened to glance my way and saw me watching her. I offered a quick, awkward wave, without even knowing if she recognized me, and then I hurried off. Maybe I should just use the back door from now on.

Wednesday, February 21 – Houston

We had a nice dinner out with teammates and friends for Leroy Burrell's birthday. He's twenty-nine. Which only recently was considered over the hill – ancient – for a sprinter. Not anymore, though. The age factor is different now.

By the time I was twenty-nine, it was pretty much a standard story to write me off as being too old to do anything significant on the track. Leroy was the new star of the 100 – and even more so the next year when he ran the 9.90 to break my world record. But then we went to Tokyo for the 1991 World Championships, and, at the age of thirty, I had the best meet of my life. I reclaimed the world record in the 100. I shared another world record as anchor in the 4 x 100 relay. And I also had the best series of my life in the long jump, passing the 29-foot mark for the first time in my career, and then doing it twice more the same night. So Tokyo put at least a temporary hold on the age issue.

Then 1992 really made people wonder. Linford Christie of Great Britain, even a year older than me, won the 100 in Barcelona, while I won the long jump and ran the best anchor leg of my career for another world record in the relay. And we continued to stretch the limits. In 1993, when Linford and I faced each other in the match race of the year, the London tabloids were pumping it up as the battle of the "Wrinklies."

Just for the heck of it, I did some research this afternoon. I pulled out a book from the 1984 Olympics, went through the roster for men's sprinters and hurdlers – total of twenty Americans – and figured out the average age. It was twenty-three. (Exactly the age I was then.) Now compare that to the U.S. team we sent to

Sweden last year. Same twenty spots, average age was twenty-six. And that's a big difference. It's almost impossible now to come right out of college and immediately establish yourself as one of the consistently top sprinters. There are too many guys sticking around and steadily improving in their post-collegiate years.

Why? For one thing, we keep learning more and more about training techniques and other factors, such as diet, that affect longevity. But even more important than that, I think, more important from a practical standpoint, athletes are sticking around longer and longer because our sport has finally reached the point where they can afford to stay around. That is one of the direct benefits of the transition from amateurism to professionalism that's evolved, slowly but surely, during my career. There have been many people in the sport who have fought against that evolution, mainly meet promoters and the governing bodies, and they've had their own selfish reasons for doing so. But I don't see how anyone could still argue that professionalism is not best for the sport. It allows the top athletes to stay around so much longer, and that's who the fans want to see. They want to see people they know.

People like Leroy. So forget about twenty-nine being the twilight of a sprinter's career. Now it's an ideal time for the biggest stars to shine.

Thursday, February 22 – Houston

There was a moment of panic this morning when I wondered if my season was about to be declared over. In fact, when Dr. Jeffrey Brown, my endocrinologist, was first telling me I appeared to have a thyroid disorder, I was much less concerned about running and jumping than I was about my basic health.

Who would even know about the thyroid gland unless something goes wrong with it? As Dr. Brown explained it, what I have is a fairly common and treatable condition. He told me that the thyroid, located in the neck, is an endocrine gland, which means it secretes hormones into the bloodstream. Thyroid hormones tell the body how fast to work and how to use its energy. Initial tests revealed that I'm hypothyroid, which means my gland is underactive.

In other words, no matter how hard I'm training, no matter how much emphasis I'm placing on proper nutrition and rest, my efforts are being sabotaged by a breakdown beyond my control. The only obvious symptom has been my body temperature. Dr. Brown measured it at just ninety-five point six degrees. I'm not getting enough thyroid hormones in my blood, so my body is all out of whack. That much I understand, but what does it really mean?

It's amazing how subtle a thyroid disorder can be. In fact, Dr. Brown said, if I had not come in for a routine checkup, if he had not taken my temperature and then ordered blood work, I might very well have proceeded through the season without ever catching the problem. It's not like you just wake up one day and your body is falling apart. It's much more likely that the condition will wear you down gradually.

The way Dr. Brown explained it, maybe I'm missing only five percent of my body's capacity to perform, which would be virtually impossible for most people to notice in their daily activities. But five percent is huge for a track and field athlete. When you're going by hundredths of a second or maybe centimeters to determine a winner, five percent could easily be the difference between not even making it to Atlanta and ending up the Olympic champion.

So where do we go from here? As little as I knew about the thyroid gland, I certainly didn't have a clue how to go about fixing a bad one. Surgery? Medication? "First we'll have to do another test," Dr. Brown said. "We need to make absolutely sure we're taking the right approach. Then we'll start you on medication, and we'll keep testing, maybe once a week, to get the levels just right."

We scheduled another appointment for Monday. Meanwhile, Dr. Brown gave me some reading material on the thyroid gland. I've already been through most of it, though, and have yet to find the answers for which I'm really searching: How long before I'll be back at full strength? What are the odds I'll be one hundred percent in time for the U.S. trials and the Olympics? Or is this really the end of my season, the end of my career?

Friday, February 23 – Houston

Someone faxed me a newspaper story about Donovan Bailey, the Canadian sprinter who won the 100 in the World Championships last year, and I was impressed with the way he's continued to represent both himself and the sport. It's no easy thing for an athlete to handle the sudden and constant media demands that come with a major breakthrough year like the one Donovan just had. Five years ago he was completely out of track and field, working as a stockbroker, and now here he is, twenty-nine years old, with everyone on him.

And then Donovan's situation is further complicated by the memory of another Canadian, Ben Johnson, who, after the controversy he created in the 1988 Olympics and the investigations that followed, might as well be a brand name for steroids. As the first Canadian sprinter of real significance after Ben, one of the legitimate favorites heading into Atlanta, Donovan is inevitably asked to make comparisons. He's often put in the position of having to defend himself — having to declare himself a clean athlete — and just because he's running for the same country Ben did.

Even the story I just read starts with that stuff: "When any track enthusiast is asked who is Canada's fastest sprinter, Ben Johnson quickly comes to mind. But Donovan Bailey is changing that. And because his rise among the world's premier sprinters has been meteoric, the question has been raised more than once if he has taken performance-enhancing drugs." It is so unfair to Donovan. So unfair to link anyone that way, with no justification whatsoever, to one of the most notorious cheaters in the history of international sport.

No, Mike and Marna Marsh were not able to stay this clean while we were landscaping.

Still, I've yet to see Donovan really snap at anyone about it. He calmly answers the same way he's been answering for months now: "Ben and myself, we're both black guys, both born in Jamaica, both competing for Canada. But the similarities end there. We're talking about two totally different eras."

Amen.

And there is one other thing I take away from this newspaper story that impresses me about Donovan. In sharp contrast to so many other people in our sport, he seems to be comfortable enough with himself to say something positive about his competitors. Too many people think they need to tear down others in order to build up themselves. I've never understood that. But Donovan seems to realize that in building up each other, we can also build up the entire sport.

Saturday, February 24 – Houston

So much for those flower-eating rabbits of weeks past. I've moved on to the next level. I spent the afternoon with Mike Marsh and his wife Marna as unofficial guest landscaper working on the yard of their new home. We did it all: digging, planting, seeding. Maybe I'm coming back in another life as a green thumb.

Or as a professional basketball player. Because once we were done in the yard, I ended up spending the evening with the Los Angeles Lakers. A local restaurant owner had invited Leroy Burrell and me to join him at the Summit to watch the Lakers play the Houston Rockets. It was the first time Magic Johnson has been in town since returning to the NBA. What our host failed to mention was the location of his seats. We were right on the floor at the end of the Lakers' bench. Might as well have suited up with Magic and Company.

What got me the most about being so close to the action was how much talking goes on during a game. Del Harris, the coach, hardly ever sat down, and all he did was walk around the bench talking to his players. Always a running commentary. He should have been broadcasting the game for radio or television. Cedric Ceballos was my main man on the bench. He played most of the game, scoring 26 points, but whenever he came out, he'd sit next to me, and we'd talk. It was interesting to get that up-close perspective. Funny thing was, soon as Ceballos was ready to go back in, he'd let the coach know, and in he'd go. I guess it's truly the generation of the athletes. At least in the NBA.

There was only one bad thing about sitting where Leroy and I were. So many people see you down there. I wouldn't want the home-town fans to think of us as traitors. Of course, we were still pulling for the Rockets regardless of where we were sitting, and they eventually fought back from behind to win a close one, ending the Lakers' eight-game winning streak.

Sunday, February 25 – Houston

One of the most relaxing routines I have is hopping on my bicycle and taking my dog, Ramses, for a run. I ride. He runs alongside me.

We usually go for half an hour to an hour a day. Sometimes we head to the park, about three miles from home, where we join all kinds of bikers and joggers and dogs. Sometimes we just make a big circle or two through the neighborhood streets. I'm sure most of the neighbors know us by now. Ramses is the one constantly checking me out to see what he can get away with. I'm the one yelling, "Ramses, out of the road. Stay on the grass." It amazes me how well he usually listens and responds.

Ramses is just a pup, a Rhodesian Ridgeback, seven months old, and very active. Always getting into everything. Always digging in places he doesn't need to be digging. But he is so friendly and intelligent. Being single with no children, I really enjoy having Ramses to look after. I'd had Rottweilers for years, and always loved having them around, but the last one, Maggie, died a few years ago, and it would have been difficult to just replace her with another Rottweiler. I thought it would be better to start all over with another breed.

I spent a couple of months doing research, reading books, talking to breeders, and kept coming back to the idea of getting a Ridgeback. The Ridgeback, which originated in South Africa, is a muscular, medium-sized dog with a short, tan coat, and, you guessed it, a distinctive ridge of hair running down the center of his back. As a member of the hound family, the Ridgeback generally has a fairly gentle temperament.

The most hilarious part of the entire research process was the day I came home from the gym and found my mother there, waiting to join me for lunch, and she was struggling to give me a phone message she had just written down. "Uh, Carl, this woman just called for you, and she's got two bitches waiting if you want to stop by and look at them." Poor mother, she had no clue the woman was a breeder and was talking about two female dogs. I will never forget that look on her face as she forced herself to repeat exactly what that woman had asked her to tell me.

Then there was this passage I read and even underlined in a book about Ridgebacks: "It is fair to say that most dogs are in better shape than most humans who own them. The reason for this is that most dogs accept exercise without objection. People do not!" Definitely something to keep in mind while we're logging our miles together on the road and in the park — me with the assistance of wheels; Ramses, named after an Egyptian king, relying on nothing but legs and his determination to keep up.

Monday, February 26 – Houston

I went to see Dr. Brown again. He believes his initial diagnosis of the thyroid problem was correct. In fact, he was able to be much more specific this time. Technically, what I have is a case of chronic lymphocytic thyroiditis, which anyone other than a doctor calls Hashimoto's thyroiditis.

The way Dr. Brown explained it, the body routinely produces antibodies to protect against the invasion of outside forces such as bacteria or viruses. But sometimes the body also produces unwanted antibodies that end up damaging otherwise healthy tissue. With Hashimoto's, it's a matter of developing potent antibodies that unleash an aggressive assault on the thyroid gland. That's when the trouble begins.

The only way to fight back is by repeatedly introducing new reserves. The standard treatment is a thyroid hormone replacement known as L-thyroxine. Dr. Brown wants to prescribe it to me, in the form of a drug called Synthroid, but first there is a major concern to be addressed. We need to rule out any possibility of another condition known as Addison's disease, which affects another hormone source known as the adrenal gland. "When you have Hashimoto's, there is also a fairly high incidence of Addison's disease," Dr. Brown said. "If we treat the Hashimoto's with L-thyroxine and you have undiagnosed

Addison's, the result could be quite severe. In fact, it could be life-threatening."

What? I was still trying to process the whole idea of a common thyroid disorder – and now he was injecting the phrase "life-threatening" into the discussion? "I'm not saying anything out of the ordinary is going to happen," Dr. Brown tried to reassure me. "But we do need to take every precaution. Once you test negative for Addison's, the treatment is pretty routine from there. But this is not the kind of thing you just jump into."

No, I'm not about to jump. I have the utmost confidence in Dr. Brown. He's extremely intelligent, deliberate, and professional in every sense of the word. I started seeing him in 1992 after a nasty sinus infection nearly wiped me out at the Olympic trials in New Orleans. It was only with his help that I was able to make it back in time for the Barcelona Games – and then go on to win two gold medals. Dr. Brown has been a friend ever since. He's helped me deal with allergies and other minor health issues – and has never once misled me. But I still have so many questions. There is so much uncertainty.

We must act soon, though. Dr. Brown said he's hoping to have me back at full strength within a month to six weeks. But it could take as long as two to three months. That would make it very difficult – almost impossible – for me to have much of a season leading up to the Olympic trials.

Joe Douglas is already making calls to get a second opinion. We'll get back with Dr. Brown in the morning. Meanwhile, I have a lot to think about.

Tuesday, February 27 – Houston

Joe Douglas made a few more telephone calls on the thyroid situation. After speaking to two more doctors, he was pretty well reassured that Dr. Brown is leading us down the right path. My comfort level has increased dramatically. We need to proceed with the test for the adrenal gland. Then I need to start on the Synthroid.

But first there is one other important step. We need to check in with the U.S. Olympic Committee and the track federations to make absolutely sure that everything we're doing is approved in advance.

The last thing I'd want to do is get in trouble for something totally innocent. As long and hard as Joe and I have worked to maintain the integrity of our sport, as much as we have fought to rid track and field of improper drug use, we're certainly not about to take any chances. Any little mistake could make us look like total hypocrites. So we'll get everything in writing. By late morning, one of Dr. Brown's assistants was faxing a summary of my case to the Indianapolis headquarters of USA Track & Field, the national federation.

Wednesday, February 28 – Houston

I'm afraid my diary might be turning into a medical notebook. I can't help it. The thyroid condition is pretty much dominating my thoughts.

I'm struggling with the idea of going to the national indoor championships this weekend in Atlanta. I'm supposed to run the 60. USA Track & Field is counting on me to be there. Nike is expecting me. We also have big plans for the introduction of our special organ donor cards. Those are all good reasons to go. But I keep thinking about one particular discussion I had with Dr. Brown.

"What are those things you start in?" he wanted to know. "The blocks?" Obviously, he's not a track and field expert. He's always enjoyed sports, but primarily football, baseball, and basketball. Dr. Brown, in his mid-forties, has never once been to a track meet.

"That's right," I said. "Blocks."

"Well, have you really been blasting out of them? Are you running out of the blocks as well as normal?"

"No. Not that I'm exactly known for my start. But, no, I don't think I've been getting out of the blocks very well."

"Classic thyroid situation," Dr. Brown said. "When you have a problem with the thyroid, it will affect the large muscle groups. It can also cause weakness in the proximal muscles around the hips, shoulders, any joints, and that will directly affect your explosiveness. You can be as strong as you want, and lifting the weights has obviously helped you, but if those muscles are not firing properly, then what good are they?"

It's strange. I've been feeling pretty good in workouts. One thing is certain, though. If I don't have an explosive start in the 60, I can pretty much forget about running a good race. So there's really no reason for me to compete Saturday. What's the point? What if I get drilled on national television? Is that the message I want to send out just weeks after finishing last in that other race?

Maybe I should just attend the meet and help promote it without competing. But how would I explain that? I don't want to talk publicly about the thyroid situation because I don't want the added distraction of my whole year being turned into a medical story. I'd rather keep it quiet, at least until after the Games.

I'm in a tough spot. I've been totally distracted since the initial diagnosis last week. Each day brings a new development with which to deal. Today I got word that the test for Addison's has been approved. I'll have it tomorrow morning in Dr. Brown's office. From there I'll either go home to relax or Atlanta to settle in for the meet. But I'm really not sure how to make that decision.

Thursday, February 29 – Houston and Atlanta

My gut feeling was that I should skip the meet, but ultimately I came to the conclusion that I really don't have a gracious way out of it. With so many people counting on me, I simply can't break my commitment.

At least I can find consolation in something Dr. Brown said this morning. I was sitting in his office with an IV line in my arm, doing that test for the adrenal gland, and I asked him if he thought I should compete at this point. "Whatever you want to do," he said. "It really doesn't matter what you're running now, because everything will soon be back to normal. Remember, we're talking four to six weeks, and then we should see the real you again."

Obviously, my confidence is way down. My emotions have been all over the place. But I keep thinking back to that one thing Dr. Brown said. *Everyone will see the real me again.* So I went to the airport and made the trip. I'll run the best I can.

Friday, March 1 – Atlanta

Anyone who knows me knows exactly where I am the day before a meet. I'm relaxing in my hotel room, resting my legs, starting to think about the task at hand. I'm certainly not out doing appearances and interviews. That's always been the rule.

(PHOTO: CONWAY-ATLANTA)

Joining me for the release of our special organ donor cards are (left to right): Jenny Spangler, Danny Mantle, and Wendy Marx.

Today was a total exception.

I was out of the hotel by eight in the morning to visit a third-grade class because a cousin of mine teaches at the school and invited me. I rushed back to the hotel for an interview with NBC, which will be used tomorrow on the broadcast of the meet. Then it was off to the Niketown store for a news conference and satellite media tour to release and promote the new Carl Lewis organ donor cards. I was there for three hours, talking, answering questions, and signing cards.

It was not the most relaxing of schedules for the day before a meet, especially these nationals, in which we'll be running three rounds in the 60. But it's also a sign of where my head is. I've been so distracted all week, wondering if I'd even be here. Plus, nationals or not, this is still only indoors, still very early in the year. Sure, I'd like to run well, but we also have to be realistic. Physically and emotionally, I'm down. This is nothing more than a glorified workout to break up the monotony of training. Once the heat of June and July rolls around, nobody will even remember who won what in February or March.

Anyway, preparation and competition aside, this was an inspiration-filled day, which always seems to be the case when we're working on our organ donor programs. The families of several local donors, people who were able to see through their own personal tragedies to help others, were kind enough to join us for the event, and donor families always offer such a powerful perspective. They always remind us of the reality that each and every day is truly a gift.

It was also great to spend time with Wendy Marx, my liver transplant friend, who seems to be doing so well again after a few weeks of ups and downs. We were also joined by Danny Mantle, one of the three sons of Mickey Mantle, and Jenny Spangler, my Santa Monica teammate, who's still shining in the afterglow of her recent victory in the Olympic marathon trials. When I signed the ceremonial number one of half a million cards we're initially distributing, Danny and Jenny served as my witnesses, which was a nice touch.

I guess it's kind of unusual to have a donor card with your own picture on it, but at least there will never be any trouble checking my identification. That's a plus.

Saturday, March 2 – Atlanta

D.A.L.

In the vocabulary of the Santa Monica Track Club, that's short for Dead Ass Last.

That was me in my opening heat of the 60. I had another horrible start and was totally out of it by 20 meters. So much for using the indoor nationals as a three-race workout. I was done after one. Not that I was expecting to leave here with a medal, but I certainly wasn't expecting this either.

Two meets this year, two times I've been D.A.L. So you can imagine the general consensus: time to completely write me off again. On the way down to my post-race press conference, one of the reporters was crowing to his colleagues that this was going to be the Carl Lewis retirement party. Another member of the pack, *Atlanta Journal-Constitution* writer Steve Hummer, was about to begin his column with this: "The King of track and field may not be dead. Although, come to think of it, a cadaver would have had the same finish as Carl Lewis." Considering the organ donor cards, it was an interesting choice of words.

Granted, I was not pleased with my race, but I was not going to

(PHOTO: AP/WIDE WORLD)

Coming out of the blocks at the indoor national championships next to Jon Drummond (middle) and Dennis Mitchell (far left). Once again, I was D.A.L.

make excuses and did not want to dwell on negatives. Actually, there was something positive to take away from the track. Other than the start, I ran better today than I did in that first meet in Houston. My time in Houston was 6.84 seconds. Here it was 6.77. But it's more than just the times. In Houston, I felt totally detached the whole race. We could have run all day and I wouldn't have caught anybody. Here, if it had been the 100 instead of the 60, I'm pretty sure I would have been able to catch the leaders.

Instead of running into the next round, though, I ended my afternoon with the NBC broadcast crew, including Carol, because the producer wanted me to help announce the sprint final. Unfortunately, our location gave me a clear look at the most upsetting scene of the whole indoor season – Leroy Burrell stumbling past the finish line and crumbling to the track with an injury. He pulled a hamstring.

Please be a pull, and nothing worse, please not a tear.

I wanted to just let out a scream – it was so painful to see Leroy down like that – but had to restrain myself because I was still live on national television. I was so frustrated. How bad was it? How much training will Leroy miss? How much is this going to affect his entire Olympic year? No matter how hard we plan and work to maintain control, we still are not machines. The whole process of training and competing at this level is entirely too fragile to take anything for granted.

Once I was off the air and walking away from the broadcast area, I felt a wave of anger. We should have just skipped this damn meet. I knew I was not ready to compete. We all knew we weren't prepared to run well indoors. There was nothing to be gained. Mike Marsh finished third – fine. But I got drilled. That does nothing but raise negative questions. And then Leroy got hurt. Where does that leave us?

Sunday, March 3 – Atlanta and Houston

So many things in this world come down to timing and perspective. In fact, it's often the timing that knocks everything else back into perspective.

Just ask Leroy. When he got back to Houston last night, he was consumed by uncertainty – no idea how his leg is going to respond to the blow it took. And he was hungry. All he wanted was a plate of food and a quiet place to be alone with his thoughts.

Then Michelle, his pregnant wife, his very pregnant wife, informed him of an urgent change in plans. She was having contractions. It was time to go. Leroy and Michelle made it to the hospital shortly before midnight. Seventeen minutes into the new day, they were joined by a healthy little son, Joshua Kareem, six pounds and four ounces, eighteen inches long, and two healthy hamstrings. Daddy Leroy was still limping around that hospital room, but now the pain in his leg seemed so insignificant, because baby Joshua was kicking up a storm.

Michelle is herself an extremely talented sprinter, a former national champion and gold medalist on the 1992 Olympic relay team, so she's already heard all the cracks about how fast her children are going to be. She and Leroy have been listening to that line of thinking since their first son, Cameron, was born in September of 1994. Of course, they'll be hearing more and more of it now that they have a second son. I mean, there's no denying it. Two boys is half a relay team.

Monday, March 4 – Houston

Good news: I was negative for Addison's disease. Dr. Brown started me on the thyroid medicine. I'll be taking .112 milligrams of Synthroid first thing each morning – on an empty stomach. The rest is up to Dr. Brown. He'll let me know when to come in for tests. If necessary, he'll adjust the daily dosage.

I don't want to dwell on any of this. I don't want it to interfere with my training. I'll do the best I can to conduct business as usual.

❖

The Sullivan Award, presented each year to the nation's top "amateur" athlete, went tonight to wrestler Bruce Baumgartner, who certainly deserves it. At the age of thirty-five, he has won just about everything there is to win in his sport, including sixteen national freestyle titles. As a fellow old-timer, the first thing I want to do is applaud his longevity.

But as a former Sullivan winner – way back in 1981 – I also want to say something about the award itself. Basically, it has gone from being one of the most prestigious in all of sport to one of the most ridiculous. Because the way things have evolved, professional athletes are now considered for the top "amateur" award right along with the true amateurs.

This year, for example, sprinters Michael Johnson and Gwen Torrence were among the ten finalists. After equally impressive performances in the 1995 World Championships, either one of them easily could have won the Sullivan. But amateurs? Please.

Top track and field athletes earn millions of dollars in endorsements, appearance fees, and prize money, and it's been that way for a long time. It simply doesn't make sense anymore to pretend we're anything but pure professionals. So take us out of the running for the Sullivan. Or maybe what we need is two separate awards. One for track and field athletes and other professionals. One for college athletes. Because amateurism really doesn't exist anymore beyond the college level. If there.

Tuesday, March 5 – Houston

Back to the drawing board. Coach Tellez and I have been talking about changes we might need to make, because obviously something is not right, and the last thing we'd want to do is pretend otherwise. We've always worked from the premise that the ability to identify problems, along with the desire and creativity to address them, is an integral component in the making of a champion. Anyone who wants to stay at the top of a sport – or a business – constantly needs to make adjustments. It's a perfectly normal part of the process for us, even after all these years of tinkering.

The immediate question is: What's keeping me from performing the way we know I'm capable of performing? We know it's not my fitness. It's not my conditioning or my strength. It's not even my speed. Those are all where they need to be at this point in the year. So it has to be something else, and the best explanation we can come up with is lack of rhythm. Simply put, I need more races. I need repetition and continuity. That's why Coach Tellez really wanted me to run those rounds in Atlanta. He wasn't overly concerned with results. He just wanted me to run more races.

It's like a basketball player shooting jump shots. No matter what kind of physical shape you're in, you need plenty of practice, repetition after repetition. That's how you find your rhythm, and rhythm is what gives you the confidence to perform your best. It is the same with trying to hit on all cylinders in a race. Without repetition and confidence, it's not going to happen.

We have to keep in mind that, for a variety of reasons, including injuries and limited training, I've competed only sporadically the last few years. I've run a minimal number of sprints. I've been in a few long jump competitions. But I've run more relays than anything else. The lack of individual competition has left me completely out of synch.

As a result, it seems the entire odyssey of this season is going to revolve around finding my rhythm in the 100. Everyone always talks about the long jump being my ace in the hole as far as making the Olympic team – and that's certainly a valid point. But I'm still nowhere near placing limits on the events in which I might compete, and I know what the 100 means to everything else I do. When my 100 is on, all the other events tend to follow suit.

So we're adjusting accordingly, putting the emphasis on the 100, and we're pushing up my outdoor season so I can get started even sooner than we had anticipated. I'm going to run my first 100 in a meet this Saturday at Rice University. Then I'll run a time trial in practice at the end of next week. And I'll probably run meets three weekends in a row after that – taking us through the first week of

April. By then we'll have a much better idea of where I'm going to be as we head into the heat of the season.

Wednesday, March 6 – Houston

Good news out of the training room. Leroy's leg is not nearly as bad as it first appeared to be – which is a huge relief – and it's already responding well to initial rehab sessions. He's getting treatment twice a day.

Leroy says he expects to be jogging by early next week and back in his regular training routine within two or three weeks. I can only hope it works out that way, because if that's all he misses, he'll still be fine.

Thursday, March 7 – Houston

A friend has been telling me: "You need to pull out some old pictures from when you were winning everything, shots of you crossing the finish line with that smile and those arms up in the air, in triumph, because you need to capture that feeling again. Do it when you're alone at home sometime. Just take a few minutes to look at those images, absorb them, think about the feelings that went with them. You know, positive thoughts. In with the positive, out with the negative."

So I finally did that. I went into a storage closet and found an assortment of old pictures. Also some awards. It's almost symbolic, what I've done over the years with pictures and awards, because I've packed most of them away, out of sight, out of mind. I've never wanted to spend too much time dwelling on the past.

But something about seeing those old pictures again put me totally at ease. It all looked so natural, like I was doing what I was born to do, and enjoying it. There was never any doubt on my face. There was never a hint of uncertainty in my eyes. Just power and confidence and joy. *Like I was doing what I was born to do.*

And those pictures made me want to feel that again.

There's a reason certain athletes accomplish great things. It's called passion. Never underestimate the great things their passion will allow them to achieve.

In the past, I claimed victories with my body, mind, and soul. This time, I'm going to do it with my heart.

Saturday, March 9 – Houston

Not that I'm going to celebrate winning the 100 in 10.50-something seconds. Not exactly one for the record books. But time was not at all the issue in my first outdoor competition of the year. The issue was moving forward with our new plan. Getting in meets. Stressing repetition and continuity. Trying to find my rhythm.

Step One was a low-key meet at Rice University. With this being the same weekend as the NCAA indoor championships, even the top collegiate sprinters from the area were nowhere to be found when we settled into the blocks. It was just me and a bunch of second-tier college kids. The conditions were far from ideal, temperature in the upper-forties, running into a headwind, but none of that really mattered because this was strictly blue-collar work. Time for the hard hat and lunch bucket. Time to punch in with the union guys.

It was a totally different atmosphere than what I'm used to. There were no reporters and television cameras following me around. There was hardly anyone in the stands. Nobody had even announced I was coming. It was just the way I wanted it. No pressure whatsoever.

All I had to think about was running. When was the last time I was able to approach a meet that way? Hmmm. I'm not sure my memory even goes back that far. It had to be in the early 1980s, and, in a sense, that's what it felt like this time out, like I was starting right back where I was fifteen years ago. Except that back then I was running all these little meets because I wanted to win them. Now I'm doing it because I have to get myself together.

The best thing about today was my mechanics in the first 30 meters. I drove out of the blocks well, and was up and running better than I was in either of the indoor meets. From 30 to 60 meters still wasn't what it needs to be – didn't keep accelerating the way I should – but at least I was turning over well enough to stay in front of the pack. It was the first time this year I felt anything like myself, and then I shut down the engines and just cruised the last 40 meters or so.

To victory.

A meaningless victory, obviously, in terms of the competition; significant, though, on a different level, and way beyond what anyone on the outside could possibly understand. On a scale of one to ten, that first indoor meet was the absolute worst, a one; second indoor meet was about a three; and this was maybe a seven. It gives me something on which to build.

Next time I'm preparing for a race, I can think back and remember what this one felt like. Most important, once I put together a few of these races in a row, a few that feel right, then I'll be able to run from memory again. Which is the way it needs to be. Too much thinking tends to hold you back. Running from memory, from instinct, is the only way to really roll.

Sunday, March 10 – Houston

Finally. A group of athletes that once again allows me to be the youngster of the crowd – my mother and her friends. They're training for the Senior Olympics. After breakfast at Mother's house, Carol and I went with her to practice. It was pretty amazing to watch. There were about twenty men and women, most in their fifties and sixties, but a few of them up into their eighties, and they were working those bodies hard.

They were throwing and running and jumping. Also smiling and laughing – really enjoying themselves. It sure makes you wonder about all the people staying home on the couch these days, and especially all the kids passing entire afternoons and evenings in front of the television. As much as it means to these seniors to be exercising on a regular basis, how in the world could any teenager or young adult justify the sedentary existence that has come to define so many of their lives?

Of course, Mother has a distinct advantage over many of the other seniors: her experience. It was her athletic talent that enabled her to get a scholarship to Tuskegee Institute in Alabama, where she met my father. He played football and also ran track, but it was Evelyn Lawler, later Evelyn Lewis, who was clearly the star. She competed in the first Pan American Games, held in Buenos Aires, Argentina, in 1951, making the final in the hurdles. She was also a favorite to make the 1952 Olympic team, but a leg injury kept her out of the U.S. trials. Then there was coaching. After moving from Alabama to Willingboro, New

Jersey, both Mother and Father spent the afternoons of my childhood coaching track and field. They each had a high school team, rivals actually, and together they established the Willingboro Track Club.

Now, how in the world all of that translates into being a sixty-six-year-old shot putter, I'm not exactly sure, but that's Mother. She's always wanting to try something new. A few years ago, she went to Phoenix for her first Senior Olympics, as a long jumper and sprinter. She never made it to the sprints, though, because on her very first jump, which ended up winning the competition, she also suffered a compression fracture in her lower back. Two years passed before she was again able to compete — and then Mother went out and won the discus. Now she's preparing for several events, including the shot put, of all things, in a meet next weekend in San Antonio. She plans to compete in about six meets the next few months.

And plans on doing well. From what I saw, they're quite a competitive bunch, Mother and her friends. I guess you could say they're shaping up to be like the Santa Monica Track Club of the seniors. Having fun. And getting the job done.

Monday, March 11 – Houston

Mike Marsh stopped me in the middle of workout and said: "Kind of a personal question, but I feel like I need to ask. What's the deal with you the last few weeks? Not the meets, but when we're running in practice, you're kind of falling back, and I've never seen you do that before."

He was right. I had been falling back, not much, but consistently. So we talked. I started by explaining the way I've been feeling. The allergies. The thyroid situation. It was not anything I'd typically get into with my teammates, or anyone else, for that matter, because I'd never want to come across as making excuses. But Mike and I have always been straight to the point with each other, so once he brought it up, I was perfectly comfortable discussing it. And then we went beyond the physical factors, into the emotional stuff.

As a result of my recent performances, Mike, like everyone else around me, keeps getting bombarded with similar questions: *Man, what's up with Carl? He's history, huh? He keeps talking about being in the Olympics, his last hurrah, but can he actually make it?*

Mike Marsh offers an important reminder. It's time to roll.

(PHOTO: ALLSPORT)

"Like you're supposed to spend the entire year as everybody's sacrificial lamb or something," Mike said. "I'm tired of people asking me about it, so I know you have to be tired of hearing it. And I get to wondering, how is all this mess affecting the way you're thinking? What if it's gotten to the point where you're just like, been there, done that, nothing else to prove anymore, so let's just go through the motions? But here's what gets me about that. That's leaning toward the lackadaisical — and that's definitely not you. Never has been."

Whew.

And Mike said he had been wondering if he should even say anything at all. The more he thought about it, though, the more he felt a sense of urgency, and once he'd started, he wasn't holding anything back.

"You don't have a choice, Carl. It's time to roll. No rationalizing. No nothing. It's now or never. Now or forget it. I don't care what we're doing, you can't be falling back. We should be running right together, just like we always have in the past."

As tough as it can be when someone hits you with an unpleasant reality, even in the form of constructive criticism from a friend, listening to Mike and absorbing his message was actually somewhat refreshing, and even enjoyable, in a strange way. All the time I've been around teammates and friends in track and field, I've always been the one pulling them aside, offering encouragement and support, trying to light a fire. Being on the opposite end of a conversation like this was totally new to me. In fact, I don't think I've ever had another athlete talk to me that way. Joe Douglas, yes, and Coach Tellez, of course. But never another athlete. Not my whole career. It would be impossible to measure how much I appreciated what Mike was saying, and even more so, the very fact he had decided to say it.

Mike has always been one to dig below the surface and make sound judgments. He is extremely intelligent. Growing up in Los Angeles, on the hard streets of South Central, he carved out a life of promise by keeping his head in the books, always reading, and he still reads more than anyone I know. I'm sure that has a lot to do with his ability to move so naturally into the cadence and substance of some textbook philosopher. Like the way he summed up our conversation at the track: "Sometimes we need to forgive ourselves for departing from the past, and then return to it."

Thanks to Mike, I'll be thinking about that.

We're adding another meet. This Saturday at Louisiana State University. Coach Tellez thinks I can use it for both the rhythm of the 100 and to continue our strength work, because in addition to the 100, Mike and I will run the mile relay with two of the University of Houston guys. So the time trial we'd planned for practice Friday is out. Baton Rouge, Louisiana, is in.

Tuesday, March 12 – Houston

We're making yet another change in the schedule. Forget what we decided yesterday. Now the LSU meet is out. The Friday time trial is back in. Because I realized this morning during workout, I'm just not all the way back yet. I think I'm still getting adjusted to the thyroid medicine, and actually I feel worse now than I did last week. I'm OK to train. But I'm not sharp. Not meet sharp. So I don't see how I'd benefit by competing right now.

Something I've learned over the years, and I've kept reminding myself these last couple months: You have to stay flexible, have to constantly evaluate and make the right adjustments. The whole process might at times seem confusing, especially when you question and explore things as much as we do, but that is both the curse and the blessing of an active mind. Ultimately, though, it is the deep foundation of trust in myself and in Coach Tellez, a foundation built on years and years of experience, that allows me to push away any doubts that creep into the mix.

In the end, everything will work out just fine. Everything will turn out exactly the way it's meant to be. That belief, that knowledge, offers a certain calmness when my radar screen might otherwise sense nothing but storms.

Wednesday, March 13 – Houston

Never in my wildest dreams would I have imagined there is actually a book called *Could It Be My Thyroid?* Not exactly one for the national bestseller list, and I certainly never would have expected to read it. But I went to a bookstore because I wanted to learn more about my condition, and there it was, written by a local endocrinologist, Sheldon Rubenfeld, who was founding chairman of The Thyroid Society. (I was amazed to see there is even a toll-free hotline: 1-800-THYROID.) I went straight home and started reading.

What I learned was extremely reassuring. I already had absolute trust in Dr. Brown, but it gave me even greater comfort when everything I read seemed to fit so consistently with all he has been telling me. No question, we are taking the proper course of action. Also, I now have an even better understanding of just how fortunate I am that Dr. Brown caught this when he did. Otherwise, my Olympic season might have been over before it even started.

Thursday, March 14 – Houston

Despite everything I've always heard and read, it turns out Jesse Owens was not the first sprinter to win four gold medals in one Olympics. There was someone else who came before him. Alvin E. Kraenzlein. Not exactly a household name. The year was 1900. The Olympics were in Paris.

All these years I've been linked to Jesse, and nobody else, for duplicating his feat of four gold medals, and I've just now come across the story of Kraenzlein for the very first time. It is briefly covered in one of those Olympics retrospective books that's been collecting dust on a shelf in my den. This morning I was flipping through the pages to see what interesting tidbits I might find. You know, History of the Olympics 101. My continuing education.

I was amazed to learn about Kraenzlein, who ran for the University of Pennsylvania. Not only was he the winner of four events in the same Olympics, but they were all individual events, as opposed to three individual events and a relay for Jesse and me. Kraenzlein won the 110-meter hurdles plus one event (the broad jump) that has been renamed and two events (the 60-meter dash and the 200-meter hurdles) that have been eliminated altogether. As soon as he was done in Paris, Kraenzlein said he was retiring from competition and would devote himself to something more serious. He became a coach. Which, of course, begs the question: Is it really possible the definition of "serious" has changed so much since then?

Friday, March 15 – Houston

We finally did our time trial. Mike Marsh and I ran as fast as we have all year, but only part of the way, and only because we messed up and then panicked.

Coach Tellez had us come out of the blocks to run 350 meters. The idea was to take a start under meet conditions while also getting the benefit of the strength work required in a longer sprint. The goal was to run a relaxed, even pace. Unfortunately, though, by trying to regulate our speed early, we totally messed up the tempo in the first 100. We went out way too slow, about 11.5 seconds. Hearing that split time being yelled out, and wanting to avoid the wrath of Coach Tellez at the finish, we immediately leaped into the panic mode. Which worked.

The second 100 was 9.9 seconds. We were flying. But after that burst, after expending that energy, we had to back off again, and ended up right where we had been for the first 100. We ran another split of 11.5 seconds.

Mike and I were close together at that point. I have to admit, I was thinking about that talk we had the other day. No way I was going to be caught dropping back again. But Mike still ended up getting me in the last 20 meters. I think his time was 39.5 seconds for the full 350. Mine was 39.9. Which was fine — especially considering how badly we handled the pace.

Clearly, though, the most important thing for me was the feeling I had during that second 100. Of course, like the anchor leg of a relay, there were none of the usual concerns about getting started, because you're already up and running. But my speed was right there when I needed it — available upon request. That added considerably to the feeling that I'm moving in the right direction. Big-time improvement.

It was a great way to end the week.

Saturday, March 16 – Houston

A couple of interesting newspaper items came in the mail from a friend who saw them and thought of me.

First is a quote from Pete Carril, the longtime Princeton basketball coach, one of the true legends in the NCAA, who, at the age of sixty-five, is stepping down after more than five hundred career wins. *The hardest thing in the world to do is to do one thing particularly well for a long period of time at whatever standards you establish.* Amen.

The second item is the beginning of a story by *Washington Post* writer Christine Brennan, who was in Indianapolis covering the Olympic swimming trials.

At lunch today at a downtown mall, Janet Evans listened to her parents and boyfriend chatter on about the way she should swim tonight's 400-meter freestyle, one of her two big events at the U.S. Olympic trials.

"Do this, do that," Evans said they were telling her. They were nervous about how Evans, now 24 and one of America's legendary swimmers, would have to swim to beat a handful of hungry teenagers.

Evans finally had had enough.

"Stop! Guys, I've done this a million times. I know what to do. Let's talk about the weather."

Yes, I can definitely relate. And there is even a happy postscript. Hours later, Evans went on to win that race and qualify for her third consecutive Olympics. Let's hear it for experience.

Sunday, March 17 – Houston

Chalk up two more victories for the Lewises. Mother won both the shot put and the discus in that Senior Olympics competition in San Antonio. And had a blast.

Monday, March 18 – Houston

Joe Douglas has been on me about my weight. He thinks I'm too big, and that the excess baggage is slowing me down. He's been saying it for weeks. But last night was the first time I became genuinely concerned, and for good reason. I stepped on the scale and it registered two hundred pounds. Sure, it was right after a big dinner, and I was back down to one-ninety-six this morning, but I've never weighed even close to that much during the season. It's hard to believe it was just last fall, a couple of weeks into that cleansing diet, that I was all the way down around one-seventy-five.

Obviously, our lifting program made me bigger, especially my upper body, but there are other factors at work. One, I've been eating too much. I kind of lost the discipline, I guess, and for no particular reason. Two, the thyroid problem, which slows down the metabolism, has had a much more dramatic impact than I thought it would.

So, as of this morning, the fight is on. Me against the pounds. I need to be at one-eighty-five or below. I need to keep that in mind at all times. I even wrote a memo on my computer, printed it out, and taped it to the door of the refrigerator, as a constant reminder. There is nothing else there, just that memo to Ruth, who has been with me for years, cleaning and cooking, and to myself, so we can't possibly miss it.

> TO: Ruth and Carl
> FR: Carl
> RE: Revised new diet

Breakfast: grapefruit juice
20 almonds

	vitamins
<u>Lunch</u>:	vegetable juice
	sandwich
<u>Snack</u>:	fresh fruit/vegetable juice
<u>Dinner</u>:	fresh vegetable juice
	dinner salad
	main course
	vitamins

Knowing me, I won't be able to stay away from the scale. I'll probably be on it two or three times a day, keeping an eye on the progress, until I'm back where I need to be. I don't think it will take more than two or three weeks.

Tuesday, March 19 – Houston

Carol and I had dinner with Greg Louganis, the great diving champion, who is in town promoting the paperback edition of his book, *Breaking the Surface.* The book made big news when it was originally published last year because it was the first time Greg spoke publicly in such detail about his struggles as a gay man, including the horrible news that he had been HIV-positive for years.

Obviously, I was very saddened to learn he had contracted the virus, but I can't say I was totally shocked. Several years earlier, I had wondered about Greg's health when I saw him at a fundraising dinner for the U.S. Olympic Committee. He seemed to be very weak, pale and thin, and almost withdrawn, definitely not the same vibrant Greg I had always known.

We had been friends with Greg since 1980, especially Carol, so we already knew he was gay. He had always been very direct with Carol about his relationships, even sharing some of the most personal details, such as the fact he had been in an extremely abusive relationship, which he later discussed in the book as well. So while others often speculated about Greg, we never had to wonder, and we were both perfectly comfortable with who he was. To us, he was a great athlete and a warm friend, someone with whom we had shared many memorable experiences as longtime members of the Olympic family.

Anyway, this was the first time Carol and I had seen Greg since he went public with his story, and we were relieved to see how well he seems to be doing. He remains as warm and funny as always. And he is still hanging in there with his health. He is putting forth an incredible effort to help reach people with such an important message – that we all better wake up about the AIDS crisis. As Greg put it so simply yet so powerfully in the introduction to his book: He is finally ready to share his story. He hopes you are ready to hear about it.

Carol asked Greg to autograph a copy of his book for her, and above his name, he wrote: "Believe in yourself!" It is his signature line from one of his favorite songs, "If You Believe," from the musical *The Wiz*, which he often played in his head while preparing to dive:

> *Believe in yourself right from the start*
> *Believe in the magic that's inside your heart*

Thursday, March 21 – Houston

Pam Buchanan, a local clothing designer with whom I've worked for years, came by the house so we could get started on new uniforms. We'll knock out something quick and fairly standard for the early meets. But then we'll be ready with something special for the Olympic trials. We always like to wear something new and different for the trials. In fact, we always like to wear something new and different, period.

Obviously, the SMTC is known first and foremost for substance. We win, and try to conduct ourselves professionally at all times. We work hard to move the entire sport forward. But we're also known for style. We care about the way we look on the track. We like to be creative not only because it makes us feel good, but also because it generates excitement. It definitely gets people talking. What's more, when we're running as a relay team, our uniforms even offer an extra dimension in making us feel like we're all in it together, which is a great feeling.

We've paraded around in some unique threads over the years. The Spiderman uniform had these crazy-looking web designs holding us together at the sides. The Nude suit, a skintight creation with strategically appointed shades of brown, made it appear as if we were wearing almost nothing at all, when in fact we were outfitted in a complete body suit. And then we had the Tux, a tuxedo-style warm-up suit. Up

Leroy Burrell strikes a pose in the Spiderman uniform.

(PHOTO: ALLSPORT)

to that point, people thought we were making wild stuff just to make wild stuff, and a lot of the old-line, conservative track people hated it. But now what could they say? Sure, the Tux was an entirely innovative look, but at the same time, what could possibly be more conservative than a tuxedo?

For a while there, the uniforms were getting so much attention we decided to go into business with them, forming an apparel company called Sports Style. It started with a mail-order brochure and a few boxes stacked in the back of an office. Before long, we had a retail store in downtown Houston, marketing deals in Europe and Japan, and orders for custom-designed uniforms from a variety of high school and college teams throughout the U.S. I always got a kick out of going to a meet and seeing some random athlete in a uniform we had designed. Eventually, though, we had to cut back, because the business was getting in the way of other things. Now Pam and I are back to creating only one set of uniforms a year— the SMTC uniforms.

I don't want to give away any secrets just yet. We're still working on the new design and need to find exactly the right material to handle the heat in Atlanta. But one thing I already know about these new uniforms— people at the trials will once again have something extra to talk about between races.

Friday, March 22 – Houston

Another extremely positive step in the 100. In the Texas Southern University (TSU) Relays, I once again made significant improvement in both the result, 10.26 seconds to win the race, and the way I felt.

The first 20 meters were as good as possible. I was out of the blocks well, accelerated well, and was right there with the top guys, which is hardly ever the case that early in the race. The only mistake I made was from about 20 to 30 meters, when I stayed too low for maybe two or three steps too long, which delayed me from really opening up as soon as I should have. But there was even something positive I could take away from making a mistake like that. I knew exactly what I had done. I could feel it. That means I'm back at a point where I can sense the difference between right and wrong, and I take that as an indication that I'm back in sync, or at least getting there. It was easily my best outing of the year. I got everything I could have wanted out of it.

The only negative came when we ran the 4 x 200 relay late in the evening. We ran pretty well, and won without much of a problem, but my left hamstring felt tight. It was perfectly understandable – it was so cold and windy by the time we ran – and there is no reason to be alarmed about something so minor. But we'll have to see about running again tomorrow. We're scheduled to run the 4 x 400, but I'll probably end up sitting out that one. It is definitely not the time to be taking chances.

Saturday, March 23 – Houston

The hamstring remained tight, so I skipped the 4 x 400 relay, but the Santa Monica crew still won easily without me, as expected. The best part of the meet, though, belonged to the high school kids. Fans of the TSU Relays always enjoy the chance to watch Olympians and collegiate athletes, but it's not until the high school relays that they really get on their feet and raise the decibel levels. There is cheering, chanting, clapping, singing, yelling, whistling – pretty much every form of noise and encouragement. It's all part of the tradition that comes when you put maybe ten thousand people in the stands for an event that has been around for some forty years. Any professional meet in the country would be thrilled to match the atmosphere. In fact, that's precisely why I've participated here every year since 1984 — the incredible atmosphere.

Sitting with Carol way up high in the stands, as a spectator, I was as fired up as I get at a track meet, all caught up in the desire and drive of those high school kids. They exhibit so much heart. Their motives are so pure. Sure, some of them are putting it all on the line in hopes of securing a college scholarship, but more of them are running simply because they enjoy it. Either way, just about anything can happen with athletes that age, totally unpredictable, which means constant entertainment. The good. The bad. The ugly. There is no way in the world anything else in track and field — Olympics or anything else — matches the thrills and spills and energy of a good high school relay.

Sunday, March 24 – Houston

Every indication was that Primo Nebiolo, president of the international track federation, was working behind the scenes to make the proposed changes in the Olympic schedule to benefit both Michael Johnson and me. And this morning we learned the changes have indeed gone through. Which is great for the sport. It is one of the most sensible moves I've ever seen the federation make.

It was kind of funny the way we learned about it, though. We were basically props in a worldwide public relations effort. Michael was in a television studio in Atlanta, I was in a studio here in town, and we were both being beamed by satellite to a meeting room in Cape Town, South Africa, where Primo was putting on a show for federation members and the media.

First came the official announcement. The schedule was being adjusted to separate the 200 and the 400 for Michael — a major change from the original plan. The new schedule offers two rest days between the final of the 400 and the first round of the 200. Under the previous schedule, the first two rounds of the 200 were on the same day as the 400 semifinals.

The schedule was also being changed to eliminate a conflict between the 200 and the long jump — which will allow me the opportunity to choose my events instead of having them dictated by the start times and days. I'm not saying this necessarily means

I'll end up doing all four events — the 100, 200, relay, and long jump. I've never said it would, never looked at it that way, and we have a long way to go before making any decision like that. But now at least the possibility exists. As I told Primo, "We're training hard every day, and dreaming every night."

In return, Primo said something that almost knocked me out of my chair. "Carl, you have been a good friend for years. I am wishing you to win four gold medals." It was extremely nice of him to say that. After all we've been through over the years, all the ups and downs of the relationship between the federation and the SMTC, that meant a lot to me. But there was also a subtext that dawned on me almost immediately. In effect, Primo was also saying: "Michael, I'm wishing you to lose." Because in order for me to win four, I'd have to win the 200, which is one of Michael's events. I don't know if Primo even realized what he was saying, or if he simply didn't care, but I'm pretty sure Michael caught it. I can't even imagine how that made him feel. I know I left the studio shaking my head about that one comment.

All week long, Floyd Heard, one of my training partners, was dropping hints. Well, not even hints. They were more like direct suggestions.

"Sunday's the day. Turning thirty."

And one of us would say: "Yeah? So?"

Or Floyd would say: "Big birthday weekend coming up."

And another one of us would say it again: "So?"

Talk about feeling neglected. Poor Floyd was sinking deeper and deeper. He was way down in the dumps. It was hilarious, the way he was moping around, thinking we were totally ignoring him, because he never once had a clue that our apparent lack of concern was actually a conspiracy. It was all part of our plan for the big surprise party tonight at my house.

There are a couple things you need to know about Floyd to understand just how enjoyable it was for us to plan something special for him, and, in the end, how much it meant to him. I don't know if there's another adult in the world who cares about birthdays the way Floyd does. The anticipation alone wears him out. And then there's the rest of the year. Floyd is one of the most loyal, trusting, caring friends you could possibly have, as well as one of the most durable and decorated members of the SMTC. He is an integral member of the family.

Floyd first made a name for himself ten years ago as the youngest man ever and the first college freshman, at Texas A&M, to be ranked number one in the world in the 200. There have been plenty of individual triumphs for him, including four national titles and a gold medal in the Goodwill Games. But the most enjoyable times for Floyd, and the most widely recognized, especially in recent years, have come as a major contributor to the success of the Santa Monica relay teams. I couldn't possibly count the number of times Floyd, running third leg, has handed me the stick to close out a relay, either the 4 x 100 or the 4 x 200. We've traveled the world together for so long, forever, it seems, and I can think of at least four times we've broken world records together: Koblenz, Germany, in 1989; Monte Carlo in 1991; Philadelphia in 1992; and Walnut, California, in 1994. But training and running together is only part of the friendship. We also spend a lot of time together away from the track.

When Floyd arrived at nine tonight, he was expecting to join me and several other people for a business meeting, something about a soft drink company that wanted us to work on a promotion. But once he turned the corner past the garage, once he saw about fifty friends standing there in my yard, Floyd started to realize he'd been had.

Surprise!

Floyd said: "I think I'm going to cry."

He was totally blown away. He hugged and kissed his girlfriend, hugged just about everyone in sight, actually, and it would have been impossible to miss the tears filling his eyes. It would have been impossible because they were sparkling right along with his endless smile. It was a night he will always remember – and so will the rest of us.

Tuesday, March 26 – Houston

Item in the newspaper: Ivan Pedroso, the Cuban long jumper who won the 1995 world championship and also earned the number one ranking for the year, had surgery to repair a torn thigh muscle. His doctor says the operation was successful and that Pedroso will try his utmost to be ready for Atlanta. But it's difficult to imagine a long jumper coming back from leg surgery so quickly, and even if he does, there's no way he's going to be one hundred percent.

That's a shame. First of all, I feel bad for Pedroso. Last year was so exciting for him, first big breakthrough year, and I'm sure he was entirely locked into the idea of being a solid favorite for his first Olympic medal. Second, on a bit of a selfish note, I'd hate for him not to be in Atlanta, because I always want to run or jump against the best people. That makes for the best competition. Also, when someone is missing, that opens the door for critics to say, "Sure, so-and-so won, but what if so-and-so had been there?"

And then I have one other reaction. When are these other athletes finally going to accept what I've been saying for years, that you have to be careful about how often you compete, that you need to stress conservation of body over expansion of wallet? You can look it up in the record books. When an athlete's ranking goes up, his number of meets goes up, because lucrative appearance fees act like a magnet. Now, don't get me wrong, I'm all for an athlete earning a good living when the timing and demand are just right, but never at the expense of staying healthy. It's a matter of short-term gain versus long-term benefits, and without question, too many athletes fail to put the emphasis on the big picture.

I've watched Mike Powell, the world-record holder, jump way too many times since his breakthrough year of 1991. No question, he's gotten off some impressive jumps and collected considerable appearance fees. But I've also seen him suffer the consequences of jumping too much, with injuries and poor performances.

Pedroso appears to be another textbook example of what I'm talking about. He's been ranked among the top few jumpers in the world since 1992, but it was not until last year, when meet promoters finally considered him a draw and Cuban officials wanted to capitalize on the exposure, that Pedroso went way overboard. He jumped in twenty-six meets, with each competition meaning up to six jumps. No doubt, he had a tremendous season. Pedroso jumped 28 feet or better in half his meets. He even jumped past the world record in Sestriere, Italy, going 29 feet, 4 $^3/_4$ inches, although questionable handling of the wind gauge meant the mark would never be ratified. But twenty-six meets? Are you kidding me? He didn't jump that many times in the three previous years combined.

By contrast, I've jumped in a grand total of eleven meets the last four years. Even during my prime, throughout my ten-year, sixty-five meet winning streak that ended in 1991, I was averaging only six or seven long jump competitions a year.

One thing for certain is that the human body was not designed to fly 28 or 29 feet in the air and then go crashing into a pile of sand. The physical beating is brutal, so injuries are by no means limited to those who jump the most. You're at risk each and every time down the runway and into the air. But common sense tells you the more you jump, the greater the odds of injury, and it's not just a matter of multiplying the risk by the number of jumps. You also have to factor in the cumulative effect, wearing down the body without proper recovery time, which greatly increases the potential for problems.

How many injuries will it take, how many missed opportunities to maximize the long-term benefits of an extended career, before people finally accept the merits of what I've been preaching for so long? This is not about seeing Pedroso get hurt and saying, Told you so. It's just about dealing with facts. You jump too often, you're ruining your career.

Wednesday, March 27 – Houston

Our workout was six 200s. Mike Marsh and I stayed right together throughout, and I felt pretty good. But it was not until we were done, once I was over talking to Coach Tellez, that I realized just how far things have come the last month or so.

Coach T said something to me for the first time: "I think you'll be ready to do all four. It's up to you, but you could do all four if you want to." He was talking about my four events in the Olympics – and I don't mean this was the first time he said anything like that to me this year. It was the first time ever. He never even talked that way back in 1984 or 1988. It was always me bringing it up, and Coach T saying, "Well, OK, if you want to. You don't have to, but if you want to...."

For Coach T, the definitive man of understatement, never one to get caught up in the hype of the Games or all the speculation along the way, saying I could do all four, especially saying it this early in the year, was a tremendous boost for me. I've always had the utmost trust in Coach T, so this was the ultimate vote of confidence. I took it as his way of telling me I'm again looking like myself. Finally.

Had he said something maybe a month ago about doing all four events, I would have thought he'd lost his mind. But now it makes sense. Things have really been coming around since that talk we had about concentration – since making that decision to push up the season and get in more races. I've had only good races since then, which has helped me conquer so many internal doubts. My recent performances have probably carried Coach T across a few emotional barriers as well.

It all comes back to confidence. There was a certain frailty I had to overcome. I don't care who you are, as good or as bad as you are in whatever you do, you gain and lose confidence according to your results. Because you're human. Now that my confidence is back, I'm in a totally different frame of mind each time I step on the track, each time I settle into the blocks.

Six months ago, no matter what I might have said to the contrary, I honestly didn't think I could win the 100 in Atlanta. I also didn't think I had to. It would be enough to make the team in the long jump, and then be able to concentrate on that one event. But now I'm back where I actually feel like I can win the 100, and as I've said before, when my 100 is on, everything else tends to follow suit.

I would never make a decision to compete in all four events just to be in them. Nor, on the other hand, would I require myself to feel like I must win all four. The only requirement I'll put on it is to know I'll be ready for a good fight to the end of each event. If I'm able to feel that at the trials, then I'll do it. I'll go for all four.

It's nothing I'm going to discuss publicly at this point. Why invite the added scrutiny? I'll just keep saying I'm undecided, which is true, but those comments from Coach T definitely have my thoughts moving in a new direction.

Thursday, March 28 – Houston

We're getting pretty good at converting the back yard into a temporary banquet facility. Tonight it was for another charity event, a dinner for the Southwest Key Program, a non-profit agency dedicated to the education and treatment of troubled youth. Instead of simply locking up juvenile delinquents and giving up on their futures, the Southwest Key Program offers an alternative path full of hope and sometimes even redemption.

It was Kirk Baptiste, a former teammate at Houston and with Santa Monica, a silver medalist at 200 meters in the 1984 Olympics, who introduced me to the Southwest Key Program a few years ago. He was developing something called the Key Olympics, which he saw as a way to reach troubled teens on concepts such as commitment, setting goals, and working as a team. Three years later, with support from the Texas Youth Commission and Probation Department, as well as contributions from events like the one we did tonight, the third annual Kirk Baptiste Key Olympics will enable two hundred kids to participate in three days of academic and athletic games that just might make a difference in their lives.

Kirk deserves a lot of credit for the way the Key Olympics have grown into such a meaningful undertaking. In finding a way to channel his own talents and experiences into something positive for others, he has also provided some of his contemporaries, including me, with a way to reach out and share something of ourselves. When I went to the initial Key Olympics with Kirk, I found myself wondering: Who really gets the most out of this? Is it the kids who might discover something new and see the possibility of something bright in their futures? Or is it those of us who get to see the looks on their faces when they realize someone else actually cares about what they are doing?

Friday, March 29 – Houston

I've been into this new routine lately, making sure that each night before I go to sleep, I take a few minutes to fill my head with something positive. It might be something technical about running. It might be something more general about track and field or the Olympics. Or I might concentrate my thoughts on a certain person, place, or idea that inspires me. It's part of a conscious effort to foster and sustain an entirely positive atmosphere in which to train, compete, and rest. Well, tonight I was lying there thinking about how dramatically recent developments have altered the entire landscape. Four things were on my mind.

Number one is the allergies. I've gone from feeling like my head is in the grip of a vise or something, so tight and congested, to feeling like everything is totally under control. Even when the air is really bad now, even when the sting of pollen is clouding my eyes, my head remains clear as a bell. It is the first time in years that I can say that.

Number two is the thyroid situation. Thank goodness we stumbled across it. Improvement has already been incredible, and, thanks to Dr. Brown, I'll soon be right where I need to be. Back to normal. Back to full strength.

Number three is the Leroy Burrell injury. It was the last thing I wanted to see, but nonetheless significant in terms of the 100. When both Leroy and I are running our best, I feel like he's the only one who should be able to touch me. But it's been four weeks now since he pulled that hamstring, and, unfortunately, Leroy is only capable of light running. Will he still be able to make it all the way back in time to be himself at the trials?

Number four is the Ivan Pedroso injury. This is considerably different than the Leroy situation, because when Pedroso and I are both in top shape and jumping our best, I still feel like I should have the edge. There is no way he should beat me. But, again, it's crazy timing, as if it were somehow determined this was another way to help clear a path for me.

The last thing I'd want to do is dwell on the misfortune of others. That is not at all the point of this exercise. I'm simply looking at changes and timing and circumstances, and the more I'm looking at them, the more I'm thinking that we're dealing with almost Twilight Zone-type stuff. Physically, I've been feeling the best I've felt in so long – and then two of my top competitors are hit with major physical problems. It's a pretty bizarre combination of events in such a short period of time.

Saturday, March 30 – Houston

In front of the temple of Zeus at Ancient Olympia in Greece, an actress dressed in the traditional sheath of a high priestess took a knee, held a torch to a concave mirror burning with the heat and energy of the sun, and lit the symbolic flame of the 1996 Games. The torch would soon be carried away on the first leg of the most publicized relay in the world – the one hundred and eleven-day journey to Atlanta. First lady Hillary Clinton was in Greece for the lighting, beaming with optimism and urging all nations to find peace and camaraderie through sport, and the festivities made for a nice television story. It was a strong reminder of just how soon the Games will be here – and how incredibly fast these first few months of the year have gone flying by.

The scene was not nearly as grand for the final leg of my blue-collar tour. Three weeks after running my first 100, I was back on the same track at Rice University for another one of those small, warm-up meets, back in the 100. Once again, I got everything I could have wanted out of it. Despite a so-so reaction to the gun, probably lost a tenth of a second right there, everything felt more instinctive this time, and I was pleased with the way I ran. I won with a time of 10.37 seconds into a headwind.

I say this is the end of the blue-collar tour because there are no more little warm-up meets after this. Next week I'll again be seeing world-class sprinters at the Texas Relays. That will be the first real test. The good thing is, I'm already past the point of feeling like I'm trying something new every week. I've been politely plugging along – quietly but effectively. Now, with the rhythm back, it's just a matter of: Let's do it again. Let's do it again.

Monday, April 1 – Houston

Weight update. It's been two weeks since I hit the panic button and put that diet memo up on the refrigerator. In addition to wearing out the juice machine, I've also been wearing out the scale. I've been checking constantly to see where I am.

And today we have...one hundred and eighty-nine pounds. Seven pounds lighter than two Mondays ago. Four more pounds to get where I want to be.

Not that it's been easy. I've fought through some hungry moments by trying to fill up on fresh juice. But I've always been fortunate about having the ability to lose weight. Like anyone else, I gain from time to time, but I've always been able to take it back off when I need to, and usually pretty quickly.

I did sneak in a little popcorn while watching a movie last night.

No butter, of course, but I guess we better keep that memo posted.

Tuesday, April 2 – Houston

One of the most difficult aspects of an Olympic year is having to say no as often as we do. We, meaning Joe Douglas and me. No, meaning we simply do not have time for everything we're asked to do. Training has to remain top priority over anything else, no matter how appealing it might be.

Some of the decisions are much less complicated than others. For example, there's no way we could possibly say yes to all the media requests for interviews. I think most reporters, editors, and producers understand that, even if they're not always happy about it. It is also impossible to attend each and every charity function that comes up – we must get a dozen requests a week – no matter how worthy the cause.

Saying no becomes most difficult when it's something unique that we really want to do. Perfect example: A legislative assistant called this

Joe Douglas, manager and friend, is with me every step of the way. Especially when we have to say no.

(PHOTO: ALLSPORT)

morning about an upcoming U.S. Senate hearing on organ donation and transplantation. They want me on Capitol Hill three weeks from today to testify about our awareness efforts. That would mean a great deal to me, having the opportunity to address Congress on an issue so important to me, but it would also mean extra travel during a critical stretch of training. That is nearly impossible for me to do at this point. So we asked, Is there any way I could do it after the Olympics? No, we were told, the date is firm. How about "appearing" at the hearing by teleconference from Houston? I would definitely do that. Well, apparently the senators do not like to accept testimony that way. So, unfortunately, it appears we're headed toward a conclusion I was hoping to avoid. A no.

Another interesting opportunity crossed my desk this morning. It is a proposal from something called The Prince of Wales's Foundation for Architecture, which plans to build what appears to be an impressive structure known as the World Athletes Monument in Atlanta. The top of the monument is designed to include five figures, representing the five continents, holding the earth above their heads in Atlas-like stances. They want me to pose as the model for these sculpted figures. But there is also a twist. The guy coordinating the project started his pitch by explaining that he was having financial problems — and wanted me to help bail him out. That, of course, raises immediate credibility questions about the entire project. Did he really want me as a model, or was that just a creative hook to ask for money? It is remarkable the number of people I've never even met who will call seeking financial support, and the angles they will use. I imagine it's pretty much the same for any prominent sports figure. But my charitable contributions will remain targeted to more directly assist real people — you know, education, health care, support for young athletes — not statues. So...another no.

In terms of pure business, one of the toughest decisions we've recently made, although it was a relatively obvious one, concerned an endorsement deal in Japan. The offer was worth close to half a million dollars. But, again, there was a sticking point. The commercials had to be shot in Tokyo. We invited them to do the shoot in Houston, but they would not budge. That pretty much made the decision for us. There is no way I could miss a week of training to go to the other side of the world — even for that kind of money. Not now. Yet another no.

Wednesday, April 3 – Houston

"Want to race?"

I hear it all the time. Never from an actual track and field athlete – but from just about anyone else. Men. Women. Kids. You name it. They're never really serious – at least I don't think so. For whatever reason, though, people all over the world have independently concluded that the single most creative thing to do when they see me up close is to challenge me to a race.

This morning it was some guy walking into a convenience store as I was leaving. "Hey, Carl, want to race?" He had a big smile on his face. "No, thanks," I said. "Tired as I am, you'd probably beat me." Which just about had him on the floor, he thought it was so funny. If only he knew how often I go through the same old routine. I know most people are just trying to be nice when they initiate it. But I sure wish they'd come up with something new every now and then.

Thursday, April 4 – Houston and Austin

There was not a whole lot of down time today.

I was up before seven to work on a column for NetNoir online service. Then I made business calls and ran errands from nine to ten. I went to workout, actually the calmest part of the day, until almost noon. Then Carol and I rushed off to the airport, where I had a meeting with the producer of a commercial we'll start shooting Sunday. The producer remained in Houston to prepare. Carol and I flew to Austin for the Texas Relays.

Carol is going to long jump tomorrow, first meet since her season opener in January, so I'm looking forward to seeing her back in action. I'm running the 100 on Saturday. But before I could really focus on that...I still had one more commitment this evening. It was another reception, along with Kirk Baptiste and Carol, for the Southwest Key Olympics.

I'll definitely want to stay off my feet tomorrow. Other than watching Carol compete, I'll be in my hotel room, resting, the way it ought to be the day before a meet. I'll be thinking about my race. Thinking about getting the job done.

Friday, April 5 – Austin

Horrible weather. Temperature in the mid-forties. Heavy wind and rain. It was not exactly a day for the beach, or to jump into the sand. So much for Carol competing in the long jump — too much risk of slipping on the runway or the board and being injured. We've all competed in less than ideal conditions when we've had to, like at the Olympic trials, but this was not the time or the place for Carol to take a chance.

She was especially frustrated because this was the second time in a row she missed a scheduled meet. A few weeks ago she pulled out with a minor hamstring problem. But you can't make a decision like this based on frustration. You have to do what makes the most sense. Luckily, Carol had one of her ever-present romance novels to keep her company at the hotel, something to keep her mind off the fact her season had once again been pushed back by factors beyond her control.

Unfortunately, it looks like this entire trip might turn out to be worthless. The weather report is calling for more cold and wind, and maybe rain, which means I'll have to make a decision in the morning. As much as I want to be in this race, first big test in the 100 against legitimate competition, the last thing I'm going to do is take a chance on blowing an entire Olympic year for an April appearance in a warm-up meet.

Saturday, April 6 – Austin

I couldn't believe it when I looked out the window and saw it was clear as could be. Cool but clear. I was looking at an invitation to run, and was more than pleased to accept.

Usually I just remember the race itself. This time I'll also remember the introduction before the 100. One, it was nice to hear such a great response from the crowd when the announcer was done listing my credentials and boomed out my name. The announcer was really laying it on — it was almost embarrassing — and the crowd here has always been very supportive. Two, I could not help but notice what Jon Drummond, one of my competitors, was doing while I was being introduced. Drummond, the top-ranked American in the 100 last year, was clowning in an adjacent lane, which was nothing new for him, but at my expense this time. He was playing the air violin, as if to say, Big deal, Carl is done and I'm about to take him out. He was also taking bows and shouting, as if the race were already his. Now, Drummond is generally a nice guy, especially away from the track, clever and talented as well, but always trying to draw attention to himself and sometimes stepping over the line of good taste. He and Dennis Mitchell, another veteran sprinter, bronze medalist in Barcelona and number one in the world in the 100 in 1994, are the two loose cannons out there. They're the antics twins — always acting up.

Anyway, I was not going to let Drummond or anyone else interfere with what I was here to accomplish. My start was OK, nothing great, nothing horrible, and at 20 meters I was in the middle of the pack, which is right where I stayed until about the 70 mark. Then I started picking off people, one by one, until I finally made it past Drummond in the last 15 meters. In other words, I was me again. Average start. Consistent acceleration. Take it away at the end. It was the same old race I've been running for years. Most important, my top-end speed was there. It's been a long time since I could say that. And I mean *years*.

But it all comes back to confidence. *You're going to be behind, but don't panic, you'll be OK. Stay relaxed. You're going to be right there at the finish.* Thanks to the blue-collar tour, that confidence was once again there for me, just the way we had planned it. I felt both the rhythm and the confidence. Man, that felt good. It was a very big race for me.

Drummond, the fiddler, was second with a time of 10.12 seconds, and was really staring me down once we were done running. It's tough to play the clown after losing, I guess, although one might even wonder about that after hearing some of his post-race comments to the media. Drummond talked about seeing the gray in my hair, said he was almost embarrassed, and then attributed my victory to his theory that I must be taking Geritol. "Forget steroids," Drummond said. "It's the Geritol."

My time was 10.10, which is as much as I could possibly want this early in the season. In fact, it's been almost two years since I've run that fast, period, without the help of a big wind at my back. Even more important was the assessment of Coach Tellez. He said it was the best I've looked from 20 meters on since Tokyo in 1991 — and that was the race in which I came from way behind to break the world record. "Don't change anything," Coach T said. "You run like that, no way possible you won't make the team."

My top-end speed is back. No more clowning for Jon Drummond (right) after we finish the 100 in the Texas Relays.

Making the team. It might as well be a mantra between now and the trials, which begin in the middle of June. The top three finishers in each event qualify to represent the U.S. in the Games. With the exception of filling spots on the relay teams, everyone else goes home. Everyone else watches on television.

Making the team. Making the team. Making the team.

We'll all be hearing plenty of that the next couple of months. Some of us will even be hearing it in our sleep.

Sunday, April 7 – Houston

Back to work — different kind of work. Because now, with apologies to Joe DiMaggio, the American original, I'm Mr. Coffee.

I spent a good part of the day in a studio, filming commercials for a Japanese coffee company named Pokka. We're introducing a new product: ready-to-serve coffee in a can, milk and sugar already included, to drink either hot or cold. It will be sold primarily in vending machines.

This had to be the most efficient shoot I've ever had with a Japanese company. We did one or two takes of each shot, and then moved on. Typically, no matter how good the first or second take appear to be, the Japanese always want more. They'll keep shooting until you simply can't take it anymore. But these were the young Japanese. Both the director and the photographer spoke English. They were much less formal and much more efficient than what I was used to, and that allowed us to move right along.

We did profile and straight-ahead shots of me saying, "I'm Mr. Coffee." We did shots of my open hand, through which the product, with the assistance of modern technology, will magically rise and appear. Finally, there were a few shots of me drinking the coffee on a victory stand. The whole production was about as simple as it gets.

Tomorrow morning, we'll finish the commercials, with training pushed back to the afternoon. Tuesday, we'll do still photos for print ads, and that'll be it for Mr. Coffee. Back to being Mr. Runner Man.

Monday, April 8 – Houston

The words, though somewhat removed by the fact I'm not directly hearing them, only reading them in a newspaper, are nonetheless chilling. They are the words of a former sprinter named Darrell Robinson, who recently tried to kill himself by drinking antifreeze. But survived.

Speaking from a hospital in Seattle, after being in a coma for five days, Darrell told a reporter: "I still don't know where I'm going. That's the funny part. People might wonder, 'Aren't you glad to be alive?' Some days I'm glad and some days I'm not sure. I came from death, and I should appreciate where I am right now, but do I want to be in this world? I don't know yet."

Ten years ago, when he was running, Darrell had the physical tools to build a bright future. He was the 400-meter national champion and ranked number three in the world. But he never had the emotional strength to stay a champion. I always thought something was missing because he had been with us at the University of Houston for a few weeks in 1982, supposedly to attend school and join the track team. But Darrell never went to class, didn't get along with Coach Tellez, and was soon gone.

Darrell Robinson was merely a passing acquaintance. At least until he sold a pack of lies about me to a German magazine named *Stern*. This was the same magazine that had so readily paid huge money for the right to publish the fake Hitler diaries. Darrell's story came out in 1989, the year after Ben Johnson made steroids such a hot topic, so the magazine was looking for a big scoop. Unfortunately, there was no correlation between going after a good story and going after the truth. *Stern*, without ever confirming his charges, paid Darrell to spin an incredible tale of drug use by a number of athletes, including me. It all went back to that brief period when he was in Houston. Of course, the allegations were entirely fiction. After years of legal fact-finding related to a lawsuit I filed against *Stern*, the litigation was resolved in a manner that was most satisfactory to me.

Still, no matter how he tried to damage my image, and for whatever reason, what I now feel toward Darrell is what almost any human being would feel. Compassion. One thing we learned after that magazine story broke was that Darrell had already contemplated taking his own life. Whatever his problems, they'd been with him for years. Which now makes it almost eerie to think back to something I told reporters when I first learned about the *Stern* piece. Before I even got into the specifics of refuting what Darrell had said, I stressed that what he really needed was not more media attention. It was psychiatric help.

I'm left to wonder: All this time Darrell has been sending out such severe distress signals, has anyone ever tried to help him? And I wonder: Will it still be possible for him to find peace with himself? I hope so. Whatever he ultimately decides to do with his life, I hope he is able to find peace.

Tuesday, April 9 – Houston

I'm sure the Pokka coffee people had seen or heard about the Pirelli ad with the high heels, the one that generated so much attention because of the shock value, because they also wanted a racy print ad, something that would get people talking. They wanted me to pose pretty much naked...other than a G-string covering my privates.

To which I said, OK, as long as it would be done in a way that says: "This is the finely-tuned body of an athlete." Not: "This is a sex machine." Next thing I knew, I was posing in the starting position, minus the Santa Monica uniform. They also did a side shot of me standing in the almost-nude, in a running position. Always something new and different to keep it interesting. I can't wait to hear what the conservative people of Japan think about this one.

Once I got to the track for workout, I was quickly reminded just how much Coach Tellez appreciates it when I'm tied up with a commercial or interview or other business stuff, which is to say not at all. Joe Douglas and I pay constant attention to finding the right balance between the business and athletic sides of my existence. Maintaining that balance is an integral part of our jobs. But Coach T has no appreciation whatsoever for the business side. He understands it, accepts and respects it, but chooses to separate himself from it. He's there for

They wanted something racy. I guess they got it.

one thing and one thing only – to prepare me for competition. "Oh, you have a shoot today? I don't care what you have. You have to train." All the subtlety of a sledgehammer. That's the Coach T I've always known and loved.

Wednesday, April 10 – Houston

One hundred days until opening ceremonies in Atlanta. The countdown continues. Not that I'm getting a whole lot of time to even think about what day it is. The schedule this week is wearing me out.

After three straight days with the Japanese film and photo crews, I was hoping to catch a break, but no such luck. Following workout and a visit to the doctor for more thyroid tests, I was off to another photography studio for an appointment with someone from *Life* magazine. It was the first time I've ever posed with my entire collection of Olympic gold, minus that one medal buried with my father, of course.

But that was not even the picture of the day. The photographer, Joe McNally, is working on what he calls a "nontraditional" study of how athletes rely on and develop different muscle groups. Which translated into this: He wanted me to pose for a shot that would make me look totally nude, thereby displaying my muscles, right along with almost everything else. I couldn't believe it! Two days in a row. Two photographers from opposite sides of the world. Very similar ideas.

This time, in keeping with the theme of the "study," I posed with one leg up on a block, leaning into the shot, one arm forward, the other back, in a running position. In the words of Mary Ellen Clark, another athlete who posed for McNally: "Tastefully done, with nothing hanging out."

Friday, April 12 – Houston

We are not running in a meet this weekend, so we did time trials, four rounds of 60 meters, with partners. Mine was Mike Marsh. Actually, we did two rounds back to back, walked a lap for recovery, then ran the last two. We did it that way because Coach Tellez wanted us to start getting into the process, both physical and mental, of running rounds.

That is the way it works in the 100 at the Olympic trials. There are two rounds the first day. Then semis and finals are the second day. It is completely different than just going out and running the 100, one race, in an invitational meet. The challenges and demands are so much greater when you're running rounds, and then, of course, the pressure of battling to make the team takes it to a whole different level. So it's good we're starting so early with the concept of rounds.

Preparing the body. Preparing the mind. One thing I know from experience – the Olympic trials will definitely require peak performance of both.

Saturday, April 13 – Houston, Dallas, Los Angeles

First half of a very Nike weekend.

I took an early-morning flight to Dallas, where I went directly to Texas Stadium, home of the dreaded Cowboys, for an event to support youth sports. It was part of the Nike P.L.A.Y. (Participate in the Lives of America's Youth) program. I also got to sign as witness on some organ donor cards while I was there, thanks to my friends at the Southwest Organ Bank, who had a booth.

Then it was straight back to the airport for a flight to the West Coast. I had a production meeting tonight. We start shooting Nike commercials first thing in the morning.

Sunday, April 14 – Los Angeles, Pasadena, Houston

It turned out that "first thing in the morning" for the Nike commercial meant being on location at a college track by 5:30. The director knew we had a lot to do and couldn't afford to waste any daylight. Which we definitely didn't. Physically, with all the running and jumping they needed for the main commercial, which will feature the long jump, it had to be the toughest shoot I've ever done. It was even more demanding than the breakdown workouts we do on Mondays. By far. So much for using the weekend to let my body rest and recover.

The amazing thing was, even after a mad dash to catch the last flight home, and then the flight itself, I feel pretty good. I'm tired, of course, but not totally wiped out. No question, my energy level is up again. It is back where it normally was before developing the thyroid problem.

With the way I've been performing in both practice and meets, and then adding to that the overall feeling that my body is once again cooperating, I can't help but think I'm headed in the right direction. There's still a long way to go. But I'm definitely headed in the right direction – which is a whole lot better than the alternative.

Monday, April 15 – Houston

We are entering the week of the deuce. My first 200-meter race of the year will be Sunday at the Mt. SAC (San Antonio College) Relays in Walnut, California, outside of Los Angeles.

We abandoned the normal Monday breakdown – 400, 300, 200 – for a series of 200s that broke us down just the same. We ran a 200, walked back to the start, and ran another. Then we had five minutes to rest before two more 200s. All of them were in the 22-second range.

I doubt I could have done that workout just two weeks ago. It was another sign that my strength is back. Recovery is the key. Even with those time trials Friday and then a monster weekend, including the demands of travel and then all that running and jumping for the cameras yesterday, I was able to make it through this morning.

I'm recovering the best I have all year. Obviously, I've been concerned about that for quite a while now, not recovering as well as I ought to be after running, so it's certainly a relief to feel like we've been able to eliminate the problem. We always have to remember, the greatest challenge of both the U.S. trials and the Olympics is running the rounds, surviving the rounds, and still being fresh for the finals. That makes recovery a huge issue. It might be the most important factor of all. That, along with confidence, and they usually come hand in hand.

Tuesday, April 16 – Houston

We're taking more of our practice starts on the turn instead of the straightaway because that alone, starting on the curve, makes the 200 very different from the 100. It's funny how people kind of assume both sprints require pretty much the same thing: running fast. True. But that also entirely oversimplifies it. The whole strategy changes in the 200 because it's such a different race.

Over the years, as much as I've run the 100, the 200 has always been like the "other" sprint for me. Without as much repetition, I often make the same mistake. I've had a tendency to run the turn, the first portion of the race, too fast. That usually puts me out front but also makes it a struggle to hold on down the straightaway against someone who spreads his energy more sensibly, more efficiently, from start to finish. The key for me, then, is to keep running hard off the turn. I still want to grab the early lead, especially because people tend to panic when they see me ahead of them, but I also want to keep it an intelligent, smooth pace. It's a fine line, but that will be my focus this weekend at Mt. SAC.

I guess I've run the 200 almost every way imaginable over the years. Right. Wrong. From out front. From behind. But this is the strongest and healthiest I've been in so long, maybe ever, so it will be interesting to see what happens. I'm looking forward to it.

This meet and then the next one, first Saturday in May, will be very important in terms of planning, because that next one will be my first long jump competition of the year. Once I've opened up in all three events, the 100, 200, and long jump, I'll have a feel for what needs sharpening. And then I'll have probably three more meets before the trials to work on any problem areas.

Wednesday, April 17 – Houston

I've never been one to examine baseball box scores in the newspaper. But Darryl Hamilton, who plays center field for the Texas Rangers, eighth season in the American League, spent the winter training with us, so now I keep checking the fine print to see how he's doing.

Obviously, I want Darryl to have his best year ever, and naturally I'm paying special attention to anything he does that involves speed. You know, chasing down a fly ball nobody thought he could reach, beating out a bunt, stealing bases. So this morning I had to laugh. Darryl had three hits and a walk in five trips to the plate. Hard to beat that. But then I noticed he was also thrown out trying to steal. For the second time in a row! Darryl has been all over the place, talk shows and newspaper articles included, telling everyone how incredible it was to train under Coach Tellez, and now he's been thrown out two nights in a row. Come on, Darryl!

Let's back up for a minute. Coach T has always helped athletes from other sports — football, baseball, tennis — and they always leave with a better understanding of how to move more efficiently, the mechanics of running the right way. One of the most dramatic examples of improvement I've seen was Andre Agassi after working with Coach T on his footwork, and there have been many others.

So what in the world is Darryl doing getting thrown out twice in a row? I mean, last year he had a leg injury and still managed to have one of the best stolen-base records in the league. Maybe he needs to return for a refresher course.

Of course, it would be great to have Darryl back, because he's such a character, hilarious, always talking smack, and he can definitely spin a tale with the best of them. All of which made him the perfect match for one of our longtime training partners, Frank Rutherford, a native of the Bahamas who won a bronze medal in the 1992 Olympics in the triple jump. Man, did those two go at it constantly. They were always making up stuff about each other, always challenging each other, always bickering. All in good fun.

It still makes me laugh when I think of the day Darryl caught Frank from behind. The whole thing started with a phone call. A bunch of us were watching the Super Bowl together, and Frank called for Darryl, just to taunt him. "Better be ready tomorrow when you come to practice, cause I'm gonna wear you out." Of course, Darryl couldn't let go of it. "I'm gonna kick Frank's butt. You watch, I'll get him before I leave."

They were relentless — right up until the big showdown, Darryl against Frank, head to head, running 400 meters. At the halfway mark, Frank was maybe three strides ahead. But Darryl kept coming, and with about 100 meters to go, he moved out to lane two, hoping to pass Frank, who was still hugging the inside lane. Darryl was really pushing it. Frank was dying. The rest of us were howling. Then we were treated to an image forever frozen in our minds: Frank turning toward Darryl as they neared the finish, and Darryl leaning past him, arms stretched in victory toward the sky, as they crossed the line.

I couldn't believe it. Darryl, a baseball player, ran aggressively enough to go get Frank, a track guy, down the final stretch. Of course, Darryl and Frank still offer different versions of what happened. But I saw every meter of it. And Darryl was the man. Now I wish he'd start getting down to second base a little faster.

Friday, April 19 – Houston

It sure is strange to be preparing for the Mt. SAC Relays without even getting ready to run a relay (only the 200 for me). We've always had such a good time running the 4 x 100 or 4 x 200 there – and have always made it our business to put on a good show. In fact, it was just two years ago that Mike Marsh, Leroy Burrell, Floyd Heard and I set the 4 x 200 world record (1:18.68) at Mt. SAC. It is a record that still stands.

Relays have always been a lot of fun for me, and not just the races themselves, but also the training and everything else that goes with being a team. Track and field is generally such an individual sport. Relays are the exception. I love that feeling of working together toward a common goal.

As the anchor man, it gives me tremendous confidence when I see my teammates building a lead, which they usually do, and I also enjoy the feeling of them depending on me to finish off the job, whether we're ahead or behind when I get the baton. I guess you could compare it with taking the last shot while the clock is running down in the NBA playoffs, or maybe stepping up to the plate with two outs in the bottom of the ninth in the World Series. It is not a time for weak hearts. Not a time for weak minds. Nothing else I do could ever match that feeling of the baton hitting my hand and the crowd buzzing with expectation.

It was just months ago that we were talking about wanting to set another world record this year. Santa Monica has held the 4 x 100 record before, and Leroy, Mike and I still share pieces of it as members of national teams (1992 Olympics and 1993 World Championships). But now we wanted it back where we felt it belonged, under the rising sun of the Santa Monica logo, right next to its brother, the 4 x 200, and its cousin, the sprint medley. That was the family picture we were trying to put together. Unfortunately, though, with Leroy still temporarily out of action, we've had to put the relays on hold.

Saturday, April 20 – Houston and Baldwin Park, California

I've always accepted the reputation of Southern California as the land of healthy living – plenty of sunshine, exercise, and vegetarians everywhere. Then how is it that after flying here and getting settled into a hotel maybe fifteen miles east of Los Angeles, close to where we'll be running tomorrow, Carol and I spent more than an hour looking for a health food store and still came up empty?

Based on what we saw, and we took several passes in our rental car up and down every busy street we could find, we're smack in the middle of the strip mall capital of America. We kept passing fast food joints, discount shopping outlets, hardware stores, donut shops, just about every variety of downscale retail you might imagine. But there was not a single health food store to be found.

Well, actually there were two. One was apparently closed for the weekend. (Makes a lot of sense. Why be open when people are most likely to have time to shop?) The other was a vacant store beneath a big "Health Foods" sign that drew our attention but proved to be nothing more than a tease. So we finally gave up and returned to the hotel. I guess I'll be running the 200 fueled by whatever we can get out of room service. It's a perfect example of why we're usually better off at home.

Sunday, April 21 – Walnut, California

My heart was pounding from the moment I got to the track. It was a totally different feeling again. Like the way it used to be.

The last few years I'd allowed myself to fall into an attitude where I was telling myself I just wanted to run well. I was hoping I even had it in me to run well. Not anymore. Now the only thought is that I'm here to win. Forget just running well. I've got to win. It is a much more productive approach.

This afternoon it carried me to victory in the 200. I ran an intelligent, smooth race, no significant mistakes, really, and won with my best time in three years, 20.19 seconds. It was also the third-best time of the year in the world, and probably the fastest I've ever run the 200 so early in a season. It was another huge step for me.

After those two last-place finishes indoors, I was written off for dead. No way I could make the Olympic team. Conventional wisdom suggested it was time for the farewell tour. Even after winning the 100 at the Texas Relays, there were still plenty of people thinking it was a fluke. After this 200, though, the reporters were singing an entirely different tune when they came down to interview me. Instead of grilling me on whether I could even make it to Atlanta, now they wanted to know which events I'm going to choose.

There had been so much snickering these last few months. *Yeah, right, Lewis will be running in Atlanta. Sure, and Jesse Owens is coming back as well. Ali is going to box again, Spitz is swimming, and....* I know it's still early. I can't afford to get ahead of myself. But it sure can be amusing the way the pundits so readily go flip-flop in whatever direction the wind is temporarily blowing. They're no different, I guess, than the political pundits on those television debate shows I'm always watching.

There was even a reporter who wanted to know if I'm really thinking about sticking around for the long jump in the 2000 Olympics in Sydney. No! Please let me make that perfectly clear. Coach Tellez was recently quoted about that – saying there was no reason I couldn't keep jumping that long. But I am not even remotely considering such madness. Let's debunk that myth as quickly as possible. I don't want anyone thinking for as much as a split second that there is even a sliver of possibility that Atlanta will be anything but my last Olympics.

Mt. SAC was also a tremendous meet for Santa Monica as a whole (even without running a relay). Mike Marsh ran an incredible race in the 100 (9.95 seconds) after only a so-so start. Floyd Heard got his Olympic trials qualifying time in the 200. And Lamont Smith, still in college, one of our promising newcomers, broke onto the scene with a personal best and the fastest time in the world this year (44.63) in the 400. The only real disappointment was Carol, who struggled in the long jump, her first outdoor competition of the year.

Monday, April 22 – Houston

Butch Reynolds, who holds the world record in the 400, is also widely known for the time in 1990 when he allegedly tested positive for steroids. Of course, Butch has always maintained his innocence, claiming he was the victim of a grossly mishandled test. His lengthy legal battle went all the way to the Supreme Court during the 1992 Olympic trials. Later, he was even awarded millions of dollars in a judgment against the international track federation, but the ruling was eventually reversed. To this day, the issues remain murky.

Unfortunately, Butch is again stirring them up by complaining about a system we all ought to be embracing. It is a fairly new process by which track and field athletes are randomly chosen for unannounced testing. Unlike the previous testing program, in which you had forty-eight hours after being notified to report and provide a urine sample, there is no longer any prior notification. There is no time for an athlete to cleanse his or her system before offering a sample. Representatives of the track federation simply knock on your door or show up at your training facility, your office, wherever, and they wait with you until you're able to fill a bottle. It is an approach for which I lobbied for years, and I am thankful we finally have it as an additional safeguard against potential cheaters.

Butch is airing quite a different opinion. After being tested at his home in Columbus, Ohio, he made it very clear he had no appreciation at all for the situation. A local television report quoted him as saying: "When they come to your door unannounced like that, it takes away your rights. It takes away your respect as an athlete."

Wait a minute here. How exactly does a clean athlete lose any rights or respect by providing a urine sample? It seems to me that just the opposite is true. A clean athlete gains something by letting the world know he or she is clean. In fact, the whole sport gains by letting people know we're clean. The only person who loses any rights or respect is someone who tests positive.

One other thing. If Butch was so concerned that the surprise appearance of a testing official was by itself such a horrible invasion of his privacy, then why in the world did he choose to turn it into a media event? Isn't the evening news a significantly greater invasion than letting in a single visitor? We're all randomly tested every now and then. However, I don't know of a single other world-class athlete who shares it with the local television station. If Butch had just filled the bottle and handled the entire situation privately, with dignity, the whole process would have passed as routine, without any public notice or discussion whatsoever. But now people are again talking about him. People are again raising issues that were long ago filed away as a dead story.

A few years back, Butch and I had a chance to speak privately about the impact of his case. He made some good points, and also some with which I disagreed. Now I want to tell him, Butch, enough already. Stop singling yourself out by complaining. Everyone else is living by the same rules, and even applauding them.

I've been randomly tested at the track, at the gym, at home, at Mike Marsh's house. It's only as big a deal as you make it out to be. There was even something to laugh about the last time I had to fill a bottle. Even though the guy collecting the sample knew exactly who I was, he still had to ask for my driver's license as proof of my identity. New requirement, he said. Still, as serious as he was about adhering to procedure, he also found it pretty entertaining that he was checking the picture on my license, like some bouncer at a college bar.

Finally, I want to say, Butch, do yourself a favor by allowing your life and your career to move on. You've been a great athlete before. Be one again. All this excess baggage about drug testing? Leave it alone. Go back to putting all your energy into training and competing. Let people know you once again as the person who holds one of the most impressive world records in all of track and field, not as some misguided crusader, this rebel against the cause.

Tuesday, April 23 – Houston

Remember what I was trying to explain a few weeks ago about how difficult it can be to say no when it's something I really want to do, and that example of having to pass on the U.S. Senate hearing?

Well, thanks to the persistence of Senator Bill Frist, chairman of the hearing on organ and tissue donation, we were able to transform that initial no into a yes. Frist finally was able to clear the way for me to testify by teleconference from Houston, with large-screen televisions carrying me live into the hearing room, and I greatly appreciated his efforts. It was an honor to address the Senate Labor and Human Resources Committee.

I've appeared at other congressional hearings over the years, primarily to support anti-drug legislation, but this was one of the most impressive sessions I've seen. Frist was himself a prominent heart transplant surgeon in Tennessee prior to entering the political arena, so his passion and knowledge brought instant credibility. Then there were several other senators with personal stories to tell. Two spoke as donor fathers. One spoke as the friend of a transplant recipient. And other witnesses shared incredibly powerful tales of both triumph and tragedy.

One of the most exciting developments on the legislative front was discussed by Senator Byron L. Dorgan of North Dakota, who is responsible for a new amendment that will require organ donor information to be inserted with every income tax refund mailed next year. That alone will mean reaching seventy million families. Dorgan said the idea came to him when he noticed that tax returns are now sent with promotional material pushing the sale of U.S. Olympic coins — not exactly a matter of life and death. Though the timing was purely coincidental, it was just hours after the hearing that his proposal sailed through a Senate vote as part of an unrelated health-insurance reform package.

Wednesday, April 24 – Houston

This was a career first. I received a personal note of encouragement from Primo Nebiolo, president of the international track federation. It came by fax from Rome.

Primo and I certainly have had our ups and downs over the years, butting heads on a number of issues concerning the rights of athletes, but the relationship has been excellent for some time. Maybe it's one of the benefits of being around so long — we've been able to reach the point where we understand each other a lot better than we did through the early years. It was nice of Primo to write, the first contact we've had since that satellite event to announce the revised Olympic schedule, and his words were extremely kind.

"I was very pleased to learn from press reports of your recent outstanding achievements on the track. Knowing the great champion that you are, we had a feeling that the athletics and sporting world had not seen the last of Carl Lewis. I can only reiterate what I told you from Cape Town: Good luck and keep believing in your dreams for Atlanta."

Looking forward to seeing you there, Primo. As I said when we last spoke, we will be on my turf this time, and the dinner invitation remains open. My treat.

Thursday, April 25 – Houston and Atlanta

I had minor surgery this afternoon to remove a small growth from my lower back. Then it was off to Atlanta for a U.S. Olympic Committee event, which will be tomorrow morning. I sure hope the pain from the incision will be gone by then.

It's been a while since I detected the growth, which turned out to be a cyst about the size of a walnut, but I have not been overly concerned about it. The doctor said something like this is not unusual for someone who exercises so much. A pore gets clogged, fluid becomes trapped under the skin, and all the rubbing and irritation eventually causes the formation of a solid mass, like a pebble. Then the pebble grows. The important thing is to get rid of it before it ruptures and causes an infection.

The incision is about an inch long, and I'm hurting more than I thought I'd be. I will not train tomorrow – a day to heal – but that was part of the plan. We intentionally did it on a Thursday so I'd have three days off. I should definitely be ready to roll again by Monday.

Friday, April 26 – Atlanta

The USOC event was two-fold. I was in the final group of athletes to be inducted into a program honoring the one hundred greatest U.S. Olympians. Then I did a press conference as part of a media summit, a preview of the upcoming Games, that drew hundreds of reporters and photographers from around the world.

The most enjoyable thing for me was spending time with the other athletes. Twenty of us were inducted, including Muhammad Ali, Brian Boitano, Bill Bradley, Magic Johnson, Jackie Joyner-Kersee, Greg Louganis, and Mary Lou Retton. But only six of us were actually here. The others were: Alice Coachman, seventy-three years old, the first black woman in the world to win an Olympic gold medal; Mike Eruzione, one of the stars of that incredible hockey team that beat the Russians and won the gold in 1980; Karch Kiraly, the volleyball player; Bill Russell, the basketball star; and Joan Benoit Samuelson, the marathon champion.

The most memorable part of the day was finally having a chance to meet Alice Coachman, who was both a sprinter and high jumper, but was best known as a jumper. I had always heard stories about her because Alice attended Tuskegee Institute shortly before my mother did. There was one year they even trained together sometimes. As a jumper, Alice won ten straight national titles and eventually set an Olympic record while winning her gold medal in the 1948 Games in London. She then went on to complete her college education, became a teacher and coach, and has always been an energetic role model for young women, especially in the African-American community. When we met, Alice immediately wanted to know how my mother was doing, which I thought was nice, and it was great to visit with such a special woman.

There was one other thing that struck me this morning: It is amazing how far my relationship with the USOC has come over the years. It definitely started out rocky – to say the least. The way the USOC insisted on treating athletes back then, it was almost like a dictatorship. There was nothing pleasant about the resistance Joe Douglas and I often encountered when we wanted to try something new, and especially when we were stressing the rights of athletes. Now, though, with new USOC leadership and a greater desire to work *with* the athletes instead of against them, there is much more cooperation and understanding.

Obviously, the USOC does not need any single athlete to believe in everything it does. And I still do not – which is fine. But I sure have been pleased about the way we have worked together on a number of projects the last few years. That gives me great hope that we will continue working together for years to come – long after I retire – and I never would have been able to say that back in the early stages of my career.

Saturday, April 27 – Houston

I've had meets four of the last five weekends, and the fifth, in Dallas and Los Angeles for Nike, was equally demanding, so I'm ready to take a stand. For rest and relaxation. That is my entire agenda for today and tomorrow.

I'm temporarily checking out. Physically. Emotionally. And even as the writer of this diary. I'll be back Monday.

Monday, April 29 – Houston

Sometimes I catch myself thinking ahead to being at the trials and the Games. More so the trials for now, but sometimes both, and what I see is a direct reflection of how comfortable I am with the way things are going. Because I can see myself winning. Not long ago, the focus was just making the team. Now, it's more than that. It's winning.

Back during the indoor season, I was never really thinking that way. It was more a case of wondering what might happen. It is only when I have a solid base of confidence, as I do now, that my mind is truly free to generate thoughts of winning.

Still, there is an important distinction here. It's great to be confident again. But there is a big difference between that and taking something for granted. I'm still not assuming anything whatsoever. Not even about making the team – in any event. There are still so many things that can happen. But it sure makes me feel better that my thoughts are no longer clouded by so many question marks. It sure is a good sign that my thoughts are once again wandering freely toward images of finishing a winner.

Wednesday, May 1 – Houston

Leroy Burrell and I shared emcee duties tonight at the University of Houston spring sports banquet, an annual event to celebrate the accomplishments of student-athletes in a variety of sports. We had a good time with it, trying to be somewhat entertaining, but also demonstrating that we'd better keep our day jobs. Because our big crowd pleaser of the evening, our Top Ten List, David Letterman-type thing, basically fell flat. What can I say? I guess we need better writers. (OK, I admit it, we did the writing ourselves, with help from Leroy's sister, Dawn, who is also a sprinter.)

With Houston preparing to make the transition from the soon-to-be defunct Southwest Conference to a new alliance of schools, our topic was Top Ten Reasons Why We Will Love Conference USA. At least we had a few that got good reactions. The best laughs came at the expense of an entire state, Tennessee, where Houston will soon be competing with Memphis on a regular basis. "Finally," I said. "A state with a worse Southern accent than ours." It was number six on the list, and maybe we should have stopped right there.

Thursday, May 2 – Houston

We're being treated to another nasty assortment of charges and countercharges revolving around the almighty Olympic dollar. It's Sponsor Clash II, and it's another battle of heavyweights. In one corner, we have the U.S. Olympic Committee and United Parcel Service, a worldwide Olympic sponsor; in the other, the U.S. Postal Service, a former member of the Olympic family, now being accused of hitting below the belt.

They're fighting about T-shirts, licensing rights, and even the delivery of mail to athletes during the Games. In a broader sense, what they're really trading blows about is one of the most cut-throat of all Olympic events, "parasite" or "ambush" marketing. It is the aggressive pursuit of direct sales or indirect advertising benefits by a company seeking to cash in on Olympic-related marketing without actually being a sponsor of the Games — keeping in mind, of course, that the price tag on official corporate sponsorship has been known to reach $40 million.

The Postal Service, which dropped out as a worldwide sponsor after the 1992 Games, was nonetheless granted permission to produce and sell Olympic stamps, traditionally a favorite among collectors. But then, without permission, the Postal Service also decided to license the sale of T-shirts bearing pictures of the stamps, as well as lapel pins, plates, and maybe a dozen other products related to the Olympic commemoratives. That is when the sponsor police stepped in and the corporate bashing began.

The U.S. Olympic Committee is telling people the Postal Service should be embarrassed by its "Olympic wannabe" approach. The Atlanta Committee for the Olympic Games is accusing the Postal Service of clear-cut parasite or ambush marketing. The Postal Service is firing right back with charges of paranoia and shortsightedness.

The upshot of it all? Olympic administrators boycotted today's official release of the stamps in Washington, D.C. Any vehicle with a Postal Service logo apparently will be banned from delivering mail in the athletes' village during the Games. And lawyers on both sides are pulling on their uniforms and getting loose, preparing to go after their own version of Olympic gold.

Once again, I am reminded of what I thought back when Visa and American Express first went at it over ticket sales: Let the Games begin! Once again, anyone following the road to Atlanta is reminded that the official color of the Olympics, wholeheartedly endorsed by both parasites and official sponsors, and stamped with the approval of the Olympic committees, is indeed the color of money.

Saturday, May 4 – Houston

My first long jump competition of the year went pretty well. Five of the six jumps were at least 27 feet (with the other one a foul), and my final mark of 27 feet, 4 1/2 inches was enough to win the Houston Invitational. I think that also makes me the world leader so far this season.

The best thing, though, was the way I felt. It was so much easier to jump, to drive aggressively off the ground, than it had been the last few years. It was so much easier now that I'm stronger and healthier than when I was straining in an attempt to compensate for inadequate strength and fitness.

Still, there was something very strange about what I did this afternoon. There are two parts to the long jump. One is the run. In my case, it is 161 feet in twenty-one strides to the board, and the consistency of my run is something on which I can almost always depend. Once we're comfortable with the way practice is going, Coach Tellez and I practically take that consistency for granted in a meet. Then there is the jump itself, the timing of the final step and the explosion into the air, which is the element that usually requires the greatest attention as I progress through a competition. Between jumps, Coach T is constantly reminding me about staying aggressive and exploding off the board.

But this time everything was reversed. The jumping mechanism was incredible. My run to the board was a mess. No matter what adjustments we tried to make, all we could do was keep shaking our heads in disbelief. We kept taking inventory between jumps and kept sharing similar thoughts. *Excellent final steps and jumps. But what in the world is going on here? What's the deal with the run?*

I always put down a check mark along the runway, usually a sneaker, 34 feet out from the board. From there I have four more strides before I jump. But today, no matter what we tried, I kept missing my mark, and in both directions, either over or under. There was no consistency whatsoever, and being all over the place like that makes it very difficult to execute those final strides and hit the board just right. Which made this the craziest long jump competition I've had in years. Maybe ever.

A few hours later, my thoughts still keep going back and forth. I'm pleased because I definitely know I'm ready to jump. I'm pleased because of how well I got off the ground and how easy it felt. But I'm also upset that I didn't jump 28 feet. That would have sent an unmistakable message, returning me to the role of favorite and putting pressure on the other jumpers. Also, it would have been like performing a service for the event, because the long jump seems to be kind of stagnant right now, and I wanted to give it a kick start.

But then I go right back to the positive again. My run to the board is something we'll be able to fix in practice the next couple of weeks. And then watch out. The way I'm jumping, I know I'll be ready for something big.

There were other significant Santa Monica happenings today.

Carol jumped the best she has all year. It still was not good enough to qualify for the Olympics. She continues to think a whole lot more about her broadcasting career than about competing. But she is making progress.

Mike Marsh ran an excellent 200. His time was 19.98 seconds. It seems that people don't want to listen, but I'm sticking with a point I've been trying to get across for months now. I don't care who you put out there in the 200, Mike is going to be tough to beat, and you better not count him out of the 100 either. He continues to go about his business quietly, nothing flashy, but he keeps getting the job done.

And then there was Leroy Burrell, who finally made his first appearance in a meet since hurting his leg. He finished last in the 100, with a time of 10.39 seconds, obviously not very comforting for someone who holds the world record. But Leroy has to remember that place and time are meaningless at this point. The important thing is he felt OK and made it through without getting hurt. Finally, he again has something on which to build. I just hope he remains patient and does not try to rush into doing too much too quickly. He still has time to come around. Patience will be the key.

Sunday, May 5 – Houston

I'm looking at something I wrote yesterday – the fact I wanted to jump 28 feet *to send a message* – and I'm shaking my head. I'm laughing at myself. Because I really try not to fall into the lazy language of sportstalk. You know, tired cliché after cliché, and "sending a message" is now right up there at the top of the list.

Every athlete, coach, and broadcaster seems to be talking about the desire to send a message. To an opposing player or team. To an entire league. To fans. To the media. To anyone, I guess, who sits around waiting for messages.

It is hard to imagine anyone outside of sports wearing out a phrase the way we do. It is highly unlikely anyone else could match the unyielding process of replication – the ability of a single sportstalk phrase to spread, like a virus, from broadcast booth to locker room to press conference, and eventually to the local watering hole, where even John Q. Sportsfan falls victim to the sheer repetition of it.

For a while, everyone was talking about *focus*. We would hear a coach saying, "Just don't think we stayed focused out there," which, when translated, really means the coach is not doing much of a job in terms of motivating the players. We would hear an athlete saying, "If we can just focus, we'll be OK," which the skeptical observer might translate into, "There are also times we simply don't care, so we lose." And here is an actual headline I once saw above a newspaper story on college basketball: "Kentucky Focuses on Focusing."

Soon after that, though, the focus shifted to stepping up. It started with the TV talking heads. "With Smith hurt, someone really needed to step up, and, boy, I'm telling you, Jones has really stepped up." I'm pretty sure that means Jones is having a good game. We knew we were really in trouble when we heard a Thoroughbred trainer discussing the lack of a clear favorite in the biggest race of the year: "One of these horses is gonna have to step up." How exactly does a horse know when to do that?

Monday, May 6 – Houston

The overall challenge of competing in multiple events, even after all these years, is still a situation where the total is greater than the sum of the parts. Because in addition to the specific needs of the 100, 200, and long jump, there is also the constant need to juggle my approach, both mental preparation and my schedule, in order to be ready for all three events. Not to mention the relay. That will come later.

This morning Coach Tellez and I had one of those juggling conversations. Remember, the plan was to open in the 100, 200, and long jump, then evaluate where we needed the most work. With five weekends left before the trials, we had a few basic questions to answer: How many more times should I compete? In what events? Should I jump again or put the emphasis back on the sprints?

It hardly seems possible, but a full month has already flown by since the Texas Relays, the last time I ran the 100, so we agreed that the 100 has to be top priority again. We feel pretty comfortable with working on the jump in practice — probably work on the run twice a week and then take a few jumps as well — and there is not a doubt in my mind that I'll be ready to jump 29 feet. But we want to save the meets for sprinting. That is where we need the most work.

So here is the plan. I'll run the 100 on May 18 in Atlanta. I'll run another 100 on May 26 in Eugene, Oregon. And then maybe I'll run the 200 in a local meet. But no more jumping. The next time I hit the sand — other than practice jumps — we will be battling for a spot in the Games.

Of course, none of this is written in indelible ink. As experienced jugglers, we still reserve the right to make any necessary adjustments once the balls are up in the air.

Tuesday, May 7 – Houston

The May 18 meet in Atlanta is one of the early stops on the international Grand Prix circuit. That alone would mean enough of the top athletes to guarantee some marquee match-ups. Add to that the fact that organizers are going all out to put on a big opening show in the new Olympic stadium — this will be the first event there — and it should be a great meet.

One thing we know for sure is that the 100 will be loaded. Carol is going to be one of the television broadcasters, and as part of her preparation, she just received a packet of meet information, including preliminary entries. The 100 might as well be an Olympic final.

I'll be facing: Leroy Burrell, the world-record holder; Donovan Bailey, the reigning world champion; Dennis Mitchell, who has been ranked number one and has won medals in both the Olympics and World Championships; Jon Drummond, the top-ranked American last year; and a few of the top newcomers, including Jeff Laynes and Vince Henderson.

Obviously, it will take a fast time to win, and I am thinking of it as a must win. It would be huge to pick off all those guys so early in the year. *Huge.* Mentally, I am starting my preparation right now. It might seem early for that. But I'm clearing out a place in my brain to start thinking about winning that race. I'm clearing out a spot so I can start filling it with positive thoughts and positive energy.

Wednesday, May 8 – Houston

No workout today. With five weeks left before the Olympic trials, we're beginning to back off on the amount of stress we put on our bodies. It is vital that we stay fresh, so the idea is to both decrease the quantity and increase the quality of our running. I've heard people call it tapering. It is also called being smart. I'll go hard again tomorrow and Friday, and then use the weekend to recover.

Thursday, May 9 – Houston

You'd think that one of us, Joe Douglas, Coach Tellez, or I, would be directly notified about any major development regarding my participation in the Olympics. Think again.

This morning I learned by way of the local newspaper that if I make it to the final of the 100 in the trials, Erv Hunt, coach of the U.S. men, is going to put me on the Olympic relay team. Simple as that. At least that is what Erv apparently said in an interview.

What a pleasant surprise. There's no way in the world Erv or anybody else would have made a statement like that just a month or two ago. Obviously, he has been following our performances and knows what I'm doing. It also tells me he understands the dynamics of running anchor. Even though my start in the 100 is not exactly the best, Erv seems to be expressing total confidence in my top-end speed. With a running start on the anchor leg, nobody should be able to stay with me. Maybe Erv wants the rest of the sprint world to think about that for a while. It's a good way for us to get in their heads early.

Clearly, though, this is not only about me and this one Olympic season. It is also about the way our relay teams will be picked for years to come. In an even broader sense, it is about the overall team selection process for both the Olympics and the World Championships.

Traditionally, the U.S. team invites the top four finishers in the trials 100 to run the relay, and the fifth- and sixth-place finishers are asked to be alternates. Of course, given the option of running alternates in the preliminary rounds, as well as the ever-present possibilities of injuries and other variables, the coach is generally afforded a certain amount of discretionary power. Unfortunately, that power has almost always been the source of ugly battles behind the scenes, with athletes, coaches, agents, and even shoe companies lobbying for certain people to get spots on the team.

With that in mind, then, this decision by Erv may very well set a new precedent. It is an extremely bold move. It is also, I think, an intelligent one. For years, Joe and I have been pushing for changes in the way athletes are selected for the major championships. We've been seeking provisions to make sure that the top people, the people fans want to see, will always be able to compete in both the Games and the World Championships. It is not enough to rely solely on one round of trials – not enough to blindly invite the top three finishers in each individual event or the top four (six including alternates) in the case of relays. We also need to include certain proven performers who might be sick, or injured, or might otherwise suffer through an uncharacteristically poor performance in a single qualifying meet.

We need a system with some leeway – a system that allows for exceptions. And not just to benefit any single athlete. It would benefit the entire sport. A few years ago, I wrote Primo Nebiolo, president of the international track federation, to share my thoughts on the subject.

I told him: "It is your party, so you should be allowed to hand out extra invitations. With national federations choosing teams in a wide variety of ways, fans sometimes miss out on seeing a top star in the most important meet of the year. That should not happen. The solution is easy. Offer an automatic invitation to anyone who won a medal in the preceding Olympics or World Championships and has met the qualifying standard, a minimum time or distance for each event. Also invite any medalist or world-record holder who has not met the standard but is considered worthy of participating. Finally, you should be able to include current world leaders in any event, even relays. After all, the whole idea is to put on the best possible show."

Think of it this way: Would Wimbledon or the U.S. Open put on a tennis tournament without inviting the top stars? Of course not. Like any other professional sport, tennis is all about entertainment. The fans of any sport want to be, and deserve to be, entertained by the best in the business.

It is one thing for me, as an individual, to learn what I need to do in order to run on the relay team in my final Olympics. It's one less thing for me to think about as we face the pressures of the trials – and I greatly appreciate that. Looking at the bigger picture, though, I am also hoping this can be used as a first step toward long-needed changes in the overall selection process for the most important events in track and field.

Friday, May 10 – Houston

There was a brief but interesting exchange with Coach Tellez at the end of practice this morning. We were talking about our plans for next week, and with that big 100 in Atlanta on my mind, I said: "We need to be ready to roll." All I got in return, though, was a stern response: "We need to be ready the 14th of June." That would be the beginning of the Olympic trials.

And Coach T just kept on walking. I mean, you'd think I had suggested we take a trip to the moon or something. He walked right on past me, away from the track, away from any chance at all that he would ever allow us to get too caught up in anything but the trials. His whole thing is: Why change anything now? Nobody will ever remember some Grand Prix meet in May. Only the trials and the Games will mean anything in the long run.

But I still want to win that 100 next week. Dare I say anything more about wanting to send a message?

Sunday, May 12 – Houston

We fired up the grill for Mother's Day dinner. Or supper, as they say

(PHOTO: GITTINGS)

As close as we are, it is always Mother's Day.

in rural Alabama, where both my mother and her mother were born and raised. My grandmother, Lurene Jenkins Lawler, is ninety years old, bless her heart, and she has certainly earned the right to call her evening meal whatever she wants. In fact, as the matriarch of a family that includes sixty-four grandchildren, great-grandchildren, and great-great-grandchildren, she has pretty much earned the right to do whatever the heck she wants.

Even play the slot machines. Nine full decades on this earth, and she still can't get enough of going for that jackpot. She constantly badgers my mother to take her to the casino. Amazing. Then again, this is a woman who would not give up driving until she was eighty-six, and only quit then because she kept having to ask whether the light was red or green. It was definitely a wise decision to pull off the road when she did – even for someone who was once recognized by the governor of Alabama for fifty straight years of driving without a single ticket.

I'm pretty sure this was the first time in my adult life that we've all been together for Mother's Day. It was just about a year and a half ago that my grandmother moved here to stay with my mother, and I see them pretty often, but this was clearly a special occasion. Carol and our brother Mack were also here. Our other brother, Cleve, who lives in Denver, was the only one missing.

We had more than enough food: chicken and sausage (none for me), along with salads, beans, fruits, and then Carol's apple pie, which she swears she made from scratch. We talked and laughed for hours. We even reminisced about the old days in Alabama. As small children, we'd visit during the summer and grandmother would always make us little poles and take us fishing. Man, my people were country.

The most memorable moment this evening came when everyone was about to go. My mother was fixing a plate to take home for my grandmother – "supper" for tomorrow – when grandmother turned to her and whispered: "You know, I really want to be around to see ninety-one." I truly believe she will be. And still trying to hit that jackpot that has eluded her all these wonderful years. Just for the fun of it.

Tuesday, May 14 – Houston

Almost from Day One of my career, it seems, most of the other top sprinters have shared a theory about the best way to beat me in the 100. Blast me early, coming out of the blocks, which has never been a strong point for me, and then just try to hang on. You know I'll be coming after you the last 10 or 20 meters, because the finish has always been the best part of my race, but hang on the best you can.

Sometimes that approach has worked. Other times it has failed miserably. But I still feel like I am the one who makes that determination. As long as I do what I am supposed to do, staying relaxed, not worrying about anyone else in any other lane, I should be fine. But when I see someone bolting out of the blocks and allow myself to be startled, temporarily forfeiting my concentration, maybe even panicking a little, if only for a split second, that can very well be the end of the race right there. But only if I allow myself to be startled. Only if I allow myself to make that mistake.

I've been thinking about that in relation to the 100 this weekend in Atlanta. One thing we know for sure: Donovan Bailey and Dennis Mitchell will definitely be trying to explode out of the blocks. They are two of the best starters — in fact, Dennis has even been known to get away with what appears to be a false start every now and then — and both are longtime subscribers to the theory that you better try to take me out early.

With that in mind, Coach Tellez and I are stressing a plan of our own. The thought of the week is: Do not react to anything but the gun. Do not pay any attention whatsoever to Donovan or Dennis or anyone else. Let them go early. Stick to your plan, and you'll be seeing them again soon enough, like at 80 or 90 meters.

I've even considered the way lane assignments might affect my thinking. In most cases, the top guys like to be bunched up in the center lanes, where we can keep an eye on each other. But this time I'd prefer to be on the outside, maybe lane seven, where it might be easier to ignore everyone else. In the trials and the Games, lanes are supposedly assigned by a combination of previous results and random draw. (I say "supposedly" because other factors might sometimes come into play.) Prior to an invitational meet such as this one, though, lane assignments are made in what is called the technical meeting. Coaches and agents offer their best arguments as to which athletes deserve the choice lanes, and then meet officials determine the starting list. Of course, there are times when they give you exactly what you want and times they pay zero attention to you, so we'll have to see about that.

Regardless, I am already encouraged by the way my start has steadily improved in practice. Today was probably the best it has been all year. Huge difference. I feel so much stronger and more explosive than I have in so long, and I'm reacting very well to the gun. The best thing of all is the way I'm driving my left leg off the front block, really firing out, which is such a key for me.

Matter of fact, this morning I was even keeping up with the guys Coach T was using to help lock me into the right frame of mind. He put two of the Houston sprinters in the lanes next to me, one playing the Donovan Bailey role, one playing Dennis Mitchell, and had them set their blocks about a meter in front of mine. The idea was to work on the feel of starting behind without being distracted. But I was getting out so well, it was not taking long at all to pull even, and then to blow by them. I know it will not be anywhere near that simple in Atlanta. But I also know I will be prepared. As long as I ignore the other guys. As long as I run my own race.

Wednesday, May 15 – Houston

News item: The Olympic committees and the U.S. Postal Service are calling a truce in the great T-shirt war. They have agreed to share profits from the sale of shirts carrying pictures of the newly-released Olympic stamps. Maybe the mail will even be delivered to the Olympic Village after all.

But there is still something wrong about this profit-sharing resolution. The whole confrontation began as a public display of the Olympic committees' desire to draw an indelible line between right and wrong. However, it is ending without any justification whatsoever for abandoning their self-defined moral ground – that is, any justification other than money. It simply appears to be a matter of boosting the bottom line. And it smells kind of bad. Like greed.

Remember, it was just two weeks ago that the U.S. Olympic Committee and the Atlanta Committee for the Olympic Games went ballistic over the T-shirts and other products related to the commemorative stamps. The Postal Service was promoting sales without any licensing agreement. Even worse, it was treading on the ground of an official Olympic sponsor, United Parcel Service, which is a direct competitor. Both points were made very strongly and without any room to compromise.

So here is what I find so offensive: Once there was profit-sharing, once there was money on the table, the Olympic committees just dropped the ball as far as protecting their official sponsor. What happened to all that righteous indignation about the issue of parasite or ambush marketing? Hmmm.

It reminds me of something I recently heard from another athlete, a play on the acronym for the Atlanta Committee for the Olympic Games. Officially, it is ACOG. Unofficially, people have been calling it A-HOG, as in the farm animal that goes oink-oink.

Thursday, May 16 – Houston

Sitting around bashing ACOG is not exactly my idea of having a good time. But it just so happens this is the second day in a row I've had a strong reaction to the incredible wisdom and sheer selflessness of those wonderful organizers in Atlanta. Yesterday I was responding merely as an outside observer. This time it is much more personal. We just learned that ACOG has stepped in at the last minute to block our volunteers from distributing organ donor cards Saturday at the stadium.

Everywhere we've been this year, meet organizers have been more than generous and kind about working with us on the donor program, and have responded with nothing but positive feedback. This is the first resistance we have encountered. It is just forty-eight hours before the event, transplant recipients and donor family members from throughout Georgia have long since set aside the day to be at the stadium, to help save lives, and the iron fist of ACOG comes crashing down on our plans. Nothing in it for ACOG, I guess, no profit-sharing from a program that has nothing to do with money, only awareness, so why bother themselves?

ACOG officials did not care one iota about the success of the donor card program everywhere else we have been. It meant nothing to them that we had gone through all the proper channels and received a firm commitment from USA Track & Field all the way back in March for clearance to hand out the cards at this meet. All they could say was: We have a policy. No handouts at the Olympic Stadium. ACOG would not even budge in response to a personal appeal from Larry Ellis, president of USA Track & Field, who is himself alive today only because he was transplanted with a new heart last year.

Joe Douglas and I have been going back and forth on how we should react. Obviously, we're angry, but how do we respond, if at all? Reporters in Atlanta have already been critical of ACOG on a wide variety of issues. Public relations has not exactly been the organizing committee's greatest strength. So do we share our experience with the Atlanta newspaper?

Part of me feels very strongly that the public should know the way ACOG throws around its weight behind the scenes. *Last minute power play by Olympics officials squashes do-good program.* A story like that might even make the front page. Ironically, with the cycle of television and follow-up pieces it would trigger, it would undoubtedly generate more exposure for organ donation than we could ever create in a single day at the stadium. Unfortunately, though, any controversy concerning the cards could also overshadow the entire purpose of what we are trying to achieve, so we're probably better off just leaving it alone.

The one thing I want to do is at least get tickets to the meet for all the volunteers who had committed themselves to handing out the cards. I know they will be very disappointed, and probably angry as well, when they hear the way ACOG has handled this. But I hope they'll at least be able to enjoy the meet. Cards or no cards, I look forward to seeing all the transplant recipients and donor family members, and once again thanking them for all that they do.

Friday, May 17 – Atlanta

You don't have to be here very long to notice the countless construction crews, the mounds of dirt and stacks of supplies piled up all over, the constant groaning of cement mixers and bulldozers. Like any other host city two months out from an event as huge as the Olympics, Atlanta is a city hard at work. It also doesn't take long to realize that the locals are in a panic. There is an overwhelming sense of urgency, with the number one question being: How are we possibly going to have everything ready in time for the Games?

Well, the people of Atlanta just have to maintain the faith and keep plugging away. Based on recent history, Olympic cities always find some magical form of power to pull off almost anything at the last minute. Maybe it's the Greek gods smiling down on the legacy of their ancient creation. Whatever it is, the incredible glow of the Games is guaranteed to be remembered long after the panic is gone. It always is. Well, there was one exception, Munich in 1972, which will always be remembered for the horror of terrorism before anything else.

But I've been trying to reassure people here in Atlanta: Almost every Olympic cycle is the same. It goes from the euphoria of being selected as the host city to the daily grind of preparation and then to the panic that comes with unyielding deadlines. Inevitably, though, the upheaval is once again replaced by celebration. Atlanta will soon be covering up all the dust with sights and sounds from around the world — and the people who live here will be collecting memories that will last a lot longer than the temporary groaning of all that heavy equipment.

Saturday, May 18 – Atlanta

It would be hard to imagine a more intense housewarming, both literally and figuratively, for the new stadium. The temperature down on the track was recorded at 112 degrees, the competition was just as hot, and the fans, filling maybe half of the 85,000 seats, were incredibly supportive. Everything about this afternoon had the feel of a big meet, something we don't get to feel very often in the States, and also a solid indication of the sizzling atmosphere we'll soon be experiencing here in the trials and the Games. The only difference for me: Next time I'll be leaning at the finish line. More on that in a minute.

The place was really buzzing for the 100. Of course, my heart was pounding like crazy, the way it always does before we lower ourselves into the blocks, but I was also able to settle down pretty quickly. I knew I was ready, and that makes all the difference in the world. I was even going to run in lane seven, right where I wanted to be, away from the big starters.

When the gun was fired, Dennis Mitchell was first out of the blocks, like a bullet, but I never even saw him until we were way down the track. It went exactly as I had hoped — no distractions. I was totally focused on my own lane. Just me and my own race.

My start was pretty much the same as it has been in practice, still not even close to the big starters, but a vast improvement for me. I was up and running pretty well, behind most of the pack, but not by too much. From 40 to 60 meters, I was starting to make my move. From 60 to 70, I was setting up for the kill. From there, I felt like I ran the last 30 meters as fast as I have since breaking the world record in 1991. Maybe even faster.

I went flying by Olapade Adeniken, the Nigerian; Jon Drummond, the top-ranked American last year; and Donovan Bailey, the reigning world champion. At the end, it was just Dennis Mitchell and me screaming toward the finish line. Which is where I should have leaned. I was coming so fast that I thought I would get him without leaning. But maybe that would be the difference. Dennis was sticking out his chest for every inch it was worth. I was straight up and down. Still, nobody had a clue who crossed the line first.

All we knew was that the unofficial time was posted at 9.93 seconds. Finally! This would be the end of all that talk about the fact I had not run under 10 seconds since 1991. All eyes went to the stadium scoreboard for the replay, but even with the slow motion and the frame-by-frame shots, nobody could really tell who won. Dennis and I congratulated each other, went off together on a shared victory lap, and then we heard the public address announcement right along with everyone else. *The winner is Carl Lewis!*

What I felt was not really anything about beating Dennis or winning this one race. We still have so far to go. No, it was more like I was finally free to absorb and process the reality that I am actually back where I need to be. No more thinking and talking about how I'm going to be back. I *am* back.

I had not even run the 100 in six weeks, but I still felt sharp and my time was once again a dramatic improvement. In addition to those early meets at Rice University, where I ran 10.50-something and 10.37, the progression has been remarkable: 10.26, 10.10, and now this, down in the low 9.9s. How could I be anything but thrilled with where I am? No more doubts. None whatsoever. I felt the warmth of the sun, the warmth of the crowd, and I was bubbling with joy.

Of course, someone in the press conference made a point of reminding me about the last time I ran in Atlanta. It was that last-place finish in the indoor nationals — the race that prompted all those career obituaries before we even had a chance to begin the outdoor season. "Sure, I was a cadaver and everything else," I said. "I mean, I don't read *everything*. But both my parents were teachers. I do know how to read. Anyway, the important thing was that I had to rebuild my own confidence from the inside out, and I've been able to do that. I feel like myself again."

Minutes after the press conference, maybe half an hour after the race itself, someone approached me in a hallway under the stadium and told me the final results had just been changed. After further study of the photo finish, Dennis Mitchell was declared the winner with a time of 9.93. I was second with a 9.94. "Should have leaned," I

(PHOTO: TONY DUFFY/TSI)

Back under 10 seconds in the 100. I am ready to conquer the world.

said. "Guess that teaches me a lesson."

Actually, I was more disappointed to learn about the wind reading. It was one tenth above the legal limit of 2.0 meters per second. In other words, it goes down as a wind-aided race, so I still don't get credit for an official time under 10 seconds. The way that phrase has been tossed around the last few years, it might as well be my middle name. You know, Carl "Who Hasn't Run Under Ten Since Ninety-one" Lewis. Man, I was looking forward to having just a first and last name again.

Oh, well. The reality is that none of that, not the order of finish, not the wind reading, really makes a bit of difference at this point. What matters most is the way I ran, the way I felt, the incredible confidence I take away from here. If I can emulate this race, I'll be in the Olympics. Simple as that.

In fact, I'll go even further. I know I can run the 100 in the 9.8s this year. Now I have to go out and do it. In the right place. At the right time.

A few other things worth mentioning:

Unfortunately, Leroy Burrell was missing again. More leg problems — and now he also has a painful blister on the bottom of his foot. With time running out, I don't see how he could possibly be at the top of his game for the trials, but I'm still hoping Leroy will find a way to make the team. If he does, it will be on sheer talent alone.

In the other big race of the day, the 200, Mike Marsh (19.88) gave Michael Johnson (19.83) a scare down the straightaway – and that was after Mike was temporarily distracted coming out of the curve. He felt a twinge in the hamstring and had to adjust for a few strides. If not for that, he would have had Michael. Don't get me wrong: Michael showed his strength by holding on for the victory. But we also saw that he is vulnerable. I still think Mike is going to beat him before the season is out, either at the trials, the Games, or maybe even both, and please don't count me out either.

Rounding out a big day for Santa Monica: Johnny Gray ran away with the 800. Of course, the thing I admire most about Johnny is his staying power. He has made it to the last three Olympic finals, placing third in Barcelona, and has held the American record in the 800 for more than ten years. And he's even older than me. Johnny will turn thirty-six during the trials. After his victory today, he declared himself the grandfather of the 800. But that's OK. He doesn't mind teaching the young guys a few things.

Finally, a postscript on the situation with those organ donor cards: Between my victory lap and the press conference, I made a point of handing out a stack of cards to people in the stands. If nothing else, I wanted to make at least a symbolic gesture.

Sunday, May 19 – Atlanta and Houston

I stayed over for an extra day to visit with relatives. One of my first cousins was playing in a city tennis tournament. Then her nine-year-old daughter had a softball game. It was a nice change of pace to be on the other side of the equation for once – me watching them instead of them watching me.

When I got home, I called Coach Tellez to discuss my race, because he had not been able to make it to Atlanta. He was off at a collegiate meet with the Houston team. As soon as we finished talking about the 100 I just ran, we shifted gears to the one I'm scheduled to run next week, and decided to make a change. I'm switching to the 200. Obviously, my 100 is in pretty good shape, and we agreed that I can probably get more out of running another 200. As usual, we never know for sure, always a calculated risk when we juggle events, but I feel pretty strongly that we're making the right move.

Monday, May 20 – Houston

It was not until the other day in Atlanta that the reality of it really hit me for the first time. I'm back in that pressure cooker we call the 100 – the entirely unforgiving quest to be World's Fastest Human. It finally dawned on me that I'm right back in the middle of all this madness.

First there is the constant stress associated with trying to make the U.S. team. Survival of the fittest. Then you set your sights on the Olympic final. And when you finally get there – if you get there – you then cross the line into the most stressful athletic situation I could ever imagine, probably the single most pressurized 10 seconds in all of athletics. The anticipation alone – relentless expectations; so much at stake – can be enough to wear you out. And then the margin of error is so painfully slim. A single mistake, even a minor one, and you lose. And then the next opportunity to redeem yourself is four long years away. If you ever make it back, that is.

Believe me, there could be nothing else like the 100. Well, maybe having to hit a free throw with no time left on the clock to put Game Seven of the NBA finals into overtime. Even with that, though, there have already been so many chances to either win or lose, an entire contest filled with ups and downs before you reach the defining moment.

Don't get me wrong. I'm not by any means assuming myself into the Olympic final. Not at all. But it's remarkable the way the mind and body work together on a journey like this. You begin by setting goals. You keep working toward them. Still, though, there is a substantial period of time during which those goals remain somewhat distant. They seem to be detached from your everyday routines.

Then it hits you all at once – like it did the other day in Atlanta – and you realize: My God, I'm actually doing this again. Am I absolutely certain this is really what I want to do? Well, of course it is. I keep telling myself that: Of course it is. It definitely requires some serious mental preparation, though.

The one overwhelming advantage I have is experience. How could the pressure this time around be any greater than it was back in 1984 or 1988? In Los Angeles I had to win the 100 to have a shot at the four golds I was supposed to win. In Seoul there was the whole thing with Ben Johnson: the individual rivalry; the U.S. against Canada; and then, of course, the extra burden of knowing that Ben was on drugs and wanting to prove I could still win with a clean body.

Even in 1992, when I was not in the 100 myself – failed to qualify at the trials – I was still caught up in the pressure cooker because Leroy Burrell was one of the favorites. It almost felt like I'd be right in the starting blocks with my training partner and friend. There was a very poignant moment when Leroy was leaving our rented house in Barcelona for the final. I looked at him wearing his USA uniform and his Santa Monica baseball cap, and I was very proud of him. We hugged, and I told him, "Bring it home," meaning nothing less than the gold medal. As he walked away, I also thought to myself: Man, I'm glad it's him and not me. He can have it. I'll be just fine with the long jump and the relay, thank you.

Now that I find myself back in the mix for the 100, though, I am also in an entirely new situation. Nothing like the pressures in '84 and '88 because there is nothing left for me to prove. I'm here because I want to be – not because I have to be. Also, no matter what else happens between now and the Games, even if I win the trials, I still don't think I'd be considered a big favorite. Maybe a co-favorite, at best, but nothing like the way it used to be. The way people saw it in Los Angeles and Seoul, if I had won anything but gold, even silver, it would have been nothing. Second or third simply wasn't good enough.

I'm still going for the gold in the 100. No doubt, that would be huge. But now I no longer feel like I *have* to win the gold. I'm at the stage in my career where any medal would be a significant achievement. In fact, this is the first time I think the public would not only accept but even celebrate the silver or the bronze. Part of it is because so little was expected of me at the beginning of the season. Part of it is the whole thing of this entire year being more about the journey than the outcome.

So many people have been sharing this road to Atlanta with me, following my progress more than ever before, and finding themselves relating to what I am trying to accomplish. Yes, I get older, just like they do. Yes, I lose sometimes, just like they do. But I'm giving it my all. I think a lot more people can relate to that than they could to some young superstar who was always expected to perform with the perfection of a machine.

Everywhere I go now, I feel and appreciate the extra support that comes from people who are somehow touched by what I am doing. Sometimes it even feels like we're all in it together – and that alone seems to take away some of the pressure. That alone helps to lessen the madness. To some degree.

Tuesday, May 21 – Houston

We're back in the uniform business. After practice, Leroy Burrell, Mike Marsh, and I visited the office of a designer who is helping us pull the Santa Monica logo into the nineties. Better late than never. I mean, that rising sun and those block letters have hardly been altered since the seventies, when Joe Douglas first adopted them as the signature of his new running club.

On the surface, our meeting this afternoon was simply about uniforms, updating and modernizing the logo with the intention of unveiling the new look next month in Atlanta. Remember, we always like to go with something new and different for the trials. The new logo displays the sun more prominently by moving it out to the right of the *Santa Monica* letters, which will now be flowing together in cursive style. Big improvement, I think, and I'm pretty sure Joe will like it. He has always been somewhat resistant to changing the logo, but now he seems to be OK with the idea as long as we keep the basic elements. (And, of course, go through the proper legal procedures to register and protect the new look.)

Below the surface, though, there was also something else I thought about this afternoon: the idea of being together as a team. Working on our uniforms always seems to intensify that feeling of pulling together as one, and that is a crucial intangible on which we rely in so many ways. No question, the sharing of energy makes each of us a better athlete. It also makes each of us a better person. No matter what we end up doing with that rising sun.

Wednesday, May 22 – Houston

My mother, Carol and I recorded an Olympic first for the Lewis family, running consecutive legs in the most publicized relay on the planet, the torch relay. We each took a turn with the flame during its twenty-sixth day on American soil. By the time of the Games, it will have been carried through forty-two states by more than ten thousand people, including a large number of people selected as "community heroes" and an assortment of past Olympians.

No doubt, the relay has become a mammoth public relations vehicle, and with all the corporate propaganda attached to it, Coca-Cola logos leading the way, I can understand why cynics might quickly dismiss it as a high-profile road show for the sponsors. But anyone who actually participates might be just as ready to argue that point. As a torchbearer, you feel the excitement of all the people lining the street, and it makes you realize that the true meaning of the relay has nothing to do with all the staged events along the way. Forget all the rallies and pronouncements and photo opportunities. What people really want to see is so much simpler than any of that. They just want to see the torch moving down the street. That is what they so readily associate with the passion of the Games.

Being able to carry that torch meant so much more to me than I ever thought it would. There is so much history involved. So much tradition. In ancient Greece, where fighting was pretty much a constant, a sacred truce was called so that the Olympics could be held in peace. Runners called "heralds of peace" were sent throughout the land to proclaim the truce and issue a call to the Games. Much later, prior to the 1936 Games, someone came up with the idea of lighting a torch and conducting a relay as a way of symbolically reviving the tradition, and the relay has been around ever since. Of course, looking back at it now, there obviously was an unfortunate irony in the fact that the 20th century "heralds of peace" were first trotted out for the Games in Hitler's Berlin.

That aside, sixty years into the torch run, I'd find it hard to believe anyone has ever been more excited about it than mother was. She might as well have been running in the Games themselves. Well, not exactly, but we'll get to that in a minute. Carol ran first. When she reached me, we used her torch to light mine, and then she ran beside me while I carried the flame maybe three quarters of a mile to where mother was waiting. We lit her torch, and then she took off with Carol on one side and me on the other, but mother was definitely the star of

Tired as she was, my mother was still able to smile after running her leg in the torch relay.

the show. All sorts of people were shouting out to her, cheering, and the television cameras recorded her every move. She was nervous but thrilled. That smile was just plastered across her face.

Then she hit the wall. That's what we call it when you run out of gas during a race. She probably went out too fast. Then she was done in by a combination of all the excitement, the heat, and the fact that the torch was much heavier than it looked (you have to run with it held out in one hand). Mother was a disaster, getting slower and slower, but she never allowed that smile to go away, even as she was asking us: "How much further? How much further?"

We had maybe 200 meters left when Carol told her: "Don't be afraid to walk if you want to. A lot of other people do." But mother was so determined: "No, no, I want to keep running. I'm going to make it." And she did. We were so proud of her. Although she was fighting to catch her breath, mother was still grinning like a cat as she helped light that next torch and we watched the flame head off toward Louisiana. That look on her face will always remain as one of my favorite Olympic memories.

Thursday, May 23 – Georgetown, Texas

I'm with Kirk Baptiste in a small town outside of Austin, doing another event for the Southwest Key Program for troubled teens. After working out, I flew here in one of those small, private planes that makes you wonder how you're even staying up in the air.

Anyway, there is something else I'm wondering about. What is the deal with people wanting autographed baseballs from athletes or other celebrities who have nothing at all to do with baseball? As soon as I walked in, someone involved with the program handed me a ball and asked me to sign it. It was the second time this week. Someone at the stadium in Atlanta also had me sign a ball. And it happens all the time. There's no way I could count the number of baseballs I've signed over the years.

Why? I mean, I understand signing a baton, a running shoe, or maybe a magazine cover, which I'm also hit with all the time, but why a baseball? What in the world does anyone do with a baseball signed by a track and field athlete? About the only answer I've ever gotten is: "It's a hobby. I collect them." OK. But do people also collect batons or running shoes signed by baseball players? Not that I'm aware of. To each his own, I guess.

Friday, May 24 – Houston

Carol has made up her mind. She is backing away from competing in the trials so she can concentrate on broadcasting.

No question, she has come a long way in terms of fitness and conditioning, but she still has further to go, and then there is the issue of finding her timing again. Having been away from the long jump for a few years, it has taken her longer than we thought it would to feel comfortable on the runway and off the board.

The other factor is career planning. The best thing Carol can do is get in as much television work as possible. She was already committed to NBC for network coverage of the trials, and then ESPN just offered her a deal to work the rest of the days. It's another great opportunity in terms of both experience and exposure.

I definitely think Carol is making the right decision. Of course, it was kind of a dream for us to go back to the Games together. But we'll still be doing that. One competing. One offering commentary.

Maybe Carol will decide to jump again next year. She's already talking about wanting to make it to the 1997 World Championships. And one thing I've known about Carol for a long, long time — don't ever count her out of something when she really wants to do it. Don't ever count her out when she fully commits herself to getting the job done. Must be a genetic thing.

Sunday, May 26 – Eugene, Oregon

No matter what kind of shape you're in, no matter how well everything has been going, sometimes you just feel flat, like it simply isn't your day. That was me this afternoon in the Prefontaine Classic. I felt like I was operating at maybe ninety percent. There probably was a bit of a letdown, both physically and emotionally, after that big 100 last week in Atlanta.

On the plus side, though, even feeling the way I did, I still managed a close second in the 200, and with a respectable time. Jon Drummond was first in 20.20 seconds. I was second in 20.22. Remember, when I won that 200 last month at the Mt. SAC Relays, I ran 20.19, and that was my best time in three years. So I still know I'm right where I want to be, and with the trials just three weeks away, that is by far the most important issue.

Now we go home and concentrate on speed work and getting plenty of rest. I had been thinking about running one more of those local meets next week, getting in one more 100, but I don't even think I want to do that anymore. We need to begin locking in both our bodies and our minds — locking them in on the trials.

Oh, one other thing I don't want to forget, something I was pleased about at the end of the race today: I leaned at the tape. After that finish in Atlanta, I actually remembered to push my chest forward this time. That could be very important in the trials, where the difference between making the team and staying home is routinely measured in hundredths of a second.

Monday, May 27 – Houston

Memorial Day. No workout because of it being the day after a meet. But far be it from Joe Douglas to schedule me for an entire vacation day.

I had a photo shoot with Annie Leibovitz, with whom it seems I've been working my entire career. Of course, the most publicized photographs we've done were those creative shots for the Pirelli advertising campaigns. But there have been numerous others over the years.

Posing for Annie is always a pleasure because she is the consummate professional. Sometimes the most talented photographers are also the most annoying because they can be so pushy, lacking any respect for the feelings of the person they are shooting. Not Annie. She has always been so considerate and enjoyable to be with, and I'm sure that has a lot to do with the type of photographs she gets. I mean, who else could get Whoopi Goldberg to pose in a bathtub full of milk?

This time Annie was shooting to complete her work on an Olympics-related book due out before the Games. I look forward to seeing it. As we say in the book business — yes, we; I'm trying to get with the program — I'm sure it will be a tremendous addition to any library. And don't forget the coffee table. Anything Annie produces will look good there as well.

Tuesday, May 28 – Houston

We went back to the track for the beginning of the end, the final stretch before the trials, which means speed work and streamlining. Everything gets shorter and quicker. An example: Whereas one of our regular workouts in recent weeks has been running six 150s, that will now go down to a series of four sprints, and much shorter, probably 90, 80, 70, and 60. In addition to increasing the speed, we'll also be paying more attention to sharpening the various components of what we're doing, such as the mechanics of the start. We'll probably have only one more workout where we run as far as 400 meters at once — we usually do that about ten days out from the trials — but even that will be at full throttle. Not that we've been messing around up to this point. Obviously, we have not been. But now it is crunch time.

One other difference will be changing the overall focus of each week. Up to now I have had the luxury of concentrating on whatever event I'd be doing in the next meet; now I have to work on the 100, 200, and long jump all at once. Coach Tellez and I have to integrate them all into the daily workout schedule, while still allowing for plenty of rest. Being fresh for the trials is an absolute requirement, especially for someone competing in multiple events.

Wednesday, May 29 – Houston

I always have to laugh about the way people treat my one silver medal, just ignoring it, as if it could not possibly stand up to its big brothers, the golds. That is, if they even know that the silver exists. Poor thing has always been the stepchild of the family. If it were human, it would still be in therapy, trying to overcome all these painful years of neglect.

The funny thing is, even though the silver represents the only time I've ever lost an event in the Olympics, I'm actually very proud of it. I'm probably the only one who realizes how incredibly difficult a race that was for me. In fact, the 200 in the 1988 Seoul Games was one of the most challenging races I've ever run. It came after the 100 and the long jump, so my body was already worn down. Even so, I ended up running slightly better than the time I was hoping to run, better than what I thought it would take to win, but Joe DeLoach, then my training partner and Santa Monica teammate, simply ran the race of a lifetime. He broke the Olympic record I'd set in 1984, and after all he had been through, a variety of setbacks and all the hard work to overcome them, he most certainly deserved it.

When we crossed the finish line, before I thought of me losing, I thought of Joe winning. That's how excited I was for him. Of course, by the time we got to the victory stand for the medal ceremony, my thoughts were starting to shift. When Joe climbed to the top of that stand, leaving me to look up at him, I was still very proud of my friend's great accomplishment but also not as happy as I had hoped to be. It would still take some time to figure out what that second-place finish really meant to me.

Anyway, I mention this now because I just got home from yet another sad experience for that lonesome silver. Some people from NBC were in town to shoot footage and interviews for feature stories that will air during the Games, and they asked if I would bring my medals to a studio so they could tape me with them. They did not specify the *gold* medals, although I assumed that's what they meant, because that's what everyone always wants. Just for the heck of it, though, I decided to bring along the silver as well, thinking maybe it would finally get its long overdue day in the sun.

Wrong. When the guy from NBC was arranging the medals just how he wanted them in my hand, I could not help but notice the silver was missing. It was still sitting on the table where Carol had set down the entire collection. Sitting there all by itself again. I can almost hear that silver pouring out its pain on a couch in some shrink's office: "Why me? What am I, a mutant or something? Why can't I be like all the other medals?"

Thursday, May 30 – Houston

What in the world is Joe Douglas doing with my schedule? It was yesterday that things started getting crazy. After workout and the session with NBC, I also had a photo shoot for an advertising campaign in Spain (sunglasses), and then I had a column to write for a newspaper in Austria. In addition to the online columns, I'm also writing for a number of papers throughout the world. I started the column last night but didn't finish until early this morning, like a college kid cramming to complete the last term paper before spring break.

Except I didn't get much of a break. I had to rush right off to a local studio for a live satellite feed to Brazil, in which I addressed a breakfast hosted by Pirelli. It was part of the big launch for a new tire. Then I went to the track, where I was greeted by a crew from *The Oprah Winfrey Show*, here to do a segment for a pre-Olympic show. They taped us working out, and then interviewed me. After that, I flew home for lunch and had to hurry back out to finish that profile piece for NBC. Then I met up again with the *Oprah* people for a session at the Houston alumni center. They wanted to shoot me in the Hall of Fame, standing by my statue, etc.

And this is the time we're supposed to be getting plenty of rest, right? The highlight of the day was when I finally got home again and headed for the pool. Part of it was just being able to relax without anyone else around, without anyone there to care who or what I am, what I think, what I say. But the real excitement was provided by Ramses, who finally jumped right in for a swim without me having to coax him in on a leash. It was the first time he has done that. Ramses was hilarious, flopping around in the water, and it was clearly the best I felt all day. By far.

Friday, May 31 – Houston

It would be impossible to overestimate the amount of support I have been feeling lately, from both insiders and outsiders, and it would also be impossible to measure how much that means to me. Ultimately, I'll still need to go out and win or lose as an individual, same as always, but it sure helps to be surrounded by so much positive energy.

I hear it from people at the grocery store. I hear it from reporters and photographers who come from around the world. I hear it from other athletes and coaches and officials wherever we go. What I'm hearing is: "Keep it up. We're with you. We'll be pulling for you in Atlanta."

People have always been perfectly nice to me, for the most part, but what I'm feeling now has gone way beyond the norm. It's like people want to rally around you the most when they know you are vulnerable. That's when they can really identify with you. They know about your age and see all these young guys coming after you. They see you go down in defeat. But then they see you fighting back again to turn that around. They almost feel like they can help will you to victory – and they want to. Not a day goes by without me thinking about how fortunate I am to be on the receiving end of such tremendous support.

It seems like it was forever ago that I finished last in those indoor races and so many people were looking at me with sad, troubled eyes, as if I had some disease or something, as if they pitied me and the plight of this horribly unkind end to my career. And then there was that day at practice when Mike Marsh pulled me aside to confront me about what the heck I was doing. Had to be years ago, right? It was the middle of March.

I think people finally started to accept that I might be in this for real after the Texas Relays, when I won the 100. After that, there was steady progress, more believers each week, but it was definitely that last 100 in Atlanta that sent people into a frenzy. The funny thing is: So many people think I won. Even though I was second in that photo finish, the way it was played in the media, a lot of people came away with the impression that I won. There have been so many people congratulating me for "winning" that race.

NBC even took that performance and turned it into an uplifting promotional piece about my quest for gold in Atlanta. They've been running it in prime time during the NBA playoffs. But the shocker of the week was when someone told me what *Track & Field News* was predicting for me in its pre-trials issue. First in the 100. First in the long jump. Second in the 200. Talk about jumping on the bandwagon. This was the same publication, the self-proclaimed bible of the sport, that just a month earlier wrote about the demise of SMTC sprinters and how I was "just whistling in the wind" as far as my plans for Atlanta.

It sure is nice to see people smiling at me again.

Saturday, June 1 - Houston

Leroy Burrell sure cut it close, but he was finally healthy and ran the time he needed to qualify for the trials, which is a big relief to all of us. He won the 100 at the Bruce Jenner Classic in San Jose, California, with a time of 10.18 seconds. The qualifying standard is 10.20.

Once again, though, yet another example of why we need to take a long look at the rules. I just don't see why someone like Leroy, or anyone who holds a world record, should even need a qualifying time. When someone at his level has been injured all season, as he has been, there ought to be an exemption to go straight into the trials. If he's still not ready to run fast, he'll get knocked out early, so who loses anything? But the way it is now, we could have forfeited a chance to have the fastest man in the world representing us in the Games. How could that possibly benefit our sport?

Monday, June 3 - Houston

We ran the last long sprint on our pre-trials workout schedule, 350 meters, and what a way to start the final countdown to Atlanta. It was the best I've ever felt at that long a distance. I'm just beaming about it.

At times this season, I have let myself get away from turning over my strides (getting my feet back down on the track) with the snap and intensity that is required. I've wasted time by drifting into almost a bounding motion, in which I'm driving hard off the ground but not getting my feet back down quickly enough. So turnover was top priority this morning.

Mike Marsh and I ran the 350 together in 38.2 seconds, which is flying – about a second and a half faster than I've run it all year and more than half a second faster than I've ever run it. My turnover was practically perfect.

Obviously, running a fast 350 like that tells me we're in shape, which means that running rounds in the 100 and 200 should be no problem at all. It also tells me that my finish in either of the sprints should be stronger than ever. And that means the world to me. No wonder I'm beaming.

Tuesday, June 4 – Houston

There is a fine line on mental preparation at this point. You want to be getting tuned into every element of the trials. But you can't afford to be *over*thinking. You never want to lose sight of the basics that got you here in the first place.

The most important thing in these final workouts is paying strict attention to details. Otherwise, you run the risk of messing up something you've been doing well all year, and then you'd start second-guessing yourself. This is not the time for second-guessing. It is the time for quiet confidence. Each day, I want to leave the track thinking, Man, that was good, everything is clicking.

This morning Mike and I took four starts, increasing the distances we ran out of the blocks from 20 to 60 meters, and they all felt perfect. Very high quality. Actually, I'll even go beyond that. It was like we were racing for real. *Man, that was good, everything is clicking.*

Wednesday, June 5 – Houston

Remember when Muhammad Ali used to talk about floating like a butterfly in the boxing ring? No way that would work in the 100. Much too slow, according to an item someone just faxed me out of a magazine. In fact, a butterfly would be dead last in the imaginary race described by *Sports Illustrated for Kids*.

A bird known as the spine-tailed swift (one hundred and six miles per hour) would fly away with the win over a cheetah (seventy mph), jackrabbit (forty-five mph), ostrich (thirty mph), sprinter (twenty-seven mph), and butterfly (twenty mph).

Of course, Ali also had the sting of a bee.

Thursday, June 6 – Houston

I enjoyed an evening of food and fellowship with the other SMTC sprinters at the home of Bill and Dot Yasko, a warm and personable couple who constantly turn to the Bible for both knowledge and strength. Bill is the preacher at Westbury Church of Christ, where both the Marshes and the Burrells are active members of the congregation. It was Mike who first met Bill a few years ago and found him to be not only a wise teacher but also a sincere and caring friend.

After dinner, Bill invited us into his living room, where we sat in a relaxed circle of SMTC family and friends. Bill talked for a few minutes about several Bible passages he found to be relevant to the Olympic experience. Then he asked us to address any spiritual or emotional needs that might be on our minds and in our hearts as we approach the trials. He invited each of us to share our thoughts aloud.

When it was my turn, I talked about how stressful these next couple of weeks will be, especially once we get to Atlanta. I asked for each of us to have the strength and the wisdom to stick together and support each other through the entire process. Some of us will be in the same events. Obviously, we will be competing against each other. But we also have to be there *for* each other. We will need each other.

Saturday, June 8 – Houston

Forget about wanting to know what anyone would do with a baseball signed by a track and field athlete. This afternoon I was out watching friends play in a local basketball tournament, and a woman asked me to sign an autograph for her baby girl. On a diaper.

This was not just a case of being without paper and grabbing the first thing she could find. This woman actually said to me: "I've been collecting autographed diapers." At least it was clean. I think. But a diaper? I didn't even ask. I just wrote my name on it and turned back to the basketball game.

Sunday, June 9 – Houston

My friend Sri Chinmoy, the spiritual teacher, called from New York to wish me well in the trials. He also offered this advice: "Find your own time to be quiet. There will be so many activities, so many distractions, so many people talking around you and about you. You must not allow others to drain your energy heart."

It was vintage Sri Chinmoy. His thoughts are so often connected straight to the heart. They flow from the heart. They lead to the heart. In closing, Sri Chinmoy suggested that I find one hour a day to be alone in silence. No television. No telephone. No teammates or friends. Just me and my thoughts and a chance to connect with a higher power.

Monday, June 10 – Houston

I went to see Dr. Brown for a final checkup before heading to Atlanta. My blood work showed the thyroid situation has stabilized right where it should be. And everything else was perfect. It's incredibly reassuring to get a clean bill of health at a time like this. Dr. Brown seemed happy for me, too. I know he's been rooting for me. He's even come out to watch me run a few times, and we've developed a strong friendship based on mutual respect. We've come a long way together since that initial diagnosis in February.

Wednesday, June 12 – Houston and Atlanta

It hardly seems possible that four years have passed since the last time we packed our bags for the Olympic trials. But here we are again. Different time and place. Same song and dance. One more shot at all the excitement and drama that comes with an all-or-nothing meet. Top three in each event get to come back for the Games. Finish fourth — no matter who you are — and you watch on television.

On the plane to Atlanta I realized that this is the most relaxed I've ever been heading into a major meet. Part of that comes from my belief that I've never been more ready to perform. That is not a feeling you can simply will into your psyche. It is either solid as a rock or it is absent altogether. I could not imagine being in a better state of mind.

Then there is one other major factor contributing to how relaxed I feel. This is the first time I don't have to win the trials in order to be successful. All I have to do is make the team. That in itself would be a huge accomplishment – and that makes me just like ninety-nine percent of all the other athletes. It is the first time in my adult life that I can actually say that. Sure, I understand that there is still going to be a spotlight on me. I know I will still be judged as either a success or a failure. But the parameters are so different now.

Once again, I am acutely aware of how incredibly blessed I am to feel such a wide range of emotions. I've been to the top of the mountain. No doubt, the view has been breathtaking. But I'm also seeing and feeling so many new things by approaching the same landscape from new angles. That in itself just might prove to be the most meaningful aspect of this whole journey. Maybe not for people on the outside looking in, but definitely for me.

Thursday, June 13 – Atlanta

I noticed something about the way other athletes seem to be acting toward me. Not my Santa Monica teammates; they're the same as always. I'm talking about people outside the club. They seem to be more comfortable than ever around me. So many of them are going out of their way to wish me well and let me know that they're pulling for me.

Why now? I think this might be the first time I'm not intimidating to them. Is it the age factor? Does that alone make me more accessible than I've seemed to be in the past? Maybe it's also that I've been opening myself up more to them. Who knows?

But it sure is nice to feel so much positive energy coming from so many people within the sport. It is such a simple thing. It is nothing more complicated than someone coming up to me in the hotel lobby and offering encouragement or expressing appreciation. But each and every comment registers with me to a degree beyond which anyone else could possibly imagine. It sure is enjoyable, sure gives me a boost, to be absorbing all this kindness and support.

❖

The starting lists for the 100 were posted late this afternoon. There will be thirty-three people in four heats. All but nine will advance to the second round. That might make it seem like the first round is just a walk in the park for the top guys – and some of the other sprinters might see it that way. I do not. I'm going out there with a specific purpose. I want to set a tone for the rounds to come.

There is a certain rhythm I'm trying to establish when I'm running rounds. I've learned over the years that when I run well early, I also run well late. I can't just take it easy early and then try to turn on all the engines in the final.

Part of running a good opening race is simply for myself. It makes me feel good about what I'm doing. But there is also an external factor. It gives my competitors something to think about as we advance toward the final.

Friday, June 14 – Atlanta

There is always a bit of apprehension leading up to the opening race. I'm trying to get comfortable with the new surroundings. I'm noticing the other guys warming up. Naturally, I'm excited that the time to run is finally here, but I'm also reminding myself how important it is to stay as calm as possible about the whole thing.

In both rounds today, I walked onto the track very relaxed, and that was exactly the way I ran. My time in the first round was 10.10 seconds. In the second round it was 10.04. If anything, I might even have been too relaxed. I got out of the blocks pretty well, but then I was not aggressive enough from about 15 to 30 meters. I'll need to be more intense in the semifinal and final.

Overall, though, I'm right where I want to be. The only guys who ran faster in the second round were Jon Drummond (10 flat) and Leroy Burrell (10.01). What an effort for Leroy after all he's been through just to get here! The next best times were run by Mike Marsh and Dennis Mitchell (both 10.07). Once again, we are looking at the same old veterans being in the best positions to make the team, and I feel very good about my chances.

I know I'm ready to go under 10 seconds. All I have to do is go out and run the way I know I'm capable of running. I want to win, and think I can, but I'll certainly accept anywhere in the top three. Like anyone else who has been training with a single purpose, I'd be thrilled just to make the team.

Saturday, June 15 – Atlanta

There was a moment just before the 100 final when my mind almost gave way to my heart, and I thought to myself: I can't believe this. I'm about to cry.

The public address announcer had just finished listing my credentials. The gold medals. The world records. Trying to make my fifth Olympic team. *Ladies and gentlemen, Carl Lewis.* And now I was hearing and feeling the roar of the crowd washing over me.

I've been thinking a lot lately about something I touched on at the beginning of the year – how I wanted to live this whole Olympic season as a victory lap for all that came before it. And I've been thinking about how dramatically that approach has already affected me. More than anything else, it has afforded me the opportunity to dwell more on the journey of the entire process than the outcome of any single competition.

It was within that context, then, that I was absorbing the support of the crowd in the Centennial Olympic Stadium. I was deeply moved by the feeling that so many people could relate to and appreciate what I was trying to do. Luckily, though, I caught myself before any tears actually flowed. I had a race to run, one of the biggest of my life, and I had to snap myself back into focus.

I kept telling myself to drive off the front block. That is always the key to a good start for me. Unfortunately, I was helpless. My right calf had cramped for a few steps in the semifinal, and now it was cramping again right out of the blocks. I could not shake the pain, and it was impossible to push off that leg the way I needed to.

Maybe I should have just stopped. Who really knows the risk of injury at a time like that? But I kept hoping. I kept running the best I could, which clearly was not good enough. I finished last with a time of 10.21 seconds, by far the worst of my four races in the trials (the best was 10.03 in the semifinal).

The top three finishers were: Dennis Mitchell (9.92), Mike Marsh (10.00), and Jon Drummond (10.01). They will represent the U.S. in the Games, and they all deserve it, because they all ran well.

They fought through the heat and pressure of four tough rounds in two days, and they got the job done better than anyone else. Simple as that.

Still, though, I could not help but be frustrated. I knew from that semifinal just how well prepared I was. I mean, I cramped the first three steps in that race, which had to cost me a few hundredths of a second, and still ran close to 10 flat. There was no doubt in my mind I would do better than that in the final, and the way people were running, I felt that anything under 10 would be enough to make the team, which indeed proved to be the case.

Of course, I was not expecting my body to boycott at a time like this. I was not factoring in the impact of that sharp pain shooting through my leg and refusing to vacate the area. But that remains the reality of it. Despite all the time and effort, despite all the hard work and sacrifices, my Olympic 100 is over before it even has a chance to begin. Just like that — with bags of ice wrapped around my lower legs. That walk off the track, that walk away from all the hopes and expectations that had been building for months, well, it definitely seemed to be a lot longer walk than it really was.

In the post-race press conference, a reporter wanted to know if I thought it was the age factor that caused me to cramp. Was I wrong to believe I could survive through four tough rounds just days before my thirty-fifth birthday? No, I really don't think age had anything to do with it. I've cramped when I was in my early twenties and I've cramped in my thirties. These things just happen sometimes, especially when you're running four rounds in this heat and humidity.

Of course, there was one other factor I had to consider: What, if any, impact might the thyroid medication be having on my muscles? Synthroid has been known to cause cramps. But I only shared this line of thinking with a close friend and then with a doctor in the drug-testing room, because I still don't want the distraction of publicly addressing my thyroid condition until after the Games. I also don't want to make excuses.

Another reporter wanted to know if I thought this was my last 100 in a major championship. No, I don't think it was. I *know* it was. Enough is enough. No more madness of the 100. But I'm still very excited about my two remaining events in these trials, the long jump and the 200. I can't wait to get back out there and compete again. Can't wait to earn a spot on the U.S. team.

Meanwhile, though, I keep filling my heart and my mind with the victories I felt both before and after the 100. The memory of that introduction and crowd reaction will always be with me. So will all the hugs and the kind words that came in the hours after the race. With the outpouring of affection I felt from so many other athletes and coaches and even some of the reporters who have covered me for years, it finally dawned on me just how powerful this season-long victory lap is turning out to be.

The private moments with other athletes meant the most of all. Of course, I spent the most time with my Santa Monica teammates, as always, but so many others made the effort to seek me out and share their thoughts. Among them: Gwen Torrence, Dennis Mitchell, Jon Drummond, Jackie Joyner-Kersee.

Almost two hours after the 100, after the press conference and drug testing, after all the fans and reporters and most of the other athletes were gone, I spent a few minutes with Jackie on the way out of the stadium. She too had just completed a tough day at the office. It was the first time she'd lost a heptathlon since 1984. With her second-place finish, though, Jackie still qualified for the Games.

We walked down an almost-empty hallway underneath the stands, with our arms around each other, kind of holding each other up, I guess. We talked about the past. We talked about the future. We knowingly assured each other that this is not quite the end. Not yet. People just don't know how ready we're going to be next month when it counts the most. We laughed about that.

We also laughed at ourselves for still being here after all these years. We laughed together about the fact we're probably the only two people in the world who have even a clue what it's taken, both physically and emotionally, to still be standing after all we've been through.

"People just don't know," I said, with a sigh.

"No, they don't," Jackie said.

And with that, we headed out of the stadium.

This is not exactly the way I planned on walking away from my last 100 in my last Olympic trials. Dennis Mitchell, who won, is on the right.

(PHOTO: USA TODAY)

Sunday, June 16 – Atlanta

Even nine years after his death, hardly a day goes by without me thinking about my father. I have this deep faith that he is somehow still watching over me. It's a comforting belief, and especially today, which is Father's Day.

As much as I respected and enjoyed my father throughout my childhood and teen years, our relationship expanded to a whole new level in my early twenties. It meant so much to me that we could finally share ourselves as adults – and we had such a good understanding of each other. But then he was gone so quickly. I was twenty-five when he died. In addition to my unspeakable sadness, I also felt almost cheated by his absence. Being without him took a long, long time to accept. Now, though, I often think about how incredibly fortunate we had been in the first place. It is scary to think just how rare it is in the black community to have such a healthy, strong relationship between a father and son. Scary, but true.

So I was deeply touched tonight by watching Michael Jordan on television after his Chicago Bulls took care of the Seattle SuperSonics to claim the NBA title. A few years ago, the murder of his father, James Jordan, was a major factor in Michael's decision to leave the NBA. Now that he was back on top of the game he loves, it was very moving to see Michael in his own moments of reflection. He had already dedicated the entire season to the memory of his father. Now he was collapsed on the floor of the locker room, exhausted and sobbing. He would soon try to describe what it meant to win the championship for his father: "I can't even put into words how sweet it is. My father meant so much to me. I know he's watching. This is for Daddy."

Amen, Michael. I turned away from the television, bowed my head, and thought about my own father. I told him the same thing I always tell him: "I'll be alright. I'll always love you, and I'll be alright."

Monday, June 17 – Atlanta

My plan for the long jump qualifying round was as basic as it gets. Just qualify. There was no need to do anything spectacular because we all start from scratch again in the final. So I just wanted to get through the preliminaries without putting too much strain on my body – and especially the legs. I was still somewhat concerned about my calf, so I didn't want to be too aggressive.

I felt good warming up, and was pretty relaxed as I stood on the runway for my first jump. But then everyone started yelling, "Watch out," and there was a moment of panic as we all dodged a wildly-thrown hammer. The hammer is a sixteen-pound ball attached by a four-foot wire to a handle. An errant throw can turn into a lethal inci-

(PHOTO: USA TODAY)

Long jump qualifying round at the trials.

dent – and actually has. I remember the time a newspaper reporter was hit on the back of the neck and killed by a hammer at a meet in California.

For good reason, then, it took me a minute or two to regain my composure before getting settled back on the runway. It is totally beyond me how, during eight days of competition, they managed to schedule the hammer and the long jump at precisely the same time. That does not make a lot of sense. But, as always, we must be ready to compete no matter what the conditions.

Anyway, the real issue was my approach to the takeoff board. I felt pretty fast on the runway, but it took me a while to feel loose, and that affected the timing and placement of my steps. I was significantly short of the board on my first two attempts, and only barely got a piece of it on the third and final jump. Still, I made it through.

The third jump – 26 feet, 4 $\frac{1}{4}$ inches (8.03 meters) – was not exactly one to celebrate. To put it in perspective, I jumped further than that as a freshman in my first national collegiate meet. But it still placed me sixth among the twelve athletes who will move on to the final. Wednesday night, we'll be jumping for real. All I'll be thinking about between now and then is how I'm going to hit that takeoff board just right, and when I do, I will not only be jumping into a pile of sand. I will also be leaping onto my fifth Olympic team. After all the ups and downs and all the hard work. Finally.

Good news on the medical front: After a few phone calls with Dr. Brown about the cramping problems, he flew here to examine me and run tests. Before leaving for the stadium, I gave blood. By the time I was back, Dr. Brown had the results. The thyroid situation remains fine. And it appears that my body is back in balance again. All the mineral levels and everything else came back just the way Dr. Brown wanted to see them. Normal.

Tuesday, June 18 – Atlanta

It is an off day for everyone, no competition at all, and the timing could not have been better. I am more than happy to have the extra rest. In fact, maybe my calf should write a thank-you note to the people who made the schedule.

Still, though, I can feel the tension building. I know there are plenty of people who figure I'm done. They saw me go down with the cramp in the 100. They watched me struggle through the qualifying round of the long jump. They factor my age into the mix. And here is what they conclude: No way I'll be able to fight back from where I am. Might as well call Dr. Kevorkian to help put my career out of misery.

But there is no suffering here. None whatsoever. All I feel is the anticipation that comes with being on the brink of something big. If the Lord had wanted me out of the Olympics altogether, He would have given me a muscle *pull* instead of a cramp. But apparently He only wanted me out of the 100. I truly believe He still wants me in the long jump. That gives me a tremendous sense of comfort as I think about tomorrow.

Wednesday, June 19 – Atlanta

It was about five minutes before the scheduled start of the long jump final — we were still warming up — when the stadium announcer warned the crowd that "a nasty patch of weather" was approaching from the west. *Approaching?* Storm clouds were already making it very dark for the early evening. And then came the thunder and lightning bolts, a few of them so close that they almost appeared to be touching the scoreboard.

Was there some sort of message being sent? First there had been that misfired hammer in the qualifying round. Now this. It makes me think of something Sri Chinmoy was telling me on the phone just a few days ago. He kept saying, "Please, please, pray not only for your success but also for your protection." In all the years I've known him, it was the first time he ever said anything like that to me — and without any explanation of what he was talking about.

But now I turned my thoughts to the importance of starting off with a good jump. If the weather was about to get crazy, I at least wanted the comfort of an early lead, because I had no idea what would be expected of us. Would they want us to keep jumping? Would they have us wait out the storm? Would they stop the competition altogether and have us come back tomorrow?

"Better get in a good one right here," I kept telling myself as the other guys were going through the first round of jumps. By the time it was my turn − I was eighth in the order − I was almost panicky. And it definitely showed. I came up well short of the board, and after falling back in the sand, my first measurement was only 26 feet, 2 ¹/₄ inches (7.98 meters). "Settle down," Coach Tellez told me. "Just relax and jump."

Maybe the other guys were pressing as well. Half of them fouled in the first round. Joe Greene was the only one with an even some-what respectable jump − 27 feet, 4 ¹/₂ inches (8.34 meters). I certain-ly would not have expected that opening jump of mine to put me in third place after the first round, but it did. Of course, there was no way any of those early marks would hold up through six rounds.

And the storm? Amazingly enough, we got only a few minutes of drizzle, and then the skies cleared, as if Mother Nature had changed her mind and decided to smile on us. We would still have to contend with inconsistent winds, but such winds are pretty much a given in any large stadium. As Coach T had reminded me, I just needed to settle down.

My next jump was much better − 27 feet, 2 ³/₄ inches (8.30 meters) − which moved me up into second place. But I still missed the board, which was the equivalent of erasing at least 8 inches (the width of the board) from my mark. This was starting to feel like that season-opening series of jumps in early May. The jump-ing mechanism itself was working well enough to win. But the inconsistency of my approach was once again giving me trouble.

I was not the only one struggling, though. Maybe it was the pressure. Maybe it was the swirling winds. Maybe it was a combi-nation of things. Kareem Streete-Thompson, a legitimate contender for one of the three spots on the team, did not even make the cut from twelve to eight jumpers after three rounds.

But there was an even bigger surprise unfolding. By the time we got to the all-important sixth and final round, Mike Powell, the world-record holder, was all the way back in sixth place. Joe Greene was still clinging to the lead with that first jump, I was right behind him with my second attempt, and Mike Conley was in third place.

Staring down that runway as he was preparing for his last jump, Mike Powell was looking at the very real possibility of elimination from the Olympic team. Mike is probably the best competitor I've ever

Reaching for every possible inch in the long jump final.

faced in the long jump, and he had been in similar situations before. In fact, he qualified for the 1988 team on his final attempt. But tonight his best effort was only 26 feet, 9 inches (8.15 meters). Was there something wrong with him? Or would he once again be capable of pulling it out at the last minute?

I watched from all the way up by the start of the runway, where I was sitting in the grass, doing some light stretching and trying to remain as calm as I could. I could not see Mike's face from where I was, but I could easily picture his usual look of determination as he rocked back and forth to ready himself for his initial steps toward the board. *Chop, chop, chop.* His run seemed to be pretty good, and then up he went off the ground, kicking and flailing for every inch he could squeeze out of the air. All I could do was wait along with everyone else for his mark to be flashed on the scoreboard. Mike folded his hands together in front of his lips, as if he were praying. He probably was. And then the mark was finally posted – 27 feet, 6 ½ inches (8.39 meters). He had jumped all the way into first place! Mike ripped his hands away from his face, threw his arms into the air, jumped and shouted with joy, and took off on one of his patented celebration runs down the track.

Nobody ever said this was going to be easy. Now Greene was in second place and I was in third, with two more guys remaining ahead of us in the jumping order. If either one of them passed me, my back would be squarely up against the wall. I'd have to do what Powell did – pull it out on my last jump. But if neither one could pass my mark, I'd be back in the Olympics.

Dr. Brown, who was watching from the stands, would later tell me he had bruised both elbows while rocking back and forth against the armrests on his seat. "I don't know how you guys get through these things," he would say. "When I was just starting out as a doctor, working in an emergency room, there was a night I had to handle two cardiac arrests at the same time. It was a lot easier than watching the long jump."

First came Erick Walder, a former national collegiate champion, who had been steadily improving throughout the evening. His reaction after climbing out of the sand made it look like he was close, and he was, but his final jump turned out to be three inches short of my mark. One down, one to go.

*This is no casual wave. Those are five celebratory fingers because I've finally made it —
my fifth Olympic team.*

Next was Mike Conley, the 1992 gold medalist in the triple jump, who had already qualified to defend his title in the upcoming Games. My mind was set on the expectation that Mike would get off a good jump and push me down into fourth place. I was already preparing for my one make-it-or-break-it jump at qualifying for the team. But what was this? Mike seemed to be pulling up on the runway, struggling with his left leg, and then he just hopped awkwardly across the board and into the sand for a...foul. No mark. I was back on the team! I'd had no clue Mike strained his left hamstring on his previous attempt. "I told my coach there was no way I could take my final jump," he would later explain. "But then the winds changed, and I thought maybe I had a chance."

But he was out. I was in. By exactly one inch. That was the difference between our best marks, both of which came in the second round. The trials are all about creating an opportunity for yourself – and now I finally had an opportunity to compete in the Games. Obviously, I was very excited. I was proud of my accomplishment. More than anything, though, there was an overwhelming sense of relief.

The long jump is the one event that has never deserted me. It's always been my favorite. And now it's the one event putting me back in the Olympics. Maybe there were people who thought I was just waving to the crowd. I was not. I was actually holding up the fingers of my right hand in a special high-five, saluting both the past and the present, each of the outstretched fingers representing one of my five Olympic teams. I did not even know it at the time, but someone would later inform me that I'd just become the first American man to make five teams.

I took off on a victory lap, but only made it about halfway around the track, where I stopped for a three-way hug with my mother and Carol, who had been waiting for me along the front row of the stands. Then I had interviews and the awards ceremony, so I temporarily lost any chance to complete the lap. I guess I'll just have to wait until next month for that.

Thursday, June 20 – Atlanta

This is the second and final rest day of the trials. It is also my transition day. It is essential that I move away from the excitement and relief of making the team and get right back into the competition mode, because the next three days will be dedicated to the 200.

Before I really started concentrating on running, though, I was able to enjoy two nice surprises. The first came during a press conference at Nike headquarters. That would normally be an entirely routine process — nothing I would even bother mentioning. But this was a special gathering. After ten minutes of standard questions and answers, the Nike people surprised me by bringing out Jackie Joyner-Kersee to join me on the stage.

That transformed it into one of the most enjoyable press conferences I've ever done. Jackie and I told the story of leaving the stadium together the other night. We reflected on all the time we have spent together in track and field. We talked about the respect we have for each other. And we laughed a lot. Jackie and I always find something to laugh about.

The second surprise came by way of telephone while I was relax-

(PHOTO: NIKE)

A nice break from competition with the First Lady of track and field, Jackie Joyner-Kersee.

ing back in my hotel room. It was a call from Hillary Rodham Clinton. I was just sitting there playing around on the Internet, the phone rang, and next thing I knew, I was chatting with the First Lady of the United States. It was very exciting because I have always admired both the President and Mrs. Clinton. I even attended the swearing-in ceremony and marched in the inaugural parade back in 1993. But I've never had any direct contact with the Clintons. And this was not one of those made-for-television deals they dial up from the White House after the Super Bowl or the World Series. This was much more personal than that.

Mrs. Clinton was calling because she'd been watching the trials and simply wanted to let me know she was a fan of mine. She wanted to offer her congratulations, and sounded so genuinely excited for me. It was really something to hear Mrs. Clinton say she is proud of what I am doing for America – and that I made her proud to be an American.

So this was not exactly the typical rest day. Never in a million years would I have expected to share it with both the First Lady of our sport and the First Lady of our nation.

Friday, June 21 – Atlanta

I'm all the way back to feeling like myself again. I'm one hundred percent for the first time since cramping in the 100. I could tell while I was warming up for the first round of the 200, and then I knew it for sure once we started running for real. I felt strong and powerful, but was also very relaxed the whole way. It was probably the best I have felt in a major meet since the 1991 World Championships.

Even the time surprised me. The whole idea was to get through the opening round without using too much energy. The way I was easing up – at about the midway point – I figured my time would be maybe 20-high or even 21 seconds. But it was 20.30. I could hardly believe it when someone in the press conference told me that. I could even hear the whispers. *Carl's not playing.* No, I'm not. *Looks like he's ready to do something again.* Yes, I am. Such as make the team in another event. I really want this one now – even more than I thought I would.

The competition is extremely tough. Mike Marsh. Michael

Johnson. Jeff Williams. And maybe there is someone else who might be capable of pulling off an upset. But the way I ran the opening round has given me all the confidence in the world.

Sure, I had to wonder a little after the 100. Would I be able to get my body back to where I could still be a factor through four rounds of sprinting? There was even a short period of time after the long jump when I debated whether I should just pull out of the 200 altogether. But Coach Tellez and Joe Douglas put the emphasis right where it belonged. They reminded me that I've worked way too hard for way too long to just give up now. In a sense, I earned the right to give it my best shot in the 200.

My whole career I've tried to stick to the same guiding principle: Never give up. Don't ever give up. No matter who we are or what we do for a living, though, there are going to be times when we need to remind ourselves of even the most basic tenets that define who and what we are. In this case, I reminded myself of two things. One, I've never been someone who just throws in the towel without a good fight. Two, one of the most exciting things in life is allowing yourself the opportunity to take risks. To risk and then fail is an entirely healthy aspect of human growth. To avoid risk and then be haunted by questions about what might have been — that would be like voluntarily forfeiting your right to experience half the emotions in the world. What a boring existence that would be.

Saturday, June 22 – Atlanta

With only an hour and twenty minutes between the quarterfinals and semifinals of the 200, a schedule that offered very little recovery time between races, I knew this was going to be an extremely challenging day. As it turned out, though, running was the easy part.

I was second in my quarterfinal and third in my semifinal. I still was not going all out — still thought it made the most sense to conserve whatever I had left for the final. But I was encouraged by the way I felt. Of course, the big news of the day was Michael Johnson running a wind-aided 19.70 (two hundredths of a second faster than the world record), which was definitely impressive. As even Michael made a point of saying, though, this is not about records. It is about making the team. As I was preparing to leave the stadium, I was very much

(PHOTO: TONY DUFFY/TSI)

Back in action for the 200.

looking forward to the final.

But then I saw Joe Douglas in a hallway outside the interview room, and he looked like he had just been kicked in the stomach. Joe unfolded a sheet of paper for me. It was the lane assignments for the final — and I was stuck in lane one. With the long and tight curve on the inside of the track, it is the absolute worst place for anyone to be in the 200 — and then my height makes it an even tougher turn for me than it is for others. It would be virtually impossible to make the team. I could run what I'd consider to be a great race in lane one, maybe 20.20 at best, and still place fifth or sixth in the final.

So now there were two of us feeling like we'd been kicked in the stomach. My initial reaction was to say: Forget it. Just tell them I'm not running. All I can do in lane one is get hurt. By trying to blast through that tight curve, I would be exposing myself to a very real risk of injury, and especially when I factor in the way my leg was feeling after those 100s. The one thing I absolutely cannot afford to do is throw away my Olympics, the long jump and maybe the relay, by trying to create a miracle in lane one.

How did I end up there in the first place? The people who run the trials — the leaders of USA Track & Field — will tell you that lanes are drawn randomly. The four runners who place first and second in the semifinals are drawn for the most desirable positions, lanes three through six. The four runners who place third and fourth in the semifinals are drawn for the inside and outside spots, lanes one, two, seven, and eight.

But the definition of *random* is certainly open to debate. We all know of instances when lane assignments or entire heats have been juggled for one reason or another, and I have always argued that there is nothing wrong with that. If we are going to put on the best possible competition, the most compelling show for the fans, we need to make sure the marquee athletes have a fair chance to perform well. I'm not saying I should have been moved into one of the best lanes. The guys who finished first and second in the semifinals earned those middle lanes. But I also do not think I should have been put in lane one.

Joe has never been one to give up without trying, so he rushed off to discuss the situation with meet officials. I went out to dinner with friends, including Mike Marsh and Floyd Heard, both of whom had also qualified for the final (Mike in lane four; Floyd in eight). While we were eating, the restaurant manager came by to tell me I had a phone call. It was Joe. One of the meet officials had offered a solution. He suggested that I switch lanes with Floyd, just swap lanes one and eight, as if it were a foregone conclusion that I'd want a friend and teammate to take the knife for me, as if I'd choose the immediate gain of making the team over a close friendship that will last long after the urgency of these trials has faded away. No way, I told Joe. Floyd worked just as hard as I did to get here.

So I figured that was the end of it. Either I run in lane one or I pull out of the race. But Joe went right back to those meet officials, and one of them eventually offered another way out of lane one. Unfortunately, the new scenario was even more offensive than the first.

I was supposed to file a formal protest requesting a review of my semifinal. I had been third with a time of 20.29. A young runner named Alvis Whitted had been fourth with the same time. What I should do, according to this meet official, is protest that order of finish. In other words, I would be asking to be moved down to fourth place. If that were done – and Joe was directly assured of a ruling in our favor – then the change between third and fourth would require another draw for lanes. That was going to be the justification to get me out of lane one. And Joe was even told that the new random draw would be arranged so that I would definitely end up in lane seven or eight.

I could hardly believe what I was hearing. This was like a bad scene out of a B-movie about behind-the-scenes shenanigans in horse racing or something. I mean, if they agreed that I ought to be moved, why had it even gotten this far? Why hadn't they just moved me on their own before releasing the lane assignments? They never would have had to concoct such a shady plan. Obviously, the proposal was dishonest. Obviously, asking to be moved down to fourth place would be totally ridiculous. No, I would not even consider it.

So now I am left to decide which is worse: Running in lane one or simply pulling out of the race. I'm stuck in a very tough spot. If I pull out, I look like a baby. *Oh, poor Carl didn't get the lane he wanted, so he just packed up and went home.* Or I look like I'm backing down from a challenge. *Sure, Carl saw Michael Johnson run that screamer in the semifinal, and now he's scared to run against him.*

This is hardly the ideal way to be spending my energy the night before the last race I'll ever run in the Olympic trials. Or will I even run? As crazy as tonight has been, all the discussions back and forth, all the frustration, I think I better wait until the morning to make that decision.

Sunday, June 23 – Atlanta

Ultimately, I decided to run, even knowing there was no way to make the team. I still wanted to give it my best effort, and I would try to be smart about it. I would remind myself to pay special attention to any twinge or cramp I might feel while running in the curve. If necessary, I would pull back slightly to help protect against injury.

Still, by the time I was leaving for the stadium, I was telling myself: Who knows? Something bizarre could happen and I could somehow eke out third place. Stranger things have happened. But I'm not sure I really believed anything other than the fact I was headed for a public whipping.

Which was exactly what I got. I had the best reaction to the starter's gun of anyone in the field (the reaction times are recorded by computer). I ran the first half of the curve very well, aggressively, but the further I got into it, the more I felt like I was losing my battle against the centrifugal force. Still, I kept pumping my legs the best I could, and eventually made it to the straightaway, which I ran very well. In fact, amazingly enough, I ended up with exactly the time – 20.20 seconds – I had set as the standard of what I thought would be a great race in lane one. It put me in fifth place.

There were several thoughts when I crossed the line. One, Michael Johnson ran the race of his life. The crowd was already erupting in response to his winning time – 19.66! – a new world record. It is never any fun to have someone run a world record on you. But I made a straight line to Michael because I wanted to offer him a congratulatory handshake. He certainly deserved it. The 200 record had been the longest-standing mark (seventeen years) in the sport, and now he would have an opportunity to complete his dream. Michael will have a shot at becoming the first man in history to win both the 200 and 400 in the same Olympics.

Also, I was happy that Mike Marsh made the team in the 200 – in addition to his spots in the 100 and on the sprint relay team. I certainly know how hard Mike has worked all year, and it always brings a great deal of satisfaction when a teammate and friend performs so well. This will be an exciting summer for Mike. He has a very legitimate shot at adding three medals to the two golds he already won in Barcelona. A collection like that would certainly elevate him into an elite handful of Olympians.

Finally, I could not help but think: Even after all these years, the leaders of this sport still never cease to amaze me. I could have had the lanes changed. As well as I ran, it probably would have made the difference as far as qualifying for the team. But it simply would have been wrong to accept either of those proposals I had been offered. As much as I wanted to make the team in the 200, especially after what had happened in the 100, I was totally at peace with my decision.

First and foremost, I wanted to stay focused on the fact I am going back to the Olympics. I am very, very proud of that. I am extremely thankful to be an Olympian again. This is not the time to sit around and contemplate what might have been. It is a time to celebrate what is still left to come.

No matter what the results, there is always a certain feeling of relief at the end of a major meet. All I wanted to do was go back to the hotel and unwind. The one thing I certainly wanted to avoid was additional stress.

So much for that. Soon after I got to my room, Joe Douglas was knocking at the door, and he was wearing pretty much the same expression I saw when he first showed me the lane assignments for the 200. There was more bad news. This time Joe handed me a one-page policy statement for members of the 4 x 100 relay pool. The running order was listed right at the top of the page – and I was not included. It was: Jon Drummond, Leroy Burrell, Mike Marsh, and Dennis Mitchell on the anchor. I was listed as one of three alternates.

Unbelievable.

For a month and a half, we have been operating on the basis of what Erv Hunt, head coach of the men's team, has been telling reporters: that I'd be running anchor as long as I made the final of the 100 here. We have never heard anything other than that. But Erv never has – not to this moment – said one word directly to me about his plans. All I had heard was through the grapevine. Everyone being considered for the relay (including me) was supposed to attend a meeting tomorrow morning, and then Erv would announce the team.

But now this. Part of my reaction is based on substance. What in the world happened? Why the drastic change? Part of my reaction is more emotional. Why would Erv issue his decision in writing without even offering the courtesy of talking directly to us? How could he be so spineless about it?

This is definitely the most upset I have been all year about anything in track and field. Well, let me clarify that: It is the combination of both the handling of the 200 and the handling of the relay team that has set me off. It is impossible for me to think of either situation as an isolated incident. After all I have seen and learned over the years, I cannot help but look at these things within the broader context of just how screwed up the administration of our sport really is.

By now, track and field should know how to conduct its business on the level of any major sport. But the bottom line remains painfully clear: Sure, some of us are now able to earn a handsome living in professional track and field; unfortunately, though, it is a world still ruled by amateurs.

How could we possibly expect any improvement when we have a national federation that still relies so heavily on the input of college coaches? I mean, that might have been OK back when the majority of Olympians were undergraduates or just out of school. But those days are long gone. It is ludicrous that we remain stuck in such a hopelessly outdated system. Does the NBA consult Dean Smith or John Thompson on major personnel or marketing decisions guiding the fate of professional basketball? Of course not. The NBA hires its own people – its own professionals.

I am so tired of banging heads with the people who govern track and field. Do they even realize that our sport is in big trouble? I wish they could finally recognize and accept that – and before it's too late. Even if we have great athletes, the inept administration of track and field can still kill it.

I am left to wonder if my usefulness to the sport has simply expired. Not my usefulness as an athlete – I know I am still capable of competing at the highest level – but my usefulness as a catalyst for change, for growth. The way I feel right now, maybe I should just throw in the towel after the Olympics. Maybe I should just give it everything I have in the long jump and then walk away from the whole scene.

Monday, June 24 – Atlanta and Houston

I really don't understand what Michael Johnson keeps talking about. He keeps telling reporters we have a rivalry and do not like each other. A rivalry? Not that I'm aware of. We hardly even compete against one another. And not like each other? We don't even know each other. Maybe he's just one of those athletes who believes in the use of animosity as fuel.

Then there is this thing he keeps saying about my unwillingness to relinquish my role in the sport to him – whatever that means. What role? I mean, I go out and compete just like anyone else does. It is not up to me to decide who the fans and reporters choose to follow. That is up to the fans and reporters. So what does Michael want me to do, just retire for him? Am I supposed to stand in the middle of the stadium with him and hand off a baton to symbolize some generational changing of the guard? I just don't understand what he wants me to do.

This morning it was the *Today* show. Bryant Gumbel interviewed me about the trials, and was digging for me to say something negative about Michael. Gumbel had obviously been prepared with the things Michael has been saying about me. But I told him pretty much the same thing I've been saying all year: that it's great for track and field to have another star. Another star creates more attention for the sport – and then the whole sport has a chance to benefit from that. Later in the show, though, Michael went on and gave Gumbel exactly what he wanted. *We don't like each other. If Carl won't give me what I deserve, I'll just have to take it from him.* All the same garbage he's been saying for months.

Is he trying to build himself up by tearing me down? Is he working from a marketing plan based on the notion that conflict sells? Is there some other way Michael benefits by trying to create a rivalry? Or has he even thought about what he is saying? It is almost impossible for me to even guess at the answers to these questions. I don't have a clue what he is trying to accomplish.

Tuesday, June 25 – Houston

I keep thinking back to that 100 in the trials, and now I'm getting angry about it. Maybe I needed to be back home, alone with my thoughts, before the frustration could really sink in. Obviously, there is nothing I can do to change the outcome, but still there is emotional baggage. I knew I was ready to make the team in the 100. I was absolutely certain of it. Yet I came up empty.

I don't want to dwell on it. It makes more sense to just let go of the sprints and concentrate on the long jump during these final weeks leading up to the Games. But I keep hearing this little voice from somewhere deep inside: *I want one more stellar 100. One more the way I've already run it this year. One more 100 the way I know I'm still ready to run.* And then I'll be comfortable just leaving it at that.

Wednesday, June 26 – Houston

Back to work. After discussions with Coach Tellez and John Lott, our strength and fitness coach, we put together a very specific plan for the next few weeks. I'll continue training on the track for both the sprints and the long jump. In addition, though, I'm also going back to some of the basics from the strength and fitness phases of our early-season training: plyometrics, medicine ball, box drills, and other exercises that will help with my explosiveness. The idea is to finely tune the fast-twitch fibers of the muscles. We need them to keep firing away the best they can.

And there is also one other benefit to getting back in the gym. I think it will help me mentally. I like waking up and going to the gym. Those early-season workouts were some of the most enjoyable and productive of my entire career. It will be nice to break up the monotony of just being on the track all the time.

Friday, June 28 – Houston

It's been way too long since the last time I added any course material to my imaginary History of the Olympics 101. This morning I was treated – courtesy of a U.S. Olympic Committee promotional piece – to an interesting list of comparisons between the first modern Olympics and the upcoming Games.

There were thirteen nations represented in Athens 1896. There will be almost two hundred in Atlanta 1996.

Three hundred and eleven athletes, men only, competed in Athens. Almost eleven thousand, including thirty-seven hundred women, will be in Atlanta.

One hundred thousand people watched the competition in Athens, with ticket prices ranging from twelve to twenty-five cents. There will be about two million spectators in Atlanta, with some paying up to six hundred dollars a piece for the best tickets.

The facilities in Athens cost about one hundred and twenty thousand dollars. The tab in Atlanta will be in the neighborhood of half a billion.

There was almost no public dissemination of results from the first Games. Some fifteen thousand media representatives from around the world will descend upon Atlanta.

One thing I know they'll be covering: a much faster race in the 100. Thomas Burke, an American, won that first sprint title with a time of 12 seconds flat.

Saturday, June 29 – Houston

The Kirk Baptiste Key Olympics finished this afternoon, and then we had an awards dinner for the teens who participated. In just three years, the size of Kirk's academic and athletic program has more than doubled to about two hundred participants. It was quite moving to witness the impact of it all.

Remember, these are juvenile delinquents who are trying to find some sort of meaning and purpose in their lives. They are not necessarily bad people, but they have done bad things, some of them very bad, and now they are seeking new beginnings. It was truly amazing to see these youngsters react with such joy to the simple fact that someone cared about them. These kids are just screaming out for attention.

You could see it in their eyes. Everyone in the program was given some kind of an award, and each time one of their names was called out, each time another youngster paraded across that stage to the cheers of both peers and adults, you could just see the pride shining out of his or her eyes. It was something every parent in America should have a chance to see. Or something every parent should have to see.

Monday, July 1 – Houston

Anyone saying I'm thirty-five years old will finally be right. Today is my birthday. I introduce it this way because so many people have already had me a year ahead of myself for so long. Even the official entry sheets at the trials kept listing me as a year older than I really was.

I think it goes back to the initial stories about my desire to compete in Atlanta. They all focused on the age factor. *Old Man Lewis will be thirty-five by the time of the Games.* With repetition, that last part was often dropped, and it was changed to just *Lewis is thirty-five.* It's kind of fun to be the same age for maybe eighteen months or even two years.

Anyway, this was probably the most low-key birthday I've ever had. After a routine morning at the track, there were some afternoon phone calls and a few presents from friends and family. But that was really it. I just felt like being alone – just wanted to relax. I'm having a pool party Thursday for the Fourth of July, which is also my brother Mack's birthday, so I've been telling everyone we'll just make it into a big combination birthday party. For both the United States and the Lewis brothers.

Tuesday, July 2 – Houston

I think almost any athlete knows when retirement is near. But I also think there must be one isolated moment or experience that finally makes it absolutely clear: *Hey, this is really it, time to go.* I always figured it would be something directly related to my performance on the track, maybe a bad race or a particularly tough day of practice. This morning I realized it was something entirely different – and that it's already happened. It was the last night of the trials, that Sunday night when I was so frustrated by the handling of both the 200 and the selection of the relay team. It took a while to sink in, but I think the frustration of that night was actually my call to retirement.

I've always wanted to make a difference in track and field, *for* track and field. I've always tried to initiate changes that would allow the entire sport to grow and prosper. But that last night of the trials made me feel like we were moving backward instead of forward. I'll always be grateful for all that the sport has offered me. I'll always be proud of the progress we have made together. But I left the trials dispirited, as if the passion I'd always felt for track and field had just been sucked right out of my veins. I really wasn't needed anymore.

Not in track and field, anyway. This all came into focus over the weekend when I participated in two events that helped me understand what I was feeling. The first was Friday night, an Urban League dinner at which I received a community service award for my work with charities. The second was Saturday, the Key Olympics program with Kirk Baptiste. I found myself thinking: This is what makes me happy, affecting people's lives, motivating others. I felt so needed again.

Lane assignments in the 200? What do I think of Michael Johnson? Do I want to be on the relay team? I'm so tired of all that petty stuff. What does any of it really matter?

Wednesday, July 3 – Houston

I made a prediction this morning. I said that Frankie Fredericks of Namibia would break the 100-meter world record (Leroy Burrell's 9.85 seconds) in tonight's Grand Prix meet in Lausanne, Switzerland. Frankie has been tearing up the track lately and has an excellent chance to emerge as one of the unexpected stars in the Games. But my prediction was wrong. He missed the world record by just a hundredth of a second (matching the 9.86 I ran in the 1991 World Championships).

It was a serious wake-up call for anyone who has been ignoring Frankie – which is easy to do. He goes about his business very quietly, almost stoically, so even though he was second in both the 100 and 200 in Barcelona, he never seems to get much attention. What a race, though. The field was loaded. After Frankie, the order of finish was: Donovan Bailey (9.93), Ato Boldon (9.94), Jon Drummond (10.00), Linford Christie (10.04), Bruny Surin (10.05), Leroy (10.05), and Dennis Mitchell (10.15).

The only one missing was Mike Marsh. Put him in Leroy's spot and that could easily be the 100 final in Atlanta. For now, though, Mike is once again demonstrating the restraint that so often sets him apart from the pack. While the other top sprinters are running all over

Europe, chasing after appearance fees, Mike is training and resting here at home. That strikes me as the wisest approach to be taking with the Olympics so soon. It basically comes down to an analysis of short-term gains versus long-term benefits — and Mike is one of the best analysts in the entire sport.

Thursday, July 4 – Houston

Carol was in charge of planning the pool party. We had about thirty people at my house, including most of our local SMTC friends, but track and field had absolutely nothing to do with the atmosphere. The Olympics never even came up in conversation. Forget running and jumping. We were happily consumed by swimming, eating, sharing stories and laughs with our friends. It was an enjoyable afternoon.

Friday, July 5 – Houston

I was planning on one final blue-collar meet this evening at Rice University. I wanted to get in one more 100 to help me stay sharp for whatever races I might run in Europe after the Games. But it turned out that Rice had canceled the meet because of the holiday weekend. I ended up running a regular workout, including two hard 60s, with Mike Marsh.

Saturday, July 6 – Houston

After having lunch with Sri Chinmoy in New York, a mutual friend of ours just called to fill me in on what was said. Sri Chinmoy was discussing my performance in the trials but then shifted into a much broader analysis of my current and future status.

"According to others, he is finished," Sri Chinmoy said. "But according to God, he will never be finished. According to his critics, King Carl has lost his throne. But according to his friends and dear ones, he is still on the throne with his crown. And even when he himself thinks or feels that he is no longer on the throne, God will still say that he is on the throne. King Carl will remain forever on his throne, even if it is not always visible to our naked human eyes. In God's Heart-Eye and in the heart-eye of aspiring humanity, he will remain eternally King Carl. That is not only my inner feeling but my absolute prediction. On the strength of my oneness with the highest Source, the highest Reality, I am predicting that he will forever and forever remain King Carl."

I hardly know what to think of such remarks. But I'll certainly try to use them as inspiration.

Monday, July 8 – Houston

This is the time we start hearing and reading the human interest stories that give texture to the Games. We learn about an American kayaker named Cliff Meidl, partially crippled by a massive shock in a work accident ten years ago. We read about a Tutsi middle-distance runner named Gilbert Tuhabonye, representing the nation of Burundi, his body covered with burn scars from a Hutu soldier's attack. We hear about the Palestinian athletes who want to carry a message of hope to Atlanta. Palestine's only previous tie to the Games came in 1972, when Palestinian terrorists killed eleven Israeli team members at the Olympics in Munich. Now two runners and a boxer will be representing the two-year-old Palestinian Authority. One of the runners, Majdi Abu Marahil, a thirty-two-year-old father of five from the Gaza Strip, says he wants to meet with Israeli athletes and speak with them in the Hebrew he learned as a day laborer at an Israeli farm.

So much for gold medals and world records. These are the personal histories that make the Olympics what they are.

Tuesday, July 9 – Houston

The U.S. relay team is starting practice in Chapel Hill, North Carolina. After a few days of training, Jon Drummond, Leroy Burrell, Mike Marsh, and Dennis Mitchell will run together Saturday in the Gold Rush International Meet at Duke University. I'm not in North Carolina because I'm not on the team. Erv Hunt, the coach, made that perfectly clear, in writing, the last night of the trials, and I've completely accepted that.

There are three other guys going to practice as potential alternates: Jeff Williams, the fourth-place finisher in the trials 100; Tim

Harden, who was fifth; and Tim Montgomery, who was seventh. Montgomery's name was not on the original policy statement circulated by the coaches on June 23, but I guess he was added to the relay pool when Joe Douglas told them I would not be attending camp.

My stance now is the same it has been since the night of the 100 final, when reporters immediately started asking me about the relay. I'll be available if the team needs me, but as far as I'm concerned, I'm totally out of contention. The long jump will be my only event in the Olympics.

Erv has talked about the possibility of running me just in the preliminary rounds, as an alternate, which would give me a chance to pick up another medal. But I've made it clear I don't think that would be fair to the younger guys. I have plenty of medals. I'd prefer to give the new guys a chance to win one. Williams is a veteran sprinter, Harden is just out of the University of Kentucky, and Montgomery is still in school, but not one of them has ever been in the Olympics, let alone won any medals. So why take that opportunity away from them? Running in the Games would be something to remember and cherish for the rest of their lives.

For some reason, though, Erv is dogging me in the press for not being in training camp. "He can't make the team right now," Erv is saying. "He's not even in camp yet." Why would I be? I've already explained my reasons, numerous times, in response to questions from reporters. I guess Erv has not publicly released the lineup he distributed to the athletes, but everyone on the inside knows that the team has already been picked.

Think of it this way: Your boss fires you because he's not satisfied with your performance. Do you still show up for work the next day? Of course not. You don't have a job, so why would you go to the office? Actually, even that comparison is slightly off. I do still have a job, the long jump, and that's what I need to be working on between now and the Games.

Wednesday, July 10 – Houston

It turns out that Erv Hunt is preparing two U.S. relay teams to run in the meet at Duke. There will be an "A" team (the actual team he named at the trials) and a "B" team (potential alternates). Erv never told me or Joe Douglas anything about running a second team. I just happened to come across a story on the Internet that mentioned it.

I'll be in the meet Saturday, definitely in the long jump and maybe in the 100 as well, so it's too bad Erv chose not to tell us about his plans. I would have happily accepted an opportunity to run head-to-head against "A" team anchor Dennis Mitchell, which is probably the precise reason Erv elected to keep me in the dark.

What if I went out there on the "B" team, got the stick a few yards behind Dennis, and then ran him down on the anchor leg? That would certainly complicate things for the coach. How does Erv avoid such a situation? Easily. He puts Chris Huffins – a decathlete! – on the "B" team. Nothing against Huffins, who is an extremely talented athlete, but I don't think the "A" team has a whole lot to worry about with a decathlete on the other team. Neither does Erv.

Thursday, July 11 – Houston

I'm trying to improve my attitude in time for tomorrow's trip to North Carolina, but I'm still having trouble with it. With each day since the trials, my emotions have drifted further away from the intensity required to compete well. I know I have to jump this weekend because I still need the work on my run to the board. But I'm almost disinterested. There is only one more competition that really matters. The long jump final in Atlanta is eighteen days away. I wish we could just get on with it.

It's strange. I'm about to enter the most important stretch of the year, one of the most important periods of my entire career. This is the time when I'm supposed to be overflowing with confidence and energy. Yet I find myself in a bit of a funk. I've been wasting too much time and energy thinking about the negatives within our sport. I need to start concentrating on the positives again. I need to keep filling myself with positives.

Friday, July 12 – Chapel Hill, North Carolina

Members of the U.S. track and field team voted this evening for our nominee to carry the American flag next week at opening ceremonies, and I just found out I was selected. It does not necessarily mean I will be the flag-bearer in Atlanta. That decision will be made in a meeting of the team captains of all sports. But I already consider it a tremendous honor to be chosen by my peers. It is hard to imagine how incredible it would be to represent the entire nation that way — leading the U.S. team into the stadium during the most memorable night of the Games.

I've already been looking forward to playing another special role in the opening ceremonies — even though I don't have any idea what it's going to be. All I know is that Billy Payne, president and CEO of the Atlanta Committee for the Olympic Games, has invited me to be "one of less than twenty-five Olympians" in a tribute to the more than seventy thousand athletes who have participated during the first one hundred years of the modern Games. The invitation came in a letter Payne had someone hand to me after the May 18 Grand Prix meet in Atlanta. It says: "In order to enhance the emotion and drama of your appearance in this historic moment, it is important that you maintain confidentiality about your selection to represent the athletes of the 1984 Olympic Games." When Joe Douglas called for more information, he was told that I should just enter the stadium along with all the other athletes. Someone from the organizing committee will approach me when I'm needed and lead me to my secret destiny.

Saturday, July 13 – Durham, North Carolina

The crowd at Duke University was incredible. There were more than twenty-eight thousand people in the stands, almost unheard of for a meet in the U.S., and it felt like every single one of them was encouraging me to get off a big jump. Unfortunately, I did not deliver. My best jump — 26 feet, 3 inches (8.00 meters) — was almost a foot less than I jumped at the trials. The field was weak, so I still won, but now I know what it's like for the body to jump when the mind is somewhere far away. It's not a pretty sight.

Actually, the jumping mechanism itself was not that bad. It was pretty much the same as it's been all year. The problem was still my approach to the board. The second half of my run was better than it's been, more aggressive, but the first half still needs work. Coach Tellez was not the least bit pleased with me. "I don't know what in the world you're thinking about on the runway," he said. "But I know you're not concentrating on the same things we've been doing in practice."

Of course, my poor results raised some legitimate questions: How could I jump so badly just two weeks before the long jump in Atlanta? What does this do to my confidence? How could I possibly hope to win another medal?

One of the reporters wanted to know if I was discouraged. My first thought was: I don't know if I care enough right now to be discouraged. But I tried to remain upbeat: "I'll be ready for the Games. The difference between now and two weeks from now is the mental focus. That's what it's going to take for me to win. That's what it's going to take for anyone to win."

The "A" and "B" teams were still warming up for the relay when I left for the airport. I was just happy to be going home. I later heard from Carol that the "A" team won with a time of 38.16 seconds. The "B" team was second in 38.50. Nobody was overly impressed with either performance.

Sunday, July 14 – Houston

I keep thinking about the talk I had with Joe Douglas just before I left the stadium in North Carolina. He knew I was down. He'd been concerned about that for a few days. So he pulled me aside.

"Two more weeks," he said. "One more competition. *One.* Maybe it seems like you've already accomplished everything you want. Maybe none of this seems like it matters right now. But these Olympics are something you'll have the rest of your life to think about. You don't want to be looking back with any regrets."

I tried to explain where my mind was, tried to explain just how much the trials had taken out of me, not physically, but emotionally. I tried to assure Joe that everything will be fine, that I'll be ready when I have to be, but nothing I said seemed to be enough for him.

"No matter what you do, you're always going to have my support," Joe said. "You know that. But I want you to think about something. If you don't think it's enough anymore to just go out and compete for yourself, then do it for those of us who can't compete. Do it for those of us who care about you but can't compete."

That really hit me. Nobody had ever said anything like that to me. Nobody ever had to. Joe was exactly right. It was the most emotional

I'd ever seen him. We hugged, and I thought he might even cry, but he didn't. All the way home, I kept thinking about what Joe had said, and I'm still replaying it in my mind.

I've also gained some perspective by taking a few minutes to look back at the entire year. I finished last in those two indoor races, but Coach Tellez and I stuck with our plan, and we overcame those early setbacks. I was diagnosed with the thyroid condition, but Dr. Brown gave me the right guidance and treatment, and we were able to handle the situation. Now this. I guess I can look at this funk I've been in as the third crisis point of the year. It's time to start dealing with it the same way I approached the others. Develop a plan. Stick with it.

I was fortunate that Joe caught me when he did, before it was too late. I've been thinking way too much about the negatives in track and field, and about certain insiders who want to tear me down. But I'm done thinking about them. The next two weeks I'll focus on the people who care about me, the people who want me to do well. I'll also make sure to think about the rest of my life — the fact that I'll have the rest of my life to look back on whatever I do in these Games.

I'm already starting to feel better. Thanks to Joe.

Monday, July 15 – Houston

Juan Antonio Samaranch, longtime president of the International Olympic Committee, has never been known for understatement when promoting the far-reaching impact of the Games. But he outdid even himself in an exchange that aired tonight during a pre-Olympic special on HBO. It was part of a segment called *The Monarch of the Rings*, in which journalist Frank Deford profiled Samaranch in his role as the unchallenged ruler of the Olympic movement.

Here is what Deford offered as an introduction: "Juan Antonio Samaranch seeks to stay above any criticism by constantly claiming that what is essentially some games, a sports TV show, is somehow imbued with spiritual properties that make it, in the favorite word, a movement, with the same sort of pious imagery that is usually applied to religion."

And here is what Samaranch then said: "We are more important than the Catholic religion."

Yeah, right.

Wednesday, July 17 – Houston

It's difficult to anticipate what I'll be feeling and thinking in Atlanta. I'm not talking about the competition itself. I figure all the sights and sounds and thoughts associated with the long jump will be pretty much the same as always. But what about everything else that defines the Games? There are a number of reasons why everything else will be so different for me this time.

The most obvious is that this is my last Games. For that reason alone, it feels so detached from the others. Then there is the fact that I'm going to compete in only one event. What will that be like? And even the geography of it – just an hour and a half flight from here to Atlanta – is playing a big role. It's unprecedented that I'm still home this close to the Games. I've always been on the road for two to three weeks already, training and competing elsewhere, getting adjusted to new time zones and climates. This time I'm even breaking the Games into two separate trips. I'll go tomorrow for two days of events, including opening ceremonies on Friday, and then I'll be back home for almost a week before the start of track and field.

Of course, the biggest uncertainty of all comes back to this being the last time around. This is the least pressure I've ever felt heading into a major competition. But how could I possibly prepare myself for the emotions I'll be feeling through my final Olympic moments, all the last-this and last-that? What will it be like to walk out of that stadium after my final Olympic competition?

I know I'm prepared for the rest of my life. It's just those first few minutes I'm not so sure about.

Thursday, July 18 – Atlanta

I've always been a believer in taking care of business before pleasure. This time I'm working in reverse order. The real business does not come until next week when I return for the long jump. For now, I'm here to take in the overall atmosphere of the Games. I'm visiting with other members of the Olympic family. I'm checking out the city. I'm enjoying myself.

It's kind of strange, though, because I feel like I'm here in two distinct roles. One is current Olympian. The other is former Olympian.

It's as if I have one foot in the door and one foot out, which is certainly a unique position for someone still trying to win a gold medal.

As a current Olympian, one of the first things I did this evening was join an incredible group of athletes for a Nike press conference to kick off the Games: sprinter Michael Johnson and pole vaulter Sergei Bubka; tennis players Monica Seles and Andre Agassi; basketball players Anfernee "Penny" Hardaway, Scottie Pippen, and Lisa Leslie; and swimmer Tom Dolan. It was a lot of talent to have in one room.

As a former Olympian, I then rushed off to a dinner for the "100 Golden Olympians" chosen by the U.S. Olympic Committee and Xerox as part of the centennial festivities. It was like being in an Olympic museum — except that the wax figures were actually interacting with each other: track and field champions Bob Beamon, Bruce Jenner, Al Oerter, and Bob Hayes; speed skater Bonnie Blair; figure skaters Kristi Yamaguchi and Brian Boitano; basketball star Oscar Robertson; swimmer Matt Biondi; and so many others. It was uplifting to be with such an impressive group of former champions who seem to be doing so well with their lives — happy, successful people.

But I also had to wonder: With all this celebration of the past, with all this energy being spent looking backward, am I still maintaining the emotion and drive necessary to keep moving forward? I have to keep reminding myself that I still have a competition coming up here. I have to do the best I can to keep my thoughts and feelings in the present tense.

Friday, July 19 – Atlanta

In the past, I've enjoyed walking into the opening ceremonies, in the parade of athletes, with people I know. In 1984 I was with the basketball players, including Michael Jordan and Patrick Ewing. In 1988 I was with swimmer Mary T. Meagher and a few of my Santa Monica teammates, including Carol. In 1992 I was again with the Santa Monica crew. This time I intentionally drifted away from my teammates so I could take in all the sights and sounds on my own. It was a special walk, blending in with all the other American athletes, watching so many people enjoying themselves, absorbing the cheers and the energy of the crowd.

Bruce Baumgartner, who earlier in the year won the Sullivan

Award as the country's top amateur athlete, had been chosen to carry the American flag. It was a fitting tribute. Bruce is our most decorated wrestler. It was also a touching way to remember his former teammate and friend Dave Schultz, who was shot and killed in January while training on the Philadelphia estate of chemical heir John E. du Pont.

Before I made it even halfway around the track, I was pulled aside by someone from the organizing committee. It was time for me to put on my "former Olympian" hat — time to honor everyone who participated in the first century of the modern Games. I was introduced along with eight other former champions, including Bob Beamon, Mark Spitz, Nadia Comaneci, and Greg Louganis. I got the most joy out of watching Bob when he was introduced. He was beaming, waving his hat and letting the cheers wash over him. It was moving to see him so genuinely excited by the way the crowd responded to him.

My conversation with Bob was one of my highlights of the night. He was supportive, as he always is, and we even talked shop for a few minutes. "I know you can still jump 29 feet," he said. "But you've been looking down at the board too much. You need to keep your head up." I told him he was probably right. Then I realized how strange it was to be having a conversation like this. We were standing there as former champions, yet we were talking about my upcoming competition. Once again, I felt like two athletes — former and current — at the same time.

Watch out for the fashion police. Leroy Burrell is on the left. Mike Marsh is on the right.

There were two other points in the ceremonies that will always stand out in my memories. First was the tribute to the Reverend Martin Luther King, Jr., including the reading of a passage from his "I Have a Dream" speech. What an appropriate message to incorporate into the festivities. After all, the Olympics are all about bringing people together.

Second was the surprise appearance of Muhammad Ali for the lighting of the Olympic flame. He was the perfect choice. There's always a big guessing game about who will light the flame. I was hoping it would be someone from Georgia. It's always nice to have that local flavor. But I was thrilled the moment I saw Ali. He was shaking with the unmistakable curse of Parkinson's syndrome. Yet he still stood tall and proud. The star of the show.

Saturday, July 20 – Houston

Thanks to the generosity of my friends Jim Bernhard and Bret Talbot of Baton Rouge, Louisiana, who offered the use of their private jet, we were able to fly right back from Atlanta after the opening ceremonies. Under normal circumstances, Mike Marsh, Leroy Burrell, LaMont Smith, and I would have felt pretty silly walking around the airport in matching coats and ties (our U.S.A. team outfits), but who was going to see us at four in the morning?

As much as I enjoyed the opening ceremonies, they were just that: ceremonies. Watching the swimming on television tonight was the first time I really felt the true excitement of the Games themselves. It was the first time I started feeling like I'm really about to compete again. I was watching alone at home, and within a few minutes, I was jumping up and down, cheering on the Americans, screaming at the television as if they could hear me.

I almost jumped right through the screen when Jeremy Linn was just barely beaten by Belgium's Fred DeBurghgraeve in the 100-meter breaststroke. Linn, out of the University of Tennessee, still broke the American record while claiming the silver medal.

Then there was Whitney Metzler, just eighteen years old, from Glen Rock, Pennsylvania. Nobody really expected much out of her in the 400-meter individual medley. She was fortunate just to be on the team. But then she went out and set a personal record, by more than two seconds, which was huge, to qualify for the final. She was so over-whelmed, she started crying. There would be no medal for her in the final – she finished eighth – but she set yet another personal record. Young Whitney accomplished what any Olympian would want to accomplish. She surpassed her best when the whole world was watch-ing. I'll always remember her as one of the first people who got me into the spirit of these Games.

Monday, July 22 – Houston

The strangest thing happened this morning between practice jumps. I was walking back along the infield grass. I guess I was just daydream-ing – and then it hit me all at once. I had this peculiar feeling that I was up on the victory stand in Atlanta. It lasted just a second or two. I didn't even have a vivid image of it. But the feeling was unmistak-able. There was nobody else on either side of me. I was all alone on top of the world.

Tuesday, July 23 – Houston

It turns out I am not the first American man to make five Olympic teams, as I'd been told during the trials. What I am is the first to make five teams in track and field. I clarified that point this morn-ing after reading about a fencer named Peter Westbrook. At the age of forty-four, he is a *six*-time Olympian. I like what he said in Atlanta after losing in his last solo appearance before retirement: "When you look at the whole scheme of things and what I've accomplished, it's almost asinine to be sad at this point. I'm not complaining." Amen.

Wednesday, July 24 – Houston

Practice has been great the last few days. I feel strong and sharp. Emotionally, I'm back into it. I'm no longer trying to force things to happen. I'm *letting* them happen. There's a big difference.

Coach Tellez and I figured out something very important this morning – and it was flat luck that we were in a situation to do so. Robertson Stadium, our usual training facility at the University of Houston, was being used for the Junior Olympics, so we had to move indoors for practice. It just so happens that our indoor track is made of a Mondo surface, as is the track in the Olympic stadium. Mondo, an Italian company, makes a very hard running surface. It's almost like concrete — hardly any give at all. That means you'll probably turn over your legs quicker than you will on another track, but you'll also lose some bounce. With so little give in the Mondo, so little reaction to the energy you're putting down on the track, your legs are doing more work than they do on other tracks.

This morning, while practicing long jump approaches, my first time on Mondo since the trials, we concluded that the loss of bounce was slightly shortening the length of my strides. My approach is twenty-one strides. But twenty-one strides were not getting me quite as far on the Mondo as they normally do on other surfaces. I've been starting my run 162 feet from the board. But this morning I kept coming up about a foot and a half short.

In almost any other situation, we'd probably be frustrated by something like this. We'd be concerned about missing by so much. But our reaction today was just the opposite. We were excited. After being perplexed for weeks by the way I kept coming up short of the board at the trials, we finally had a reasonable explanation. It was probably just a matter of being on the Mondo.

So we're making a change. I'm going to start my run a foot and a half closer than I have been. Of course, we'll still make adjustments based on the wind and other variables in Atlanta, but I'm going to start at 160 feet, 6 inches. It's amazing that we would stumble across such a significant discovery just five days before the finals of my last event in the Olympics, and only because we were forced to practice inside, but I've always believed that such things happen for a reason. My confidence keeps building.

Thursday, July 25 – Atlanta

This time I'm here to take care of business. I arrived early in the evening and settled into a hotel room. After dinner, I had several brief meetings with Joe Douglas and others. Then I spent a few hours watching the Games on television. My turn is just three days away. The long jump qualifying round is Sunday. The final is Monday.

Friday, July 26 – Atlanta

Mattress Mac (a.k.a. Jim McIngvale) is back at it again. It was just months ago that he got behind our indoor meet in Houston, the first Gallery Furniture Games. Now he wants to bring the entire Olympic Games to Texas in 2008. The first thing he did was cut a deal, including the use of thirteen thousand pieces of furniture in Atlanta, to become an official sponsor of the current Games. That paved the way for him to set up a "Texas House" in the well-situated Atlanta Chamber of Commerce building, just off Centennial Olympic Park, and now he's opening the doors for all sorts of "Texas 2008" promotions. The guy never stops selling.

One of the wisest things he did was enlist the help of Mary Cullen, one of my closest and most loyal friends in Houston, to organize a big bash tonight for members of the International Olympic Committee. There are not many people who know how to throw a party the way Mary does – first-class from start to finish. She invited me to help talk up my adopted home state, so I went for about an hour of rubbing elbows with the I.O.C. folks.

One of the highlights was meeting Larry Hagman, J.R. Ewing in

Mary Cullen surrounds us with the flavor of Texas 2008.

(PHOTO: PETER HEIMSATH)

the television show *Dallas,* who was there because of his scripted ties to Texas. That's not what drew me to him, though. For one thing, I'll always associate him with *I Dream of Jeannie* (playing Major Nelson) before any other show. But the real reason I wanted to visit with him was my interest in organ donation and transplantation. Hagman is one of the best-known transplant recipients in the world. His life-saving liver transplant made headlines everywhere last year, so it was great to see and hear how well he's doing. I spent a few minutes with Hagman and his wife on the roof of the Chamber of Commerce building, overlooking the wild celebratory scene in the park below us. We sipped soft drinks and talked about our donor awareness programs. Hagman struck me as someone who is very happy to be alive.

Saturday, July 27 – Atlanta

I got up in the middle of the night to use the bathroom – don't know exactly what time it was – and decided to turn on the television for a few minutes. That usually helps me go back to sleep. Not this time.

The first time I heard the word "bomb" it did not really register. I was still in a fog. Then I heard it again. They were still trying to sort out the details, but there had been an explosion in Centennial Olympic Park at about 1:20 in the morning, apparently a pipe bomb. It was just a few hours after I'd left that rooftop overlooking the park – just a few hours after I'd been looking out at thousands of people enjoying the music, the fountains, the vendors, and each other.

There was a concert going on, some rock band called Jack Mack and the Heart Attack, when the bomb went off. At least one woman was dead, and maybe a hundred people were injured. They were still being carried away on stretchers. Everyone was trying to figure out what the hell had happened – and why. An act of international terrorism? Who knows? I'm certainly not playing down the severity of the situation, the cruel and horrible impact on so many people, but it just doesn't seem like the incident was massive enough to be the work of organized terrorists. It sounds more like the act of some isolated idiot. But why? What could anyone possibly gain by doing something like this?

Of course, the International Olympic Committee and local organizers were faced with a very difficult question: Would the Games proceed on schedule? The answer, yes, was announced in no uncertain terms. There would be even greater attention paid to security. The Olympic flag would be lowered to half-staff. But the Games would not yield to some lousy coward sneaking around in the dark. The Games would go on.

It's impossible not to think about all the people affected, both the victims and their families. They're in my thoughts and prayers. As an athlete, though, I need to keep my emotions in check. The long jump starts tomorrow. I have to keep thinking about that.

I was sorry to see Jackie Joyner-Kersee forced out of the heptathlon with a hamstring injury. She started the morning with the best time in the hurdles. Unfortunately, she also suffered a spasm in her already-injured right leg. NBC showed it over and over, and it never got any easier to see the pain on her face. Bobby Kersee, her husband and coach, eventually came out of the stands to pull her from the competition just before the start of the high jump. "The husband in me finally overcame the coach," Bobby said. "It was very emotional. I've never cried over athletics before."

My brother Cleve and a few friends came by the hotel tonight to watch the 100 final with me. Based on what I had seen in the preliminary and semifinal rounds, my prediction was Frankie Fredericks of Namibia first, Ato Boldon of Trinidad second, and then a fight for third. Of course, that was without knowing how to factor in the impact of what I call finalitis, a big-meet affliction brought on by the incredible stress of it all. It's not that you choke. It's just that some people try to do more than they can.

By the time the race was finally started — legally started, that is — the stress level was even higher than usual, due to several false starts. Linford Christie, the defending champion, was the first to leave too soon. Then Boldon jumped the gun. We were witnessing the very reason I've always wanted to change the rule for false starts. The way it is now, with forgiveness on one false start per customer, too many people are consistently trying to take advantage. They're trying to get away with a guessing game instead of waiting for the gun. I think we need to change the system so a sprinter is eliminated the first time he jumps too early (the way it's done in both high school and college meets) and then we'll have a more honest competition. The way it turned out, Linford was eliminated anyway, because on the third attempt for a clean start, he once again jumped the gun. Linford disputed the ruling, causing quite a scene by refusing to leave the track for a few minutes, which was very unfair to the other athletes. But he was gone.

Finally, after that, there was a clean start, and then the race of a lifetime. Boldon looked good out of the blocks, as he usually does, but spent too much energy in the first 50 meters. He fell apart at the end. Fredericks also started out in pretty good position, but then he pressed, looking totally different than he did in the earlier rounds, much tighter, a classic symptom of finalitis. That allowed Donovan Bailey, running the perfect race, strong but relaxed, to come flying through the pack in the last ten meters — with a new world record! 9.84 seconds! It was one hundredth of a second faster than the previous mark set by Leroy Burrell. Fredericks was second (9.89) and Boldon was third (9.90) in the fastest one-two-three finish in history. Unfortunately, Mike Marsh was never really in it, running a respectable 10 flat but finishing fifth.

An interesting thought crossed my mind while I was watching Bailey carry the Canadian flag on his victory lap. All five foreigners who finished the race, including the three medalists, had trained in the U.S. under American coaches. Everyone wants to know what's wrong with American sprinting the last few years. No question, we have our own problems, but we're also preparing everyone else to beat us.

Soon after Cleve and my friends left the room, I pulled out my long jump shoes, checked to make sure the spikes were in just right, and then placed the shoes on a chair. I put a pair of socks with them. Then I picked out a uniform and folded it neatly over the back of the chair. Tomorrow it's my turn to compete.

Sunday, July 28 – Atlanta

My plan was the same as always for a qualifying round in the long jump. The automatic mark to advance into the final was 26 feet, 5 inches (8.05 meters). I wanted to jump at least that far on my first attempt. That would help my confidence. It would also keep me from being out in the stadium longer than I needed to be. With fifty-two people competing for twelve spots in the final, three rounds of qualifying jumps were going to take forever. The best place for me would be back in the hotel, resting for tomorrow. At least that's what I figured before the competition began.

My first attempt was well short of what I wanted. The run felt pretty good, but I was way over my checkmark and had to shorten my last steps before jumping. Obviously, I'm not going to jump well when I do that. The measurement was 26 feet, ¼ inch (7.93 meters), almost five inches off the automatic qualifier. No problem. I'd get it on the next one.

Ivan Pedroso of Cuba, the 1995 world champion, was back from his thigh injury, and had an automatic qualifier on his first attempt. Mike Powell, the world-record holder, was already walking away with a qualifier. And the other American, Joe Greene, the bronze medalist in Barcelona, had the best opening jump of anyone, 27 feet, 2 inches (8.28 meters).

I waited just over an hour, sitting, stretching, walking, trying to stay loose, before it was my turn to jump again. And then I had another bad run. Maybe I was subconsciously reacting to being so far over my checkmark on the first attempt, because I was not nearly aggressive enough. My steps were totally off as I approached the board, so I just ran through it, and was flagged for a foul. Now I was really in trouble. With two rounds completed and only one jump to go, I was all the way back in eleventh place.

Then guys I'd never even heard of started passing me in the standings. A Russian. A Frenchman. Another Russian. A Belgian. The names were not even important to me. What mattered was the fact that I was now in fifteenth place, three places shy of advancing to the final.

I was one mistake away from my last experience in the Olympics turning into the worst performance of my career.

This wait before my final attempt was becoming one of the longest of my life. I kept hearing people shout encouragement from the stands.

I turned away from the long jump to watch the first semifinal of the men's 400. I paced back and forth behind the runway. I sat. I stood. I took a short, easy run, trying to stay loose. I did some leg kicks. Then I watched the second semifinal of the 400, though I'm not sure how much of it I was actually taking in.

At one point while I was lying down on my back, resting on my elbows, I thought back to Jackie Joyner-Kersee pulling out of the heptathlon yesterday, and I thought about the dramatic feature on her that NBC used to close its broadcast. Jackie's departure was commentator Dick Enberg's "moment" of the day, and now I found myself thinking: *Wait a minute. I do not want to be tonight's Enberg moment. Not for ending my career like this.*

I thought all the way back to last August, those early training sessions, all the hard work with Mike Marsh, Leroy Burrell, Floyd Heard, and the rest of the crew. I specifically thought about the medicine ball. How many times did we throw that thing around the gym? We worked way too hard for me to end the Olympics this way.

Finally, almost three and a half hours after we first walked into the stadium, it was time for my third and final jump. I stood on the runway, bending over, hands on my knees, eyes closed, and I kept telling myself to relax. The main priority was avoiding a foul, so I had already moved back a little. I could hear myself thinking: *This will not be my last jump in the Olympics. No way.* I reminded myself to count the steps on the runway. When I hear each step getting faster, that helps me feel the rhythm I want, which in turn helps me to stay relaxed.

I straightened up, stared down the runway, tugged at my singlet and then my shorts, licked my lips, stared some more, and then I was off. *One, two, three...* I could tell I was off to a good start, and it turned into my best run of the night. I felt fast and strong, and knew I was in good shape leaving the ground. In the air, I knew I had the jump I needed. And then I heard the roar of the crowd. We all waited together for the measurement. When it was posted — 27 feet, $2\frac{1}{2}$ inches (8.29 meters) — we all celebrated together. I had jumped all the way into first place!

Just like that, I went from total elimination to complete confidence. Of course, we'll all start even again in the final, but this was a huge boost. In fact, qualifying the way I did gives me even more confidence for tomorrow than I would have had if I'd just gone right out and qualified on the first jump. Now I know I'm ready to jump well when I need it the most, and I know there's still more distance left in me. I haven't even hit the board yet. That's eight inches right there.

Walking out underneath the stadium, a friend stopped me, looked me dead in the eye, and said, "You're going to win this thing." I said, "Absolutely." It's the best I have felt about my jumping in a long, long time.

Monday, July 29 – Atlanta

With six rounds of jumps in the final, there was more room for error than we had last night, but I really didn't want any of that do-or-die stuff this time. The idea was to pick up right where I left off. Given the way the final was structured, I wanted to be in the lead after three rounds. That's when the field is cut to eight and the order of jumping is shuffled to benefit the top guys. The leader at that point gets to jump last in rounds four through six. The guy in second jumps next to last, and so on, in reverse order of the standings after three rounds. Jumping last is an obvious advantage, like batting in the bottom of the ninth inning in a baseball game, because you know exactly what you need to do. Nobody can sneak up behind you and snatch your prize.

Once again, though, my first attempt was way off. I missed my mark and ended up running through the pit for a foul. My second attempt was better – 26 feet, 8 1/2 inches (8.14 meters) – but still nowhere near what it would take to win. Actually, I was surprised to still be as high as third place at the end of the second round. Emmanuel Bangue of France was leading with a jump of 26 feet, 10 1/2 inches (8.19 meters) and Mike Powell was second with a jump of 26 feet, 9 3/4 inches (8.17 meters). But nobody was really doing much. Now was the time to make my move.

I thought I might have been trying too hard on my first two attempts, so I told myself to just enjoy the third one. I still wanted it to be the pivotal jump of the night, the one that would allow me to jump last in the order through the next three rounds, but if I could just

Stretching out on my third jump.

(PHOTO: LORI ADAMSKI-PEEK)

think about enjoying it, maybe that would help. There can be a fine line with the intensity of a major competition like this. No doubt, you need to be extremely focused. But you also don't want to be so intense that you're getting away from what you normally do. So I stood on the runway before my third jump, twenty-one strides from the board, and told myself: "This is not a jump to win the Olympics. It's a jump to compete well. It's a jump to enjoy."

The first few steps felt great. The rest of the run was even better — and then I actually hit the board. When was the last time I did that? Someone later told me that I drifted off slightly to the right, but I did not notice it at the time. I guess I was too busy enjoying myself. It hardly even felt like I hit the sand.

I bounced right out of the pit and turned back to see what I had done. No question, it was the biggest jump of the night. I collapsed to my knees, by the side of the pit, and then fell forward, chest and cheek against the ground. The roar of the crowd didn't feel like the response of eighty-two thousand fans. It felt like the warm embrace of eighty-two thousand friends. My mark was finally posted on the scoreboard alongside the runway: 27 feet, 10 $^3/_4$ inches (8.50 meters). The place went crazy. I went crazy. It was my longest jump at sea level in four years, since the Olympics in Barcelona. I don't know who was the

(PHOTO: ABAKASH)

The measurement is in. And I like it.

(PHOTO: NANCY ANDREWS/THE WASHINGTON POST)

most stunned: the other jumpers, the crowd, or me. I was in first place by more than a foot.

The waiting would be entirely different now. Last night it was a matter of waiting to determine my own fate. Even with all that tension, I still felt like I was in control of the outcome. This time it would be waiting to see what everyone else was going to do, wondering if anyone else could equal or surpass my mark. I almost had to laugh at myself. You usually want your Olympic experiences to last forever. This one I would have been more than happy to end right then.

But there was a lot more jumping to be done. I watched Joe Greene go 27 feet, ¹/₂ inch (8.24 meters) to move into second place, pushing Bangue to third and Powell to fourth. I watched Ivan Pedroso, the defending world champion, walk off, eliminated after three rounds, clearly not in shape after the injury he suffered in March. And I watched a parade of fouls. That's what happens when you're way out front and everyone else is trying to squeeze every last inch out of the board. You start seeing fouls.

There was a moment between jumps when it dawned on me that this could easily be the last jumping competition of my life. *As long as my lead holds up, why ever jump again? Why not just retire from the event and stick to running for one more year?* Then I remembered what happened last time I had similar thoughts in the middle of a competition. It was during the 1991 World Championships in Tokyo. I already had two jumps over 29 feet, the first two of my career, and I was thinking: *OK, you get the world record on this next one, you win the gold medal, you walk off into the sunset.* In the very next round, Powell had the jump of his life, breaking both the world record and my ten-year winning streak. And changing my career plans.

Powell was certainly on my mind again this time. He's always capable of popping a big jump. But there was something strange about the way he was acting. He was so uptight, so stressed out, frowning and cussing and throwing things. It was like all the rest of us were here to compete to the best of our abilities, but Powell was here only to win the gold medal. It had to be his. Otherwise, he'd think of himself as a complete failure. That's a mighty heavy burden for an athlete to put on himself. In the fifth round, Powell fouled for the second time in a row, and apparently strained his groin in the process.

Everyone else kept fouling or coming up short as well, until James Beckford of Jamaica jumped into second place with a mark of 27 feet, 2 $^1/_2$ inches (8.29 meters) on his last jump. Beckford had been looking good on the runway all night, so it was nice to have him done. No more need to be concerned about him.

That left only three more guys with a shot at me. Powell, still hurting, fouled yet again, just crumbling into the pit this time, lying face down in the sand, crushed by both the physical and emotional pain. Then Bangue, the early leader, had a weak effort. And so it came down to Greene. He already had a lock on the bronze. He seemed to get off a pretty good effort – but then the official at the board started waving his red flag. Foul! It was over! I was the Olympic champion!

It was the biggest moment of my entire career. No way anything else could possibly top it. It is the most thrilling victory I've ever had. It is the one I've been able to share with the most people. It is the most meaningful. By far.

I ran down to meet Greene coming out of the pit. We hugged. Then it was just me and the crowd. Me and my friends. No more wondering. No more worrying. The time was finally here.

One more victory lap.

It would definitely be the most enjoyable lap of my life.

I started toward the stands. Someone threw me an American flag. And then I was off. I stayed in the grass between the track and the stands. I wanted to share this with every single person in the place. How in the world did all these people get into my dream? I went over to Jesse Jackson, who was waving from the front row, and gave him a hug. There was a huge message lighting up the scoreboard: *Carl Lewis has joined Al Oerter as the only athlete to win four gold medals in one event.* I saw an old friend, Sam Mings, founder of Lay Witnesses for Christ, a group with which I've been associated for years, and went over to hug him as well. Someone threw me another flag, so now I had one for each hand. I waved the flags to the crowd. I held them against my chest, squeezing them. I draped them over my shoulders. I hugged Beckford, who seemed to be extremely happy with the silver. I hugged one of the officials. I

probably hugged just about everyone.

And then the lap was complete – but I was not done yet. I still wanted a piece of this night that I could always keep as a reminder. Maybe in a jar. Up on a shelf. So I stopped one last time at the pit, kneeled down in the sand, and started scooping with my hands. It was like being a little kid again, playing with Carol, building castles in the sand while our parents were teaching the older kids how to run and jump. But this time I walked off with a plastic bag full of sand. Golden dust.

The most enjoyable lap of my life starts with one flag (left) and ends with both hands full.

(PHOTO: ABAKASH)

EPILOGUE

The reporters started in on me almost immediately after I walked off with my bag of sand. "With your ninth gold medal, you're now tied as the most decorated athlete in the history of the Olympics." Three others won nine golds: distance runner Paavo Nurmi, the Flying Finn, who competed in the 1920s; Soviet gymnast Larissa Latynina, who competed from 1956 through 1964; and American swimmer Mark Spitz, who dominated in 1968 and 1972. "So what about the relay, Carl? Will you be going for number ten? Do you want to run? Should you be put on the team ahead of someone who beat you at the trials?"

Never mind the fact that I had just accomplished the only goal I had set for myself in Atlanta. Never mind that the relay team had been picked weeks earlier — and that I'd already made numerous public comments accepting that fact. Never mind that I had not even packed any sprint shoes for the Games. Never mind that all I really wanted to do was enjoy the rest of the week as a spectator. None of that seemed to matter anymore. All that mattered was the desire to create a good drama. The media folks wanted a soap opera.

No matter how many times I was questioned about the relay, my responses were pretty much the same: "Sure, I'd love to run if I'm asked, if I'm needed." I guess I committed the horrible sin of telling the truth. "Who wouldn't want to compete one more time in front of such incredible fans, and in my own country? But I've totally accepted what the coaches have decided, and I'll continue to support the team. The one thing I want is for the U.S. to win the gold. With the tradition we have, we should always win the relay, especially when we're running at home."

I never once said I *should* be on the team, never once asked Erv Hunt or any other coach to put me on it. In fact, Erv and I never even spoke to each other. Not once. Erv asked Joe Douglas if I would join the team at practice in case I was needed. Dennis Mitchell, the team captain, asked me to do the same. So I had a pair of shoes delivered by overnight mail, and I went to practice. Once I was there, though, Erv made it pretty obvious he had no intention of using me. Whenever I got close to him, he put his head down and walked the other way.

The relay is always the last night of track and field. That allowed for five days of the soap opera. *Carl Lewis and the relay. Will he or won't he?* It might as well have been: *Who shot J.R.?* After a few days of being bombarded for information, Carol finally wrote the words "I Don't Know" on a piece of paper and pinned it on her blouse.

People were divided into two camps. One side was saying to give me the baton. I was the most experienced anchor man in the world. With a running start, I was still as fast as anybody. Plus, all the attention of trying for a tenth gold would be good for track and field. The other side was saying to forget about me. I lost at the trials. I did not attend the relay camp. I was washed up.

I could certainly understand the difference of opinions. But the media coverage truly baffled me. I was accused of "lobbying" for a spot on the team by conducting a "campaign" through the media — even though all I ever did was answer the questions I was asked. But the so-called lobbying campaign was a mild accusation in comparison to some of the others. There was "speculation" that NBC was pressuring the coaches to put me on the team — supposedly a power play for ratings. There was "speculation" that Nike was going to pay off another member of the team to let me run in his spot.

And then there was the most insulting theory of all: that Leroy Burrell, with a bad right Achilles, was just faking an injury to open up a spot for me. Leroy was understandably upset that anyone would question his integrity. He worked very hard all year to overcome several injuries. He's the best second leg in the history of the relay. It was ludicrous, and totally insensitive, to think he would just throw in the towel. "Where do these people come up with this stuff?" Leroy asked me. "I'm going to just give away my shot at an Olympic medal? How many of them are going to give away their stories when they're about to win a Pulitzer Prize?"

Common sense had nothing to do with any of this. Neither did restraint. Newspapers all over the country made front-page news out of the relay. There was even a U.S. congressman, Ron Wilson of Houston, who wrote President Clinton and talked about a petition

drive to get me on the team. Maybe *Atlanta Journal-Constitution* columnist Prentis Rogers, who covers the media, had just the right explanation for the feeding frenzy: "There's nothing like a little controversy to
recapture the interest of an Olympic audience that by now may be
growing just a bit weary of watching the Games."

Two days before the relay, *USA Today* easily claimed the
overkill-of-the-Games award by publishing six stories on what it
called my "last-minute bid for a record-breaking tenth gold medal."
Unfortunately, the debate kept getting louder because Erv would
never really make a decision. I'm not saying it was an easy decision,
especially with so many people watching to see how he would handle it, but good coaches make tough decisions all the time. That's
what makes them good coaches.

Even the day of the relay itself, the coaching staff kept sending
mixed messages. At 12:43 in the afternoon, Charlie Greene, one of
Erv's assistants, left a recorded message for Joe Douglas in his hotel
room: "Would you please have Carl at the warm-up track at 5 p.m.?
Final decision – I repeat, the final decision on whether or not Carl
will be running – will be made an hour before the finals."

Ten minutes later, Dennis Mitchell called me in my room. He
said he wanted me to run. He was going to do everything he could to
speak up for me at the warm-up track. But I stopped him right there.
I said: "Dennis, I'm absolutely fine with not running. You have to
understand that. This is me talking. This is not the newspaper or the
television. I've never asked to run. You know that. So don't feel like
you have to say or do anything for me. You've done a great job as the
leader, holding the guys together through all this mess. Just do what
you have to do. Get ready to run. I'll be there to support you. I'll be
at the practice track to wish everyone well. I'll be in the stands cheering for you."

At 3:15 in the afternoon, Al Baeta, another of Erv's assistants,
called Joe and told him the decision had been made. I would not be
on the relay team. Of course, the coaches would later make a point
of telling the media that the decision was made in a team meeting
once we were all at the practice track. I don't know why they told the
story that way – maybe to make it look like the team voted against
me while I was standing right there – but that simply was not the
case. The decision had already been made to replace Leroy with Tim

Harden, a newcomer to the international scene. With the exception of Harden for Leroy, the U.S. team would be exactly the team Erv had listed on that policy statement he distributed the last night of the trials. It would be: Jon Drummond to Tim Harden to Mike Marsh to Dennis Mitchell.

A few minutes before boarding the bus from the warm-up track to the stadium, Dennis pulled together all the athletes: the four guys who would be running, plus Leroy, Tim Montgomery (who ran in the pre-liminary and semifinal rounds), and me. Dennis said he really want-ed all of us to share the victory lap together. He wanted Leroy, Tim, and me to meet the rest of them down on the track. I said, "No, no, Dennis. No way in the world I'm getting in the middle of that. I'll see you downstairs when you're done. But this is your day." As I was walking away, I had another thought: I could not believe these guys were already planning how to celebrate. Shouldn't they be concen-trating on running?

The next thing they knew, they were watching the Canadians cel-ebrate their victory. Donovan Bailey, the 100 champion, and his team-mates won with a time of 37.69 seconds. Dennis and Company were a distant second in 38.05. Harden was clearly the difference. At one point, he fumbled with the baton. Canada's Glenroy Gilbert outran him by thirty-four hundredths of a second. That left a difference of just two hundredths on the other three legs.

We'll never know for sure what would have happened if I had run. There are plenty of people who think we would have won. There are plenty of others who think I was fortunate not to have been a part of it. They figure I was spared the embarrassment of los-ing. Whatever the case, I do know I broke a world record getting out of that stadium as soon as the race was over. No way I was going to stick around for interviews and let the reporters use me for another episode in their soap opera.

Even with the relay controversy swirling around me, I was still deter-mined to enjoy my last few days at the Olympics, and I did. For the first time in my career, with only the long jump on my schedule, I had the opportunity to see a few events other than track and field. I espe-cially enjoyed watching the diving with Hillary Rodham Clinton, who was in town for the day and invited me to join her. I found her to be very warm and likable. Of course, I would have loved to talk politics, but it wasn't the time or place for that.

My other favorite was the women's tennis. I've always enjoyed tennis, both watching and playing, but this was especially fun because I was sitting with the Spanish delegation for a doubles match featuring Arantxa Sanchez Vicario and Conchita Martinez. It was so funny to be using the little bit of Spanish I know. We were all cheering together: "Sí, Arantxa. Sí, Conchita." Even Bud Collins, the colorful broadcaster, joined us for a while, and we had a blast. It was the most fun I had all week.

Then there was a memorable morning with old friends from the U.S. Olympic Committee. I was with them because gymnast Kerri Strug and I were being honored as recipients of the prestigious Olympic Spirit Award. I will always remember the short film that cinematographer Bud Greenspan showed in celebration of my achievements. It was very emotional. In closing, Bud attributed my longterm

(PHOTO: WHITE HOUSE)

My first time as a spectator, with diver Mary Ellen Clark, left, and Hillary Rodham Clinton.

Sharing the Olympic Spirit Award with gymnast Kerri Strug.

(PHOTO: JOHN DICKERSON)

success to the following approach: "Never look to the ground for your next step. Greatness belongs to those who look to the horizon."

❖

Someone in Atlanta asked me what I would write as my epitaph. It was an interesting way to contemplate the end of my Olympic career. But it was difficult to come up with a response. It's not like walking away from my final Olympics means my life is about to end. At least I hope not.

My career is not even over yet. I still want to compete in a few meets next year. I'm also excited about my days after track and field. I've been in this sport, this business, my entire adult life, so I'm really looking forward to new experiences. There will be no more need to plan everything around training and competition. There will be no more media microscope on everything I do. There will be so much more time for friends and family and fun, so much more time to help in the community, so much more freedom.

I'll increase my involvement with the same causes I've been supporting for years, especially organ donor awareness and the Best Buddies program. I'll also be more involved in politics. I don't want to be an elected official. I do want to offer my help both locally and nationally on a wide variety of issues. My involvement with track and field? I'll always do whatever I can to help with the University of Houston program and the Santa Monica Track Club. Those will be my priorities.

And that epitaph? Ultimately, my legacy will be defined by others, as it should be. But I do hope I'll be remembered for more than just medals and records and statistics. I'd like to be remembered for what I've done to move track and field forward as a professional sport. I'd like to be remembered for my fight against the use of performance-enhancing drugs. I'd like to be remembered for my passion. I'd also like to be known as someone who had an impact on redefining the limits of longevity in track and field.

Still, this longevity thing will go only so far. Amazingly enough, I've actually been asked if I might consider competing yet again in the next Olympics, Sydney in 2000. One more time at the age of thirty-nine? Not a chance. Maybe I'll be in Australia doing television commentary or other work. But the only thing I'll be running is my mouth.

I'll always have plenty to smile about when I look back on my last Olympic year.

(PHOTO: HOCHI SHIMBUN)